D0984528

NATIONALISM AND
MINOR LITERATURE

THE NEW HISTORICISM:
STUDIES IN CULTURAL POETICS
General Editor, Stephen Greenblatt

NATIONALISM AND MINOR LITERATURE

JAMES CLARENCE MANGAN AND THE EMERGENCE OF IRISH CULTURAL NATIONALISM

DAVID LLOYD

University of California Press
Berkeley · Los Angeles · London

University of California Press
Berkeley and Los Angeles, California

University of California Press, Ltd.
London, England

Library of Congress Cataloging-in-Publication Data
Lloyd, David, 1955–
  Nationalism and minor literature.
  (The New historicism : studies in cultural poetics)
  Bibliography: p.
  Includes index.
  1. Mangan, James Clarence, 1803–1849 — Criticism and
interpretation.   2. Ireland in literature.
3. Nationalism and literature — Ireland.   4. Ireland —
Intellectual life — 19th century.   5. Canon (Literature).
6. Culture — Political aspects — Ireland.   I. Title.
II. Series: New historicism.
PR4973.Z5L56   1987   821'.8   86-30920
ISBN 0-520-05824-0 (alk. paper)

Printed in the United States of America

1   2   3   4   5   6   7   8   9

Chapters 1, 3, 4, and 5 are based, though in substantially revised
form, on articles appearing respectively in *Cultural Critique* 2,
no. 2 (1986): 137–69; *Irish University Review* 14, no. 2 (1984):
178–90; *Comparative Literature* 15, no. 3 (1986): 271–83; and
Dispositio 7, nos. 19–20 (1982): 141–62.

For Joan and Oliver Lloyd

Contents

Preface

> A chronicler who recites events without distinguishing between
> the major and the minor ones acts in accordance with the
> following truth: nothing that has ever happened should be
> regarded as lost for history.
>
> Walter Benjamin,
> *Theses on the Philosophy of History*

The French traveler and radical friend of Alexis de Tocqueville,
Gustave de Beaumont, remarked in 1839 that although Ireland
was a small country, its problems raised questions of major
importance for the social and political concerns of the time in
Europe. If it remains true that Ireland's history offers peculiarly
significant paradigms for developments in Europe and elsewhere,
this is no doubt due to its anomalous position as at once a
European nation and a colony. In consequence of its geographical
proximity to England, Ireland underwent, earlier than any other
colony, a process of hegemonic domination which was as ex-
perimental as pragmatic. Successive imperial measures taken to
discipline and control this recalcitrant colony transformed it into
a testing ground for state apparatuses later adopted both within
Britain and throughout the Empire. Equally, of course, the
contradictions inherent in hegemony assisted in the emergence of
a nationalist movement powerful enough to lead one of the first
successful independence struggles within the British Empire, a
struggle which in turn became a model for other colonized nations. The context in which modern Irish nationalism began to
emerge, alongside the impact of that context on the specific forms
taken by nationalist ideology, is a principal object of this study
and one of the points at which it seeks to contribute to a fuller
understanding of the political and cultural effects of colonialism.

The significance of Irish history for other colonies or post-
colonial states lies not, however, in some possible level of identity

between such disparate geographical and historical situations, but rather in the account of one particular set of reactions to the attempt by an imperial power to produce identity as the cultural counterpart to the material and political homogenization of its subject peoples. Reduction to a single common form for human identity is the end that hegemonic colonialism is forced to pursue in the face of the multiplicity of resistant cultural and social forms contained within any empire. The power of nationalism lies in its countering of an imperial model of identity, for which the colonized people represents a primitive stage in a universal history of civilization whose apex is the colonizing power, with another, formally similar model that seeks to forge an oppositional identity from within. The larger argument of this book is that while nationalism is a progressive and even a necessary political movement at one stage in its history, it tends at a later stage to become entirely reactionary, both by virtue of its obsession with a deliberately exclusive concept of racial identity and, more importantly, by virtue of its *formal* identity with imperial ideology. Ultimately, both imperialism and nationalism seek to occlude troublesome and inassimilable manifestations of difference by positing a transcendent realm of essential identity. The limitations of an oppositional nationalism become apparent in post-colonial states where political unification around the concept of national identity obscures continuing exploitations of class and cultural difference, and where the aim of a cultural education that retains its hegemonic forms continues to be the production of subjects fitted to the requirements of global economic imperialism.

The cultural production of ethical subjects in conformity with a Western type provides the subjective conditions for the perpetuation of economic dependency in post-colonial states. It was the specific aim of Irish nationalism to produce such subjects in opposition to British stereotypes of Irish immorality, with the result that the exploration of the potential for resistance and for alternative social models that might have been produced dialectically out of the very damage suffered by a colonized people has largely been ignored. During the period in question here, crucial by virtue of its formative influence on later nationalist ideology, the nationalist intellectuals' lack of real political power entailed the necessary mediation of their ethical demands through cultural rather than political forms. The Young Ireland movement of the 1840s inaugurated a cultural tradition that conceives the responsibility of literature, and of other cultural forms, to be the production and mediation of a sense of national identity.

The cultural field accordingly becomes a primary site of struggle both before and after independence in Ireland, though with different implications in each case. Part of the present study examines the emergence of nationalist aesthetic culture in Ireland and its dependence on models derived from imperial narratives of cultural development. The other part examines the differences from nationalist aesthetics that emerge in the writings of James Clarence Mangan, an exact contemporary of and occasional participant in the Young Ireland movement. Mangan's writings have always been recognized as relating uneasily to Irish nationalism, particularly given its demand for a literature devoted to the production of an authentic Irish identity. He has generally been considered as a failed exemplar of nationalist writing, and his failure or minor status is most often attributed to his historical position: his writing is minor by virtue of the minority status or "underdevelopment" of Irish literature at that time. My contention is, rather, that the "failure" of Mangan's work should be seen in terms of its recalcitrance to the demands of nationalist as of imperialist aesthetics for the production of a major writing in conformity with a canon whose function is to produce identity. Mangan's is a minor writing, but a minor writing in the positive sense of one whose very "inauthenticity" registers the radical non-identity of the colonized subject.

If Mangan's writing has remained largely unread, this is at least in part due to the enormous power of canonical assumptions concerning "proper" literary values. The various literary strategies examined in this book contradict those assumptions time and again, a fact which has given rise to Mangan's relegation to minor status and to his reputation as a talented but "unfinished" writer. It has, nonetheless, been occasionally observed that certain of Mangan's practices appear to prefigure writing strategies more usually associated with modernism — the use of the persona, false translation, patterns of allusion — and, more specifically, that he seems to belong in a tradition of Irish writing that would include James Joyce and Samuel Beckett. The common ground of these otherwise entirely disparate writers would lie in their critical stance with regard to nationalism and its "identitarian" thinking. Perhaps only in the wake of a critical modernism that has "allowed" such writers is it at all possible to read the complexity of Mangan's quite devious work.

Mangan's writing terminates in the impasse that seems inevitably to afflict any writing that finds itself, in the historical absence of any viable political alternative, constrained to adopt a negative critical position. The rise of nationalism to political dominance would have left Mangan with few options for resistance other than the elusiveness that seems now his most striking characteristic. But the practice of history is not only concerned with the analysis and explanation of those forces that actually came to dominate, but also with the rediscovery of the possibilities in any period that might otherwise be occluded or lost. As Walter Benjamin puts it in his *Theses on the Philosophy of History,* it is the task of the historical materialist "to brush history against the grain."

In post-independence Ireland, the historical "victor" has clearly been a politics predicated on the constitution of national identity, with as its consequence sixty years of conservative republican rule and the perpetuation of economic dependency. The ideological importance here of identity thinking as a means to legitimate a politics largely indifferent to differences other than those defined by the continuing partition of the island leaves no doubt as to the necessity of historical practices that explore such occluded alternatives and extend the critique of myths of identity. A philosophical project that may appear, in "metropolitan cultures," to be an apolitical intellectual luxury is here a task preliminary to any rethinking of radical political options.

Any doubts as to the continuing necessity of such a project were allayed when, in the year when this book was being commenced as a very literary doctoral dissertation at Cambridge University, a new journal appeared that was to become for a period the most important intellectual organ being produced in

Ireland. This journal, *The Crane Bag,* took as its project the provision of a cultural "fifth province" that would seek to transcend political differences and produce "a new unity" of an explicitly aesthetic kind. The continuity of such a project with Irish cultural nationalism became only more apparent when its second issue, entitled *A Sense of Nation,* was devoted to the question of Irish identity. The very posing of political questions in such terms persists as an intellectual stumbling block in Ireland, as in other Third World countries. Fortunately, the trajectory of *The Crane Bag* over the past ten years is symptomatic of a recognition of the bankruptcy of those terms, as its interests shifted from questions of identity to the exploration of global colonialism in relation to Ireland and to the critique of contemporary Irish ideology. It is hoped that this study will make some contribution toward that kind of reorientation of intellectual and political concern, as well as providing further materials for the critique of the political function of aesthetic culture beyond the specific context of Irish literary and cultural history.

Acknowledgments

Although this book appears in a series entitled "The New Historicism," I should acknowledge a prior debt to the tradition of English Marxist historical criticism, represented most immediately for me by the work of Raymond Williams and of John Barrell, the latter of whom, as Director of Studies in English at King's College, Cambridge, influenced my thinking in ways I increasingly come to recognize. The efforts of such critics to reconstruct "the dark side of the landscape" in a variety of contexts had no small influence on my understanding of the nature of literary studies and encouraged me to engage upon this recovery and critique of Irish cultural history. The list of others to whom I am indebted would be embarrassingly long were it not for the continual pleasures of the intellectual exchanges which it represents. Without the persistent support and encouragement of my dissertation supervisor, Tim Cribb, this study would never have been possible. I would also like to thank André Lefevere of the Universiteitsinstelling, Antwerp, Patrick Rafroidi of the Centre d'Etudes et de Recherches Irlandaises de l'Université de Lille, and Robert Welch of Leeds University for their hospitality and critical assistance at various points in my research. As is any student of James Clarence Mangan, I am profoundly indebted to three scholars: to Rudi Holzapfel, for his pioneering *Check List of Printed Sources;* to Jacques Chuto, for his invaluable and exhaustive bibliography of Mangan's writings; and to Ellen Shannon Mangan, for her research into Mangan's life. I am further indebted to Jacques Chuto for the extraordinary generosity with which he has provided published and unpublished articles, information, and invaluable criticisms over the past few years. For the uncovering of many details of Mangan's life available only in Dublin, as well as for much additional information, support, and encouragement, I am grateful to my parents, Joan and Oliver Lloyd, who have saved me repeated expeditions on elusive and often fruitless trails. More recently, my colleagues at the University of California, Berkeley, have been a uniquely supportive source of encouragement and stimulation. I would like to thank especially Paul Alpers, Mitchell Breitwieser, Cathy Gallagher, Stephen Greenblatt, Abdul JanMohamed, David Miller, Masao Miyoshi, Franco Moretti, Brendan O Hehir, Jim Porter, Robert Tracy, and Paul Thomas, whose variously oriented but uniformly attentive readings have been an enormous assistance in clarifying and extending the argument of this book. For financial assistance that enabled me to complete a substantial part of the revision of my doctoral dissertation, I am indebted to the University of California, Berkeley. For their generous and attentive readings, which enabled me to make the final revisions to the manuscript a less painful affair, I am grateful to Louis Renza and an anonymous reader. Avi Rapoport and Eric Miller have been, at different times and with remarkable forbearance, of incomparable assistance with the typing and correction of the manuscript, and Jane-Ellen Long edited the whole with incomparable accuracy and insight. I am equally grateful to Mary Ann O'Farrell for undertaking the thankless task of indexing. To all I owe a debt. Finally, without Nora Pauwels' manifold contributions this book might never have been.

Abbreviations

The following abbreviations of the titles of primary sources for Mangan's life and writings are used in this book. Not included are abbreviations of secondary texts cited extensively in individual chapters: these are listed in the appropriate endnotes.

A	James Kilroy, ed., *The Autobiography of James Clarence Mangan* (Dublin: Dolmen, 1968).
AG	"Anthologia Germanica, 1 – 21," a series of translations from the German, published in *DUM*, 1835 – 1845.
Duffy 1908	Charles Gavan Duffy, "Personal Memories of James Clarence Mangan," *Dublin Review* (April 1908): 278 – 94.
DUM	*Dublin University Magazine*, 1833 – 1850.
IA	The "impersonal autobiography," a third-person autobiography, written by James Clarence Mangan, signed "E. W." [= Edward Walsh], "Sketches of Modern Irish Writers: James Clarence Mangan," *Irishman,* 17 August 1850, pp. 27 – 28.
Life	D. J. O'Donoghue, *The Life and Writings of James Clarence Mangan* (Dublin: M. H. Gill, 1897).
LO	"Literae Orientales, 1 – 6," a series of translations from the Arabic, Persian, and Turkish, published in *DUM*, 1837 – 1846.
McCall	John McCall, *The Life of James Clarence Mangan,* facsimile ed., introduction by Thomas Wall (Dublin: Carraig Books, 1975; orig. pub. 1882).

NLI   National Library of Ireland Manuscript Col-
               lection.

Poems 1859   James Clarence Mangan, *Poems,* ed. and intro-
               duction by John Mitchel (New York: Haverty,
               1859).

PPM 1849   John O'Daly, ed., *The Poets and Poetry of Mun-
               ster: A Selection of Irish Songs by the Poets of
               the Last Century,* trans. James Clarence Mangan.
               1st ed. (Dublin: John O'Daly, 1849).

PPM 1884   C. P. Meehan, ed., *The Poets and Poetry of Mun-
               ster: A Selection of Irish Songs by the Poets of the
               Last Century,* trans. James Clarence Mangan,
               Irish text rev. William Hennessy. 3rd [*sic*] ed.
               (Dublin: James Duffy, n.d. [= 1884]).

Price   James Price, "Gallery of Contemporary Writers,
               Nos. 2, 5, and 6: James Clarence Mangan," *The
               Evening Packet* (Dublin), 22 September 1849, 11
               October 1849, 3 November 1849, n.p.

RIA   Royal Irish Academy Manuscript Collection.

TCD   Trinity College Dublin Manuscript Collection.

Introduction

CELTIC LITERATURE AND THE ASSIMILATION OF THE MINOR

The life of James Clarence Mangan (1803–1849) coincides almost exactly with a period of seminal importance in the formation of modern Ireland, falling between the Act of Union of 1800 and the great famine of 1845–1849. The most prolific period of his writing career, the decades of the thirties and forties, coincides, moreover, with the emergence of Irish nationalism in the wake of the Catholic Emancipation Act of 1829. The growth of that movement through the tithe wars of the thirties and the repeal agitation of the forties culminated in the misconceived and abortive Young Ireland rising of 1848. Mangan's life is thus framed by two unsuccessful rebellions: that of Robert Emmett in the year of his birth, which represented the last struggles of the United Irishmen, and that of Young Ireland, which, while spelling the effective end of the movement itself, nonetheless enshrined its ideals in a mythology potent in later versions of Irish nationalism. The difference betweeen these rebellions marks a crucial shift in the ideological grounding of the struggle for Irish independence. The Enlightenment universalism of Wolfe Tone's politics, largely inspired by the French Revolution, gave way to a Romantic nationalism that was at least in part driven by the need to overcome the discrepancy between Tone's enlightenment ideals and the Gaelic Catholic sentiments that motivated the revolt of the peasantry in 1798. Forging the spiritual unity of the nation as a prelude to the struggle for independence became the goal of Young Ireland, a shift in political strategy which, as we shall see, reflected the affinities between Irish nationalism and its European counterparts.[1]

The same period marks the emergence of a self-consciously Irish literature in the English language, which differs from that of such eighteenth-century Irish writers as Swift, Goldsmith, Sheridan, and Burke, who were not, for all Yeats's mythologizing, primarily concerned with their Irish origins or, more importantly, at all concerned with defining Irish identity. Mangan, on the other hand, is the contemporary of a variety of writers whose works are taken to inaugurate a distinctly Irish literature in English. Thomas Moore, William Carleton, Samuel Ferguson, Thomas Davis, John and Michael Banim, Gerald Griffin, and J. J. Callanan are all writers whose work, for all its "minor" status, is engaged in the project of redefining Irish identity historically and psychologically as well as politically.[2] What will become apparent in the course of this study, however, is that the presence in this list of an Ulster Protestant Unionist, Samuel Ferguson, is not the anomaly it might at first seem, for the project of self-definition is not one confined to the nationalist camp, but is shared by unionists and indeed by English cultural theorists.

A fuller account of the genesis of Irish nationalism and unionism in relation to the British state follows in Chapter 2. For the moment it is sufficient to remark that the period taken to be that of the origins of Anglo-Irish writing coincides with the transition from a mode of English colonial domination characterized by direct legal and military coercion to a hegemonic phase in which imperial rule depends increasingly on the incorporation of the formerly excluded native population into the apparatuses of the state. The emancipation of the Catholic population forms a necessary part of the transition to hegemony, as is indicated by the gradual, if slow, increase in the number of Catholics in administrative functions through the nineteenth century.[3] What is more, the nationalist movement that emerged together with Anglo-Irish literature is itself as dependent on the apparatuses of the British state for its dissemination as it is on the English language and culture which informs its articulation.

This contradiction, as the subsequent history of Irish politics might demonstrate, helps to explain the extent to which Irish nationalism has itself become a means of maintaining British cultural hegemony even after political independence. If Irish nationalism instantiates the conflicts or contradictions necessarily produced in the creation of a relatively autonomous native elite for the purposes of imperial hegemony, it is simultaneously symptomatic of the limits imposed on nationalism by the circumstances of its genesis. Accordingly, a large part of the interest of this period of Irish history derives from the fact that Ireland, due to its proximity to the centers of imperial power, underwent the transition to hegemonic colonialism at a far earlier point than any other colony, with the result that its experience may be suggestive for understanding that of other Third World countries.

The development of a self-consciously Irish writing is required by the nationalist project of forging a distinct Irish identity as a means to unite not only the native, Gaelic Irish, but also the various communities of Protestant "planters," with a culturally deracinated Catholic intelligentsia. The goal of creating a politically *unifying* concept of Irish identity demands the virtual reconstitution of Irish literature as it were *ab origine*, forcing a development that would theoretically have been the normal course of a national literature uninterrupted by colonial power. In such a literature all Irishmen could trace a common origin in the very commonalty of the history of their differences.

Insofar as the political task of Irish literature is conceived in these terms by nationalists, and indeed by many unionists, a certain "minor" status is written into the literature of this period. Representing quite programmatically the infancy of a literature that in a sense never existed, it is defined by its minority, having yet to mature to majority status. Irish literature of the early nineteenth century is accordingly minor in the commonplace sense of having yet to produce a canon of recognized major works, but that minority is assumed to be a necessary stage in the artificial evolution of a national literature comparable to that of the developed European nations. For the nationalist drive is to represent Ireland's right to self-determination through the forging of a canon of works that will represent the distinctive nature of Irish identity, thereby proving what even the great Italian nationalist Mazzini denied them for precisely cultural reasons — their *essential* right to a separate national destiny. This desire to produce a canonical, "major" literature and the consequent adoption of a specific matrix of concepts through which the nature of the canonical is to be defined ironically bring Irish nationalist theoreticians of culture into line with a conception of the canon and, more generally, of aesthetic culture that is intimately linked to the legitimation of imperialism and to that mode of internal political hegemony, liberal democracy, which corresponds within the nation-state to global imperial domination. If, incidentally, a formal alignment also appears between nationalist and unionist programs, this is precisely because the latter is itself developed as a means of exercising or of maintaining hegemony.

Another mode of minor writing could nonetheless emerge from the same set of historical circumstances, one in every respect opposed to what Gilles Deleuze and Félix Guattari have dubbed the dream of fulfilling "a major language function."[4] But in order to define the characteristics of this other minor literature adequately, as in order to understand the extension of hegemony through nationalism itself, it is necessary to understand the historical emergence of a particular matrix of qualities according to which major or canonical works are themselves defined to the exclusion of a minor literature. We must also examine the ideological function this institution performs in spite of its ostensibly apolitical nature.

It is not, of course, that distinctions between "good" and "bad" literature have not been made in periods before that with which we are here concerned. It is, rather, that one needs to grasp the criteria that determine the constitution of a canon at any juncture, and to grasp those criteria in relation to the general ideological forms that legitimate domination in any given historical moment. For the most part, recent writing on the question of minor literature has tended not to emphasize the historical determinants of the institution of criticism, according to which the distinction between the major and the minor work is posited. This is the case with Louis Renza's recent study, *"A White Heron" and the Question of Minor Literature*, whose introduction valuably traces the definition of minor literature within critical discourse from Frye through Bloom and Jameson to Deleuze and Guattari.[5] For in delaying discussion of the *political* function of the evaluations he critiques, Renza defers analysis of the ideological function of the canon and therefore also blurs the distinction that continually haunts his work, that between a radically minor literature and one that is still seeking to "fill a major function."

But where Renza's work merely comes short of the necessary analysis, the work of the currently most influential American theorist of major writing is thoroughly obscurantist. For Harold Bloom's theories of the "anxiety of influence," remaining totally subordinate to an existent canon, are unable to do more than blandly note the historical coincidence by which the phenomenon is only to be traced in writers of the post-Enlightenment period.[6] Failing to locate historically the conditions of the particular mode of subjectivity that is required as the object of his quasi-Freudian theory, Bloom's accounts of the agonistic development of autonomous personality merely recapitulate, with strenuous pathos, accounts of individual development that can be traced back to precisely the period from which Bloom would date the origins of the anxiety of influence. Since, in this initial form, the typology of individual development implies and is contained by a universal history of the race, Bloom's obliviousness to this relationship mystifies the virtually organic degeneracy that he envisages to be the lot of poetry and permits the unreflective ethnocentricity and authoritarianism of his theory. Historical obliviousness of this nature may self-servingly enhance the comfortable allure of producing esoteric doctrine, but only at the expense of entirely obscuring the political function of culture.[7]

To produce an adequate theory of minor literature in any sense of the term, it is necessary to analyze historically the politics of culture. Deleuze and Guattari's work goes some way toward engaging this issue, though impressionistically and largely only synchronically. What they valuably indicate, however, is the extent to which recent interest in the question of "minor" literature recognizes the prior emergence of a combative field of literature that is expressly political insofar as the literature of the Third World, of "minorities" or formerly marginalized communities, calls into question the hegemony of central cultural values. A retrospective, even belated, analysis discovers in articulating the political structure of the canon the terms of an aesthetic culture that have already been negated by a new literature.

ARNOLD AND CELTIC LITERATURE

For the sake of clarity, it is perhaps helpful to state at this point that the term "culture" will be used throughout as implying its relationship to a general idealist conception of aesthetics and of aesthetic education or *Bildung:* aesthetic culture is not to be understood merely as the cultivation of a taste for the beautiful, but as invoking a concept of man in general as producer of form, and as producer, in particular, of the forms of himself through an aesthetic labor that transcends specific economic or political determinants. That is to say, aesthetics posits the universal formal identity of the human. This general understanding of culture envisages it as both the *domain* of reconciliation and as an instrument *productive* of reconciliation. It will be seen to involve a particular concept of representation that is at once aesthetic and political and that involves crucially a notion of historical development that provides the rationale for both the integrity of the canon and the integration of the State.

Matthew Arnold's *On the Study of Celtic Literature* is neither the first nor the last text that subordinates a colonized people's culture and literature to the major canon by stereotyping the essential identity of the race concerned. Indeed, as we shall see later, his work already renovates a mode of Irish unionist thinking that was perhaps best represented by Samuel Ferguson in the 1830s. Both their arguments start from their refusal to contemplate the fragmentation of the Empire by the "separation" of its Celtic domains. At the same time, however, *Celtic Literature* rejects coercion as a remedy for the refractoriness of the Celt. It seeks, rather, to formulate a via media between these two poles. Both coercion and separation as solutions depend on an identical proposition that at once asserts and perpetuates the notion of difference. In each case, the Celt is irredeemably other, recognizes himself as other, and, in the struggle for national identity, clearly turns the effort of self-definition around the assertion of his radical otherness to the Empire. In the case of coercion, the other is to be repressed within the imperial state, returning perpetually, to the quiet desperation of the conservative, as a disruptive force which can only be met with violence, since its own violence is the expression of an *essential* otherness to civilization. In the case of separation, difference is recognized and expelled, diminishing the whole of the Empire as the cost of preserving its identity and unity.

Arnold's via media, passing through the transcendent domain of aesthetic culture, aims, rather, at producing identity, a process that may be long-drawn-out but will be, precisely as a process, reconciling in its effects. As he puts it summarily at the end of the introduction:

> Let the Celtic members of this empire consider that they too have to transform themselves. . . . Let them consider that they are inextricably bound up with us, and that, if the suggestions in the following pages have any truth, we English, alien and uncongenial to our Celtic partners as we may have hitherto shown ourselves, have notwithstanding, beyond perhaps any other nation, a thousand latent springs of possible sympathy with them.[8]

The argument, which commences from a de facto bondage of the Celt to the Empire, is that coercion that is not an obtrusive imposition can be converted into sympathy, that bondage can be converted into the bonds of a kinship that is at once deeper than and prior to actual differences.

Arnold's argument revolves, in other terms, around the notion of assimilation in the fullest sense of that word. Assimilation, in its common if not its earliest usage, implies precisely the bonding of Celt and Empire that Arnold asserts to be inextricable, and the term suggests that the process is one in which the smaller part is absorbed into the larger whole. The digestive metaphor implicit in the word embodies the relationship of power and consumption involved. It suggests equally the kind of transformation of the colonial subject, his breaking down or disintegration, that is the necessary prelude to his total identification with or absorption into the imperial state. Arnold seeks to elude the submerged violence of the term by constantly invoking the root meaning of the word "assimilation" precisely where his intent is to expose common roots. For Arnold's desire is as much to assimilate the English to the Celtic as the Celtic to the English. The process, it appears, will be reciprocal, as Celt and Englishman will come to like one another if they are shown how originally alike they are and if they seek to develop that obscured likeness. In the process of assimilation, of course, it is still the case that the Celt will be absorbed into the political English Empire, which in turn will be made more complete by the absorption of what had formerly seemed alien and different.

It becomes important at this juncture to note a slippage in the oppositions that structure Arnold's text, a slippage which is crucial and enabling for the full development of his narrative argument. His argument throughout is structured around a mobile series of interrelated oppositions based on concepts of essential ethnic types. These include, of course, the Germanic or Teutonic and the Gallic, the Latin and the Greek, and the Hellenic and the Semitic, as well as the oposition between Celtic and English which we have already observed.[9] The most important of them, for Arnold's purposes, distinguishes between Anglo-Saxon and Celt, and it is here that the slippage referred to occurs. Politically speaking, Arnold is concerned with how to effect the assimilation of the Celt into the English Empire, yet through the greater part of the argument, the term Anglo-Saxon is substituted for English with a number of effects that are both rhetorical and narrative in form.

Arnold's racial discriminations depend on an ethnography and a philology whose narrative formalizes a set of distinct racial essences that provide — to invoke the organic metaphor always implicit — like seed to plant the principles upon which the distinguishing characteristics of any race evolve:

> Modern science is equally interested in knowing how the genius of each people has differentiated, so to speak, this common property of theirs; in tracking out, in each case, that special "variety of development" which, to use Mr. Nash's own words, "the formative pressure of external circumstances" has occasioned; and not the formative pressure from without only, but also the formative pressure from within.
>
> (*SCL*, p. 325)

In the play of difference and identity, the essential racial "genius" is both secretly operative in producing differences between races and legible in the actual characteristics by which racial identities are known.

In the case of the Celt, that essential and differentiating quality is defined by Arnold as "sentiment":

> *Sentiment* is . . . the word which marks where the Celtic races really touch and are one; sentimental, if the Celtic nature is to be characterized by a single term, is the best term to take. An organization quick to feel impressions, and feeling them very strongly; a lively personality therefore, keenly sensitive to joy and sorrow; this is the main point.
>
> (*SCL*, p. 343)

But it is not simply that the Celtic genius is sentimental; along with that sentimentality goes the Celt's readiness "to react against the despotism of fact," a phrase that Arnold translates from Henri Martin and repeats ad nauseam throughout. Implicit in this negative quality are a number of related characteristics. In the aesthetic domain, the Celt has not sufficient grasp of measure, of the architectural capacity, to produce a sustained work of art, and is confined to the production of elaborate impressionism. In the domain of "material civilization" it is, Arnold remarks, "the sensuousness of the Celt proper [that] has made Ireland"; with the equally sensuously based achievements of the Greeks and Romans, we have only to compare "the Celt's failure to reach any material civilization sound and satisfying, and not out at elbows, poor, slovenly, and half barbarous" (*SCL*, pp. 345 – 46). Ineffectual in aesthetic and material culture, the Celt is equally "ineffectual in politics" (*SCL*, p. 346), and it is here that Arnold arrives at the crux of his argument.

Their incapacity for sustained formative work having been made manifest in the aesthetic sphere, which already provides the criteria by which formal development is seen as the measure of political maturity, the Celtic peoples must perforce subordinate themselves to peoples whose "genius" is more politically, formatively, directed. Whereas the Celt's individuality is swallowed up in sentimental devotion to leaders, it is precisely the propensity to *self*-discipline that assures the retention of individuality by the Anglo-Saxon type even where he submits to the restraining force of the law. In the fullest sense, the Anglo-Saxon type furnishes the essential qualities that are the civil substrate of the modern state. Temperamentally defined by "energy with honesty," the Anglo-Saxon represents the energies of progressive industrialism, founded on practicality or, in opposition to the Celt, "matter-of-factness": he is driven by the individualistic dream of self-creation through labor.

It is important to stress here that the Anglo-Saxon type can provide only the substrate of the modern state and that the discipline to which the Anglo-Saxon is willing to subordinate himself must come from elsewhere. For the Anglo-Saxon race does not represent the whole into which the only partially formed Celts must be absorbed; the Celtic, indeed, must complement the Anglo-Saxon by infusing that sense of mystery and sentiment which the humdrum Anglo-Saxon lacks. It is precisely in the synthesis of the two opposed racial types that a more inclusive whole will be produced. The greater whole that is to be produced in such syntheses approximates progressively to a state that Arnold defines ethnically or philologically as the "Indo-European" and culturally as "imaginative reason." The latter of these terms emerges in *Culture and Anarchy* as the spiritual disposition that is to be cultivated in the domain of culture.

The necessity of assimilating Celt and Anglo-Saxon is thus governed in Arnold's argument by considerations that exceed the immediate and practical desire to offer a solution to "England's difficulty in ruling Ireland" (*SCL*, p. 392). It is predicated on a fuller schema that invokes an ethical progression of both race and individual toward an ever more harmonious condition, which will come to be defined as the state of culture. An aesthetic notion of the telos of historical evolution thus governs Arnold's ethnography insofar as it is directed from the start toward the production of such a "state of culture." In this state, difference is transcended not so much by its annulment as by reconciliation, since the "imaginative reason" refuses any relationship to its objects that would be based on either separation or coercion. It involves precisely a subordination of the self to the state of facts in order that the self should come into greater self-possession. It involves, as Arnold constantly stresses in *Culture and Anarchy*, the ability to "see things as they really are."

But the significance of the "science of origins" for Arnold is precisely that it claims to provide not only an account of things as they really are, and in that case will be augmented by the simple act of applying itself to the study of the Celt, but, moreover, an account of the "tendency" of things, elucidating at once how things have been and what things will become. Concerned on the face of it with the question of difference or differentiation, philology emerges finally as the science of identity. As Arnold puts it: "Science has been and will long have to be a divider and a separatist, breaking arbitrary and fanciful dreams of a premature and impossible unity. Still, science — true science, — recognizes in the bottom of her soul a law of ultimate fusion, of conciliation" (*SCL*, p. 330). Actual difference is formally reduced to a mode of identity by way of a similar differentiation out of the same root. Thus, even when concerned with differentiation, this science of origins knows always that it is at bottom concerned with the reproduction of an identity and is governed by a law of fusion that operates at once retroactively and projectively.

Arnold draws on a teleology that seems persuasive by virtue of its familiarity and by the apparent possibility of generalizing it from the individual to the species as a fundamental law. The teleological form of things is the movement from an undifferentiated origin through differentiation to a state of reconciliation that self-consciously repeats the unity and identity of its origin. If the process of differentiation is envisaged as a diminishment through fragmentation, it is in turn productive of the greater self-possession of the ultimate state of unity, which will, as we have seen, be the fulfillment of aesthetic cultivation. Pending this, neither Celts nor Anglo-Saxons can in themselves represent a complete state: both are fragmentary by virtue of their differentiation out of the common root, the Indo-Aryan race. But in the end, what is realized in their synthesis is simultaneously the faculty of "imaginative reason" which was already the defining quality of the Indo-European as opposed to the Semitic or the Mongolian type.[10] Furthermore, and the full imperialism of Arnold's thinking is implicit in this aspect of his argument, the English race, when fully realized as the reconciliation of these disparate strains, is itself the synthetic approximation to the Indo-European root.

It is an aspect of the temporal form of Arnold's argument that the nature of Englishness appears, at first, only as an approximation to the Indo-European, a synthesis which has yet to be completed, and second, that such total Englishness has only been realized occasionally. It is here that the function of prefiguration emerges as crucial in the aesthetic domain. The object of philology is, of necessity, the written, and it is accordingly always in literature that it locates the essential and defining genius of a race.[11] Seeking the evidence of the synthesis that constitutes the English race, it is to literature that Arnold turns, only to find that the degree to which his examples are representative of the English genius as a whole rises in direct proportion to their canonical status. If Byron manifests a predominance of the Celt's "Titanism" in revolt against the despotism of fact and is accordingly found wanting ethically for the same reason that the Celt is, Shakespeare, by virtue of seeming to synthesize the qualities of so many different racial elements in his work, provides the most total expression of the reconciled strains of English genius. Each writer's work, to a greater or lesser degree, prefigures the ultimate unity or synthesis of ethnic types in the production of which his works participate both as evidence and as influence. The aesthetic work, exactly to the extent that it is a product of "imaginative reason," represents in itself a unity that is prior to it while at the same time, by drawing together disparate ethnic characteristics, prefigures the future self-reflexive realization of that unity. The more entirely a work fulfills these requirements, the higher its canonical status is held to be; the minor work, on the other hand, derives its negative valence, almost theologically, from its distance from the integrated identity it ought to embody and prefigure.

For Arnold, literature is the purest expression of the character of any nation, and through aesthetic criticism he can identify momentary reconciliations of the different components of the English race and Empire that suggest the possibility of their ultimate total harmonization; through the influence of literature, in turn, the reconciliation here prefigured will be produced in its total form. More deeply implicit in this argument is an aesthetic conception of history as a narrative of the production of an harmonious state of culture. This coincides with a congruent conception of aesthetic history, the history of forms or genres as a progressive evolution from the simple to the complex, from the savage or barbarous to the civilized. This universal history of the race is replicated in the history of the individual in the course of his cultivation into the "best self," that self in which the individual's identifications are with the interests of the state, itself ideally representative of the general interest of the race.

Writing in the 1860s, Arnold has at his disposal a discursive configuration in which philology, ethnology, and historiography are linked with aesthetic criteria in a manner so entirely assumed that it never seems necessary for him to reflect critically upon his premises. A full treatment of this configuration would necessitate a political history of German idealism, whose influence on nineteenth-century thinking throughout Europe in both political and aesthetic theory is immeasurable. Here it will be sufficient to address the question through the work of Friedrich Schiller, whose founding role for German aesthetic thinking was recognized already in his own time by Hegel, among others. Schiller's work is particularly important here in that, like Arnold in his turn, his appeal to aesthetic cultivation is a direct response to the desire to forge a unified German state out of its historical disunity.[12]

AESTHETIC EDUCATION
AND THE IDEA OF THE STATE

It is no accident that the aesthetic history that structures and justifies Arnold's evolutionary ethnography is reminiscent of Friedrich Schiller's essay *On Naive and Sentimental Poetry*. Schiller's argument, as extensively and variously disseminated in Britain as elsewhere in Europe, provides the canonical form for the vision of an historical development of humankind from a postulated epoch of harmony or identity with nature, through the self-conscious or "sentimental" awareness of difference, and toward an epoch of regained harmony that is posited as being all the more valuable for its ideal and ultimately unrealizable status. The form of *On Naive and Sentimental Poetry* is further canonical by virtue of the dual status of its narrative: on the one hand, this narrative is historical, postulating an actual transformation of human consciousness between the period of classical Greece and the Europe of the 1790s; on the other hand, the narrative is allegorical or typological, explicitly furnishing an idealized picture of human consciousness that is not necessarily congruent in every stage with actual history or with the characteristics of the writers of any given historical period. It is doubly typological. Human history prefigures the form of each individual's history in the course of his maturation; but in turn it is the maturation of the individual that provides the adequate figure for the course of human history. Each in turn is congruent with the development of aesthetic categories or genres which are seen to express discrete stages in the maturation of human consciousness from naïveté to self-consciousness.

If *Naive and Sentimental Poetry* is figurative in this dual sense, its "master allegory" is furnished by the virtually contemporary *Letters on the Aesthetic Education of Man*, the prescriptive form of an argument that in the other essay appeared as a diagnostic.[13] For in *On the Aesthetic Education of Man* Schiller is concerned to establish the preeminent necessity of aesthetic education in the effort to create the rational political State. Confronted with the political turmoil of his time, Schiller is concerned with "that most perfect of all works to be achieved by the art of man [*mit dem vollkommensten aller Kunstwerke*]: the construction of true political freedom."[14] But in doing so, his attention is turned not to political theory in the most obvious or common sense, but to the establishment of the principle "that if man is ever to solve that problem of politics in practice, he will have to approach it through the problem of the aesthetic, because it is only through Beauty that man makes his way to Freedom" (*AEM*, p. 9).

Schiller's stated goal or, rather, that which he attributes to aesthetic work, is the restoration of man's wholeness in order "to restore by means of a higher Art the totality of our nature which the arts themselves have destroyed" (*AEM*, p. 43). What is crucial to his argument is the assertion that the rational State can only be created once "the split within man is healed, and his nature so restored to wholeness that it can itself become the artificer of the State" (*AEM*, p. 45). Aesthetic education *and* the

State it will produce are to harmonize the relationship of the individual with society and to harmonize the individual within himself by restoring his ethical relationship to the essential nature of humanity of which the rational State must be an expression. Aesthetics performs this function by virtue of representing the common property of human beings, just as Arnold's "imaginative reason" stood as both the "Indo-European" ground that defined the common property of differentiated races and the means to reproduce itself as the common property of all men in the ultimate state of culture.

The aesthetic, both as object and as experience, constitutes a common property of man in two ways. It is, at first, a common property by virtue of being not an object of desire, but an object of contemplation: "Contemplation (or reflection) is the first liberal relation which man establishes directly with the universe around him. If desire seizes directly upon its object, comtemplation removes its object to a distance, and makes it into a true and inalienable possession by putting it beyond the reach of passion" (*AEM*, p. 183). In this sense, by opening up a sphere in which appropriation is impossible and in which the paradigm of human freedom is expressed, the aesthetic relation prefigures the ideal republic of the rational State. But if it is the case that "only the aesthetic mode of communication unites society, because it relates to that which is common to all" (*AEM*, p. 215), this is so because aesthetic experience is subjectively also a "common property" of man: it is an inalienable possession precisely because it embodies the essence of the human, because it is the only relation in which the individual and the essential concept of the species are identical: "Beauty alone do we enjoy at once as individual and as genus [*Gattung*], i.e., as representatives of the human genus" (*AEM*, p. 217).

We encounter again here the notion of the *representativeness* of the individual when he is engaged in aesthetic work or experience. We find here also a problem, but a problem in the form of a contradiction that is constitutive of Schiller's aesthetic theory. For aesthetic experience is a common property of the human species only as a pure potential, and it is an essential part of Schiller's argument that aesthetic feeling may not be developed at all in the savage and is scarcely more than embryonic in the barbarian or in the bourgeois. Once again, the history of the generic individual repeats a history, explicitly ideal but nonetheless grounded in ethnological prejudices, which is that of the species. But it is precisely in the still contingent assertion that the savage or the sensuous man is as yet unable to experience the aesthetic that we can grasp the logic of representation that determines the political function of aesthetic theory in a way that is more than contingent.

The theory of aesthetic experience that Schiller develops depends entirely on a formalization through which alone it can come to be an essential and universal human property. Through this formalization, the individual experience is evacuated of its specific content so that the individual can become representative of the genus. This is of course essential to Schiller's argument insofar as the rational State can only come about with the willed self-subordination of each individual to the general will. But in this respect also the prefigurative aspect of the aesthetic relation, its establishment as a *possibility* of a state of freedom, and the representative nature of the aesthetic individual become identical. The representative individual is at once the type of the human species and the embodiment of the aesthetic state in which the unity of the human experience is expressed as an ideal:

> Each individual human being, one may say, carries within him, potentially and prescriptively, an ideal man, the archetype of a human being, and it is his life's task to be, through all his changing manifestations, in harmony with the unchanging unity of this ideal. This archetype, which is to be discerned more or less clearly in every individual, is represented by the State, the objective and, as it were, canonical form in which all the diversity of individual subjects strive to unite.
>
> (*AEM*, p. 17)

The rational State and the aesthetic experience in which the individual becomes representative of the species or of the human archetype are seen as identical. The archetypal or representative man is thus to be understood as the fulfillment of the stereotype as well as its opposite. For where the stereotype is an image of the primitive as already differentiated into a partial or fragmentary form, the archetype represents the total essence of the human by virtue of its purely formal identity.

In one of the earliest theoretical elaborations of the social function of aesthetics in the bourgeois state, therefore, the concept of the State and the concept of aesthetic culture are seen to be in a far more than contingent relationship. Nowhere is this clearer than in the ideological function and effect of the concept of the representative man in both aesthetic and political theory. Both the idea of the harmonizing force of aesthetic culture and the concept of the State as the expression of the unity of the human race arise in response to the need to provide, theoretically at least, a means to reconcile the inevitably conflicting and potentially anarchic forces of bourgeois civil society. The ideology of bourgeois individualism depends on the positing of a society composed of prior and autonomous individuals defined by their differences. In order to posit this, however, it is essential to define freedom purely formally and in abstraction from specific conditions; to define freedom, that is, in *aesthetic* terms. The effect, which may be seen at once as contradictory and as constitutive of bourgeois ideology, is the creation of a single type for human individuality in which the specific differences that might characterize human experience are annulled. The totalizing drive of culture and its need of central standards demand that the essence of the human be seen as universal and that whatever deviates from that central archetype be seen as incompletely developed historically rather than as radically different.

The form of thinking that thus interlocks the political and the aesthetic within the concept of representation, and legitimates that concept by an overarching universal history that defines the achievement of freedom as an evolutionary process, is entrenched in British cultural and political theory at both its liberal and its conservative pole. In *On the Constitution of Church and State*, a text inspired by anxiety as to the possible effects of Catholic emancipation on the integrity of the Empire and therefore profoundly influential on Irish unionist thinking, Samuel Taylor Coleridge argues for the continuity between the ethical representativeness of the clerisy and their capacity to "draw out the latent man" in every individual, thus converting the native into the citizen. The argument is framed within the "long duration" of man's evolution from savagery to civilization and of the gradual approximation through history of the constitution to its "idea."[15]

In turn, John Stuart Mill argues in *Representative Government*, a text recognizably influenced by Coleridge's thinking, that the form of representative government is the highest ideal toward which the historical evolution of the human race is directed, thereby justifying the colonial administration of peoples defined as savage or barbarian in the interests of their more rapid development toward self-representation. But within the state that has already attained the stage of representative government, that narrative is replicated within the framework offered by the theory of culture. Men of culture are accorded a greater voice in the election of representatives on the grounds that they are already in themselves, by virtue of their cultivation, more representative: they are able to rise above private interests in the ethical recognition of the general interest. Ironically, this argument emerges in the chapter entitled "On the Representation of Minorities," which thereby succeeds in redefining actual minorities as preeminently that numerical minority of the educated who determine the cultural norms by which, in effect, ethnic and sexual minorities as well as the working classes are excluded from full political or cultural participation.[16]

Thus Arnold, considering himself as representative aesthetic man, is by no means alone in considering himself entitled to represent both Celt and Philistine to themselves and to each other: he embodies the formal and prefigurative realization of their ideal and *arche*typal unity, while they, stereotyped as partial, and still submerged in either a sensuous or an overly purposive relation to their objects, are as yet unable to represent themselves. Aesthetic history, in which the aesthetics of politics is grounded, plays a crucial ideological role in underwriting the history of the gradual realization of that formal essence, which exists as potential from all time, through the increasing subjectivization of aesthetic experience. The history of the species (*Gattung*) is a history of genres (*Gattungen*). And if that history is also the history of the production of reconciliation, it is the production of reconciliation in the State envisaged as the "canonical form in which all the diversity of individual subjects strive to unite." It is the history of canon formation. The canon is not merely analogous to the State, nor is it a contingent product of an arbitrary attempt to establish order and hierarchy to perpetuate the mediation of values. A major literature is established as such precisely by virtue of its claim to representative status, of its claim to realize the autonomy of the individual subject to such a degree that that individual subject becomes universally valid and archetypal. The subjection of the reader to this canonical form, the alienation of his or her autonomy in the aesthetic work, is as intrinsic an element of the functioning of a major literature as is its perpetuation of the concept of the autonomous subject as the essence of the human. It is to the simultaneous critique of both these aspects of a major literature, to the critique of the politics of aesthetics and of the aesthetics of politics, that any minor or minority literary theory and practice will have to be directed.

DEFINING MINOR LITERATURE

The foregoing analysis makes it possible to sketch a paradigm of the characteristics of a major work of literature. The first characteristic, which largely determines the rest, is that the major work should be in some manner directed toward the production of an autonomous ethical identity for the subject. This demand is realized in the narrative mode manifest in the novel, most evidently in the bildungsroman, but also in the implied narratives of transcendence in the lyric poem which, perhaps precisely because of its suppression of apparent narrative, furnished the critical center of literary theory until relatively recently.[17] Alongside the narrative representation of the attainment of autonomy emerges the requirement that the work itself be autonomous, both self-contained and original, where the latter term implies the re-creation at a higher level of the original identity of the race. For the reader of such narratives, the ethical disposition is elicited precisely through identification, which allows both the "extension of sympathy," in George Eliot's famous phrase, and elevation above private interests through taking the place of another.

Accordingly, since ethics involves the capacity to judge as from the perspective of archetypal man, and since the aesthetic experience is the mode in which that perspective is most purely achieved, the writer as writer appears as representative man, and the work as a representation of representative human experience. Hence it is that the question of the writer's moral disposition, which largely preoccupies Victorian poetic theory, is always addressed through the work and never through the actual life of, say, Shelley or Burns. For it is exactly insofar as the writer represents not only his own private experience but "elementary human passions" that he becomes both representative and canonical.[18]

The definition of the major work consequently rests on the double meaning of the expression "common property." In the first place, it represents the common properties, the essential passions, of human beings, implying the universality of the forms of human nature. In the second, since the representation of common human nature is implicitly ethical, the major work asserts its disinterest, to borrow Arnold's term. The aesthetic domain within which the major work takes its place transcends political, racial, and class differences but it is, as we have seen, precisely from this disinterest or indifference that it gains its hegemonic force. Predicated on the notion of universality, this aesthetic both legitimates and transmits the ethnocentric ideology of imperialism. In its very postulation of an eventual reassimilation of the racial or sexual other through historical development, the canon of culture permits and enacts the exclusion of that other as being a not yet fully realized form of humanity. Culture, moreover, gives the law for the form in which that humanity must — always asymptotically — approach realization.

Clearly enough, then, the primary feature of any literature that is to be defined as minor is its exclusion from the canon, an exclusion that may on the face of it be as much on the grounds of purely aesthetic judgments as on those of racial or sexual discrimination. Here one has the standard conception of minor literature as one that emulates but does not fully attain the qualities of a canonical literature. Accordingly, the literature of a minority group — most classically for this study, the literature of a nationalist minority — may well be minor in this standard sense, insofar as it seeks explicitly to embody the characteristics that constitute a major literature. It is possible that by default, as it were, and by virtue of its failure to achieve the autonomy that is required for canonical status, this literature may reveal some of the features that will be given as characteristics of a minor literature. Nonetheless, the negative possession of these features does not make it a minor literature in the stricter sense of the term.

If exclusion from the canon and, by extension, from the "canonical form" of the State gives the first condition for a minor literature, the second and definitive condition is that this literature remain in an oppositional relationship to the canon and the state from which it has been excluded. This opposition exceeds mere specularity insofar as the forms of its articulation call into question the very terms in which a canonical literature is defined. Thus the first characteristic of a major writing, the production of narratives of ethical identity, is generally refused in minor writing. Two examples may help to clarify this distinction. In Kafka's *The Castle,* a text central to Deleuze and Guattari's understanding of Kafka's minor status, K. ardently pursues recognition in the form of a social function (as a *functionary*). In a major novel, the narrative would tend to culminate in the achievement of K.'s desire, but here it is perpetually frustrated, with the effect that his identity as the land surveyor remains always in question and his identification with the functionaries of the Castle is never achieved. It is one of the minor felicities of this text that K. is in consequence continually referred to and addressed as "childlike," as a minor. Another example, doubly appropriate given the writer's displaced position as a "white negro" as well as a woman writer, would be Jean Rhys's *Wide Sargasso Sea*, in which the identity of Bertha Mason, *Jane Eyre*'s imprisoned madwoman, is written further and further into dissolution in a narrative that effectively reverses Jane's attainment of ethical autonomy in Bronte's novel. Common to these two minor texts is their refusal to constitute the narrative as productive. *The Castle* circulates around its eponymous destination with none of the sub-narratives ever succeeding in bringing K. closer to his goal or the reader to the "truth." *Wide Sargasso*

Sea refuses equally to produce an alternative identity for Bertha/
Antoinette that would save her from her "original" destiny.
Neither narrative leads anywhere, while at the same time it is the
very retention of a project aimed at securing identity that in both
cases creates a disjunction between the desire of the characters
and the effect of the text. This last feature, to which we will return,
is characteristic of the parodic mode of minor literature.

Neither the writers nor the central figures of either of these
texts accordingly make any claim to representative status. If in the
first place that lack of representativeness is the product of the
biographical alienation of a German-speaking Czech Jew or of a
Creole woman in a post-colonial Caribbean, what is crucial to
this definition of the minor status of their writings is their
common perpetuation of non-identity in their writings. That
neither narrative culminates in identifications, racial, sexual, or
social, that would stabilize identity prevents them from becoming
representative in the sense outlined above. Again, this refusal of
identity in each case circulates around an equivalent refusal to
ground the possibility of identity on the recovery of origins, a
strategy that evokes a critique of that narrative paradigm of major
literature, the reproduction of an original or essential identity at
a higher and self-conscious level.

If such minor narratives imply a critique of narratives of
identity, they equally refuse to represent the attainment of the
autonomous subjectivity that is the ultimate aim of the major
narrative. This refusal in the domain of what is represented is
replicated on the level of the modes of representation, insofar as
the minor text adopts writing strategies that are in some sense
defined by their dependence on prior texts. Those strategies
include parody, in the strict sense of a writing that is in a relation
simultaneously of dependence and opposition to its original;
translation, where it emerges as anti-philological in not returning
to the originating moment of its original; and citation, in the form
of an intertextuality not characterized by anxiety. Thus, for
example, it can be seen that both *The Castle* and *Wide Sargasso
Sea* can be conceived of as parodic, insofar as both depend on their
disjunctive relation to prior novelistic models — in the latter case
quite specifically — in order to "make sense," but neither seeks to

constitute an autonomous identity in transcendence of their initial dependence. Each of the modes of writing outlined above will be discussed at greater length in the context of Mangan's practices; it is only necessary here to stress that each immediately calls into question the mediation of autonomous objectivity through a continuously self-identical voice. Minor modes of writing, as the utterance of those excluded from representation, tend to undermine the priority given to distinctive individual voice in canonical criticism. They adopt, instead, modes of writing that are non-original and anaclitic even in their parodic mimicry of the major work, and in doing so commence the questioning of the founding principles of canonical aesthetic judgments.[19] The radical potential embedded in the critical stance of a minor writing is to be traced in the fact that, due to the interlocking with political and ethical domains that underlies the apparent autonomy of the aesthetic, a critique of the aesthetic opens out continually onto a critique of the assumptions that support the bourgeois state and legitimate its domestic and imperial hegemony.

A minor literature so defined overlaps in many respects with what has become known as modernism, and in most respects with post-modernism, as is evident given the examples just adduced. This overlap requires us to make a further set of distinctions within both these taxonomies of modern literature. If minor literature belongs in the general field of modernism, it does so only as the negative critical aspect of modernism. In other words, wherever the writer continues to conceive the work as playing in some sense a prefigurative and reconciling role, that work remains, whatever its stylistic features, assimilated to a canonical aesthetic. Hence modernists such as Eliot, Pound, and Yeats clearly belong within a major paradigm by right of the claims to transcending division and difference that constantly inform their works.

This ascription evidently initially has to ignore the difficulties these writers have in maintaining such claims in their historical moment, and to overlook the "minor" stylistic features to which they constantly have recourse. But these stylistic features, as well as the frequent histrionics that accompany the assertion of the transcendence of the aesthetic domain in such writers, are symptomatic of a crisis of canonicity that is definitive of modernism itself. That crisis arises out of the gradual marginalization of aesthetic culture, a marginalization largely due to the democratization of education and of politics as well as to the massive growth of the recreational culture industry. Marginalization is, however, also inscribed in the very logic of the representative "alien" that typifies the discourse of culture, just as its displacement by so-called mass culture may appear as a grotesque parody of the demand of men of culture for the assimilative extension of culture to the masses. In a sense, aesthetic culture is overtaken by the success of its own project: the "recreation" industry, in which the specialized worker sheds his economic identity in order to identify democratically with the masses, comes to fulfill the cultural project of recreating an essential human identity in a domain that transcends economic and political differences. If this leaves the "unacknowledged legislators" with neither function nor constituency, it is only too frequently their resource to turn to a mode of politics in which the aesthetic and the political are most completely identified, that is, fascism. The political efficacy of fascism resides in its promise of individual self-realization through total identification with the race at just the moment when the autonomy of the individual can be perceived to have been eroded, along with civil society, by the emergence of corporate power. Accordingly, reactionary modernism turns to fascism in order to shore up an aesthetic that has been superseded by the achievement in the economic sphere of that homogenization which it sought ideally to produce in an ethical form.

Radical modernism has been conceived as the critique by art of the institution of art, a definition that would certainly hold for its extreme manifestations in dada and surrealism.[20] In the general field of modernism, minor literature emerges as writing out the marginalization that afflicts aesthetic culture, and as extending, in writing it out, that condition of marginality. Rather than shore up the notions of subjectivity that underpin canonical aesthetics, and rather than claiming still to prefigure a reconciled domain of human freedom in creativity as even surrealism does, a minor literature pushes further the recognition of the disintegration of the individual subject of the bourgeois state, questioning the principles of originality and autonomy that underwrite that conception of the subject. In doing so, it plays out the contradictions that afflict late capitalist society through its paradoxical modes, refusing to offer the possibility of reconciliation. Minor literature adheres constantly to a negatively critical attitude.

Among the contradictions thrown up by the bourgeois state is that effect of hegemony already noted, namely, that the extension of colonial hegemony requires the creation of an educated native elite without the guarantee that mastery of the instruments of domination will assure assimilation. In the political sphere this has entailed the national liberation struggles of this century and the production of structural dependency as a further extension of hegemonic control. In the domain of culture, the effect of hegemony has been to produce a writing of the colonized that increasingly calls the coherence of the canon into question. What the current crisis, both for canonicity and for the definition of the object of literary studies, involves is the deferred recognition of the end of the canon itself as a viable normative institution. That crisis registers, if only symptomatically, the end of a conception of subjectivity that minor literature itself narrates. If minor literature brings us to the end of that conception of subjectivity and of representation, which is also its own conceptual limit, it may be that in turn the emergence of a Third World and post-colonial literature begins to constitute a literature of collectivity for which the canon as an institution and representation as a political and aesthetic norm would be irrelevant. Such a literature would entail the end of a minor literature just as it entails the end of canonicity, ironically at the very moment at which it has become possible for both to become distinct objects for criticism.

Minor literature belongs intrinsically to the literature of the period in which the democratic nation states emerged, and continually marks its limits and crises. This study focuses on a minor writer whose career represents a remarkably early instance of minor writing. It will become apparent that the reasons for this early manifestation of features that are often related to modernism—and in Mangan's case have explicitly been so related—lie in the special conditions created by Ireland's situation as a

European colony that entered its hegemonic phase early, and in the manner in which the peculiar exigencies of Irish nationalism caused a highlighting of the political function of aesthetic culture. It is in some senses a polemical act to retrieve Mangan's writings from their traditional relegation to canonically minor status and from their identification with Young Ireland nationalism. It is hoped that that polemic will mark the limits of readings based on canonical assumptions at the same time as it contributes to the demise of the canon as an instrument of cultural hegemony.

I

The Lives of James Clarence Mangan

THE BIOGRAPHICAL CANON

The coincidence of Mangan's life with the emergence of Irish nationalism, not to mention his occasional involvement in this movement, makes him a figure of evident importance for any attempt to understand the early history of Irish literature in English. His writing was, however, by no means confined to or always in conformity with nationalist concerns, and he published in journals that represented a range of political viewpoints. At various periods in his life he was associated with *The Comet,* an anti-tithe newspaper of the 1830s; the *Dublin University Magazine,* the organ of Tory unionism; and such Young Ireland journals as the *Nation* and the *United Irishman.* This ubiquity has enabled his appropriation by a series of biographers to instantiate their particular visions of proper Irish political or religious views, and occasionally to represent Ireland itself in struggle and in failure. At the same time, however, his very ubiquity makes Mangan elusive of such appropriations, with the result that none of the extant biographies provides an account of his life that can accommodate its often contradictory or inconsistent details. A preliminary work of critical biography is therefore required to displace the canonical image of Mangan, thereby clearing the ground for a fuller understanding of the relationship between his life in its historical context and his writings.

There is no lack of previously published accounts of Mangan's life. Rudi Holzapfel's *Check List of Sources* alone lists no fewer than thirty-eight articles and books that are primarily biographical in nature, and no doubt many others have escaped attention in small and little-known periodicals.[1] A difficulty of a different order has faced every one of Mangan's biographers, consciously or not, as John McCall noted as early as 1882: "They all invariably treat of the same main features of our poet's clouded career, chiefly made up from [John] Mitchel's work, stray paragraphs in penny magazines, and old newspaper extracts well known before to the reading public, while they leave the great Mangan's life, as one sublime whole, as great a myth as ever" (McCall, p. 3). Despite the appearance of D. J. O'Donoghue's major and reasonably trustworthy *Life and Writings of James Clarence Mangan* in 1897, McCall's charge remains substantially true.[2] A self-sustaining tradition of Mangan biography has emerged, in which each new production draws on its forebears with only slight factual variation, and rarely with any critical distance from the material on hand. Indeed, since McCall, very few new facts have come to light concerning details of Mangan's life. The few variations in the biographies appear to have emerged on account of differing prejudices rather than from a deliberate reappraisal of the few facts that can be corroborated and do not need to be balanced against possible bias, as do the individual testimonies of Mangan's acquaintances and friends. There are no journals, no regular records of payments, and scarcely any family records. A number of letters, mostly addressed to Charles Gavan Duffy, editor of the *Nation*, survive in the National Library, Dublin (NLI MS 138, fols. 6–20); some letters to James McGlashan, publisher of the *Dublin University Magazine*, are quoted extensively by James Price in his *Evening Packet* articles and by D. J. O'Donoghue in his *Life*, but probably the majority of Mangan's letters are as yet untraced. Furthermore, the extant letters belong without exception to the last four years of Mangan's life and are of little help in trying to establish his circumstances at crucial earlier periods. For his earlier life, as even O'Donoghue found (*Life*, p. xxi), one is obliged to rely on McCall, whose material, though often painstakingly researched, particularly with regard to the early Dublin periodicals, is equally often inaccurate.[3] However, some consensus exists over his statements concerning the circumstances of Mangan's family and his early life, which can be verified to a limited extent from existing public records. Beyond these sources there is little to rely on, and in the end it seems most likely that large areas of Mangan's life will remain undocumented.

The problem for the critical biographer is that in the case of Mangan one is quite clearly dealing with a mythology, in the sense of a body of accounts whose structure conforms in the first place to a certain type rather than to researched fact. The various lives of Mangan are by and large reconstructions based on fairly meager data and betray considerable investment in the perpetuation of the myth of "poor Mangan." Even O'Donoghue, though generally restrained and sober in his speculations, has a tendency to fill up the "vacuum and obscure gulf" (*Poems* 1859, p 11) of portions of Mangan's life with an unsubstantiated fabric of economic and psychic destitution, despite having sufficiently demonstrated how little evidence there is for Mangan's poverty.[4] Given the extent to which such a myth determines his biographers' readings of the few facts that can be relied upon and their speculations regarding those that cannot, it is essential to pare down the material we have to the most basic outline in order to highlight the transformation of fact into myth. Since the idea of the suffering poet recurs frequently in Mangan's writings (and in turn gives impetus to his biographers' speculations about his life), such a paring down helps to indicate the degree of deliberate appropriation involved in both autobiographies and biographies.

That Mangan indeed registered a chronic sense of psychic wretchedness throughout his life is scarcely in question, though it is of course difficult to ascertain how far a literary posture is involved here. Chronic as his psychic pain may have been, it is constantly associated by Mangan's biographers with hypothetical economic and material deprivation. In the last few years of Mangan's life — the worst, also, of the Irish famine — his condition was certainly desperate. Due to his political sympathies, according to some accounts, he lost his job in Trinity College library, while the suppression of the *Nation* and the *United Irishman* may have made his financial situation yet more precarious. Duffy claims that as a result of Mitchel's having published a letter of Mangan's offering him full support "for the achievement of our national independence," the writer "never had another day's tranquility or comfort. He lost his employment, he lost his self-respect, and for the few months that remained he became the shocking spectacle of weakness and degradation which inconsiderate critics have applied to his whole life."[5] In a letter to McGlashan, Mangan himself refers to this as the "darkest period of [his] life," and in another letter, written in an extremely shaky hand, begs Duffy to come, as he is "utterly prostrate." The extent of and reasons for Mangan's destitution will be discussed further on, but Duffy's point needs to be stressed: most of the material for Mangan's life dates from this last decade, and most of his biographers knew him only during these latter years. Their accounts of his life as a whole tend to be darkened by the shadows cast back from this period.[6] Furthermore, these last destitute years coincided with a crucial event in Irish history, the Famine, and with the political ferment that accompanied it, providing further reason to represent the poet as a fervent Irish nationalist at the last, as a devout Catholic despite his frailty, and as suffering for these convictions. The varying emphases of his biographers represent quite clearly their own specific investments, political, religious, or literary.

Mangan's own prose autobiographies are interesting in exactly this respect, written as they are at the end of Mangan's life but dealing primarily with his youth. The most important of these is the autobiographical fragment written for his friend and confessor, Father C. P. Meehan. Its exact date of composition is unknown, but as Mangan refers in it to his "Italian story of 'Gasparó Bandollo,'" published in the *Dublin University Magazine* of May 1849, it is unlikely to date from much before this time and probably belongs to the last months of his life.[7] The other, which also contains interesting material in the form of one of the few explicit self-criticisms of his work that Mangan provides, is what O'Donoghue refers to as the "impersonal autobiography," written as part of a series in the *Irishman* entitled "Sketches and Reminiscences of Irish Writers" and published posthumously in August 1850 (*IA*, pp. 27–28). One letter to McGlashan, on internal evidence probably written about May 1847, contains a long paragraph of autobiographical self-justification that agrees substantially with the others.[8] All, however, are heavily colored by his recent suffering and are not always consistent with one another. The autobiography attributes the origins of Mangan's chronic ill health to overwork as a youth in the scrivenery, aggravated by sharing a hospital bed with a leper; the letter ascribes it to the same cause, but this time aggravated by "that evil habit which has since proved so ruinous to me"; and the "impersonal autobiography" to a much earlier episode when he was sent out in the rain by a "hair-brained" [*sic*] girl to buy a ballad from a street singer. None of them is entirely reliable in even the most basic facts. In the autobiography, for example, Mangan claims to have been enrolled in Michael Courtney's Academy in 1820, when he was already seventeen and by his own account in the same autobiography would already have been at work for two years in the scrivenery. The letter to McGlashan similarly removes several years from his age, claiming that he was fifteen at the time of his father's financial ruin — given as 1824. Meehan refers to the autobiography as "the merest *Rêve d'une vie*, with here and there some filaments of reality in its texture" (*PPM* 1884, p. xxiv) and joins a celebrated footnote to Mangan's description of the "hovel" his family occupied in Chancery Lane (*A*, p. 19): "This is purely imaginary; and when I told Mangan that I did not think it a faithful picture, he told me he dreamt it" (*PPM* 1884, p. xli).

But though Mangan's biographers recognize the fantastic nature of his autobiographies, they all exhibit a tendency to take on something of his extravagance in the treatment of the material variously available and to add their own myths to Mangan's own. Mangan's autobiographies are singularly lacking in political commentary or in religious discussion beyond the immediate question of his own damnation. His biographers tend nonetheless to adduce religious and political positions with a confidence that Mangan's writings and actions scarcely permit and that other commentators frequently deny. The most significant and influential of Mangan's early biographers in this respect is John Mitchel, Young Irelander, editor of the extremist *United Irishman*, and later editor of the first American edition of Mangan's *Poems*. His introduction to this volume is a distinctly political biography. Mangan stands out against the imperialism of British criticism, which "completely . . . gives the law throughout the literary domain of the semi-barbarous tongue in which I have now the honour to indite." As Mitchel sees it,

> Mangan was not only an Irishman, — not only an Irish papist, — not only an Irish papist rebel; — but throughout his whole literary life of twenty years he never deigned to attorn to English criticism, never published a line in any English periodical, or through any English bookseller, never seemed to be aware that there was a British public to please. He was a rebel politically, and a rebel intellectually and spiritually, — a rebel with his whole heart and soul against the whole British spirit of the age.
>
> (*Poems* 1859, p. 8)

The duality ascribed to Mangan, between his shabby outer life and the inner and higher life of his spirit, "one well known to the Muses, the other to the police" (*Poems* 1859, p. 14), is explicitly the image of an Ireland outwardly oppressed but secretly, spiritually, alive, "for his history and fate were indeed a type and shadow of the land he loved so well" (*Poems* 1859, p. 15). Mitchel's purpose is to emphasize this duality at every point, and he accordingly produces the most heavily colored of any of the canonical accounts, stressing Mangan's destitution, drug addiction, and physical deterioration on the one hand, and his gentleness, political commitment, and "spirituality" on the other. Factually, the biography has little to offer that is not better documented elsewhere, the more so since Mitchel only knew Mangan in the last five or six years of his life. In other terms, the importance of the biography lies precisely in its extravagant typology — a point to which we shall return — and in the fact that its republication as the introduction to O'Donoghue's centenary edition of Mangan's poems has made it the most widely disseminated and canonical image of Mangan that exists.

Similar typological features also emerge in the biography prefixed to the third edition of the *Poets and Poetry of Munster* (1884) by Father C. P. Meehan, a priest of nationalist sympathies who wrote for the *Nation* under the pen-name "Clericus." Here, however, Mangan's degradation is posed against his depiction as a gentle and amiable sinner striving to keep within the folds of the faith, but in his "waywardness and irresolution" (*PPM* 1884, p. xvii) often going astray. Once again, Meehan's acquaintance with Mangan dates from the later years of his life, and, as with

Mitchel, the quasi-obituaristic status of the account provokes reservations concerning the strictness of his attachment to the facts. The next important version is John McCall's brief *Life* of 1822. His intimacy with the Dublin journals circulating during Mangan's early writing career and the detailed research recorded in several manuscript notebooks in the National Library give some reason for cautious attention to his deductions and assertions concerning Mangan's early years.[9] In many cases, particularly with regard to Mangan's parents, he is the only printed source available for the period. Even here, however, he is occasionally demonstrably wrong and has a tendency to flesh out good stories — such as the ballad episode mentioned above — without warrant. Though less emphatically, he shares some of the nationalistic and religious prejudices of Mitchel and Meehan. His sources in public houses seem at least to provide him with an oral tradition concerning Mangan's social life, as, for example, in his descriptions of occasional evenings the poet spent in the Wexford Street saloon with the novelist William Carleton and other writers (McCall, p. 26). Such accounts may stand as a useful corrective to the more puritanical extremism or evasiveness of other biographers.

Another corrective, though in the opposite direction, is provided by Charles Gavan Duffy, editor of the Belfast *Vindicator* and the *Nation*, and a personal friend of Mangan's at the same period as Mitchel and Meehan. Like the waning ardor of his nationalism, his sobriety is often due as much to propriety or to the length of the interval that elapsed before the writing of his account as to any more trustworthy grasp of biographical details.[10] The letters addressed to him from Mangan provide, however, the most useful single index of Mangan's state, physical and mental, at this time.

O'Donoghue's *Life*, the most substantial biography of Mangan to date, draws largely from all of these writers as primary sources, and is so far a trustworthy or untrustworthy account. He is considerably more committed to an objective study, and his conclusions seem on the whole the most judicious. Similarly, his accounts of Dublin housing conditions in various places where Mangan is known to have lived and his records of wages generally payable for Mangan's various employments are more useful than previous biographers' vague assertions of irredeemable poverty. However, as in the case of McCall, it is difficult to establish finally how much of his information is based on hearsay, more or less reliable. He quotes a number of accounts provided specially for his biography by contemporaries of Mangan, but these are frequently based on current rumor and on memories stretching back some forty years in many cases.

All of Mangan's biographies are thus affected to varying degrees by the problem that a lack of reliable information provokes reliance on an oral and undocumented tradition that gains the status of fact and is then transmitted as such. One is, in effect, approaching the interpretation of a hagiographical canon, which not only seeks to omit or discredit much counter-evidence but appears at times to involve a tradition without verifiable sources. In such a case, it is always the structuring of the myth and its relation to the ideological interests that produce it that are of final importance. In the elucidation of those relations, the very areas of doubt concerning the facts behind the myth are frequently crucial aids to interpretation insofar as they throw the reconstructive play of the biographer into relief.[11]

THE FAMILY FORTUNES

Mangan was born in Dublin at 3 Fishamble St. on 1 May 1803, second son of a schoolteacher, James Mangan of Shanagolden, County Limerick, and of Catherine Smith, originally of Kiltale, County Meath. Despite a tradition, stemming at least from John O'Daly's brief biographical sketch prefatory to the first edition of the *Poets and Poetry of Munster*, which places their marriage in 1801, the father and mother were in fact married on 22 April 1798 in the parish of Saints Michael and John, and within a year had had one son, William. This first son has also gone unnoticed by subsequent biographers, who unanimously refer to Mangan as the eldest child. Born on 22 February 1799, William appears to have died in infancy, since a fourth son also christened William was born on 20 June 1808.[12] The father's background is difficult to assess due to the paucity of available information, but

O'Donoghue refers to him as "a man of some education and refinement" (*Life*, p. 2), while McCall describes him as "one of those ripe Munster scholars" (McCall, p. 3). Mangan's father would, it appears, have received his own education and perhaps taught in the informal "hedge schools" to which, as a result of the Penal Laws, the Catholic peasantry resorted. By all accounts these schools, for all their provisional nature, could furnish an excellent education in the classical and Gaelic traditions. It is clear from the writings of the time, particularly those of William Carleton, that the hedge schoolteacher tended to be held in some respect in the rural districts and to nurse considerable ambitions if he emigrated to the city.[13] Here may lie some of the reasons for the young Mangan's respect, however grudging, for his father's "princely soul" (Price, 22 September 1849), an attribute, according to Carleton, of many a hedge schoolmaster. McCall further speculates "that it was from this parent the son inherited that great natural poetical talent which he in after years displayed" (McCall, p. 3). Little more is recorded of the father, except that in marrying Catherine Smith he married into a grocery and spirits store at 3 Fishamble St.

Mangan's mother had come to Dublin "to superintend the business arrangements of the shop" (McCall, p. 3) on behalf of her recently widowed aunt, a Mrs. Farrell. The exact date of her move to Dublin has proved impossible to establish, but otherwise far more of her background is known than of that of the father. Her father was John Smith, "a respectable farmer and grazier at Kiltale near Dunsany, Co. Meath" (McCall, p. 3). The farm remains in family hands to this date, one of the farmhouses still much as it was in Mangan's time, a building of some substance. As graziers, the family would have been little affected by the slump in corn prices that followed the Napoleonic Wars, and during the Famine itself, in July 1847, they were capable of supporting Mangan during a six-week period of retreat after he had had a serious quarrel with his brother William in Dublin.[14] The family is indeed typical of a number of middle-class Catholic families of the time, whose prosperity grew, toward the end of the eighteenth century, out of the allied stock-rearing and provisions trades, which were among the few profitable occupations permitted to

Catholics under the Penal Laws.[15] In this particular case the trades were very closely allied, as the Smith family had long supplied the Fishamble Street grocery and continued to do so at least until the time of Mangan's death, shortly after which the prosperous business passed into the hands of cousins of the Smiths, named McNally.[16] One is dealing then, in the first year of Mangan's life, with a middle-class family of trading and farming stock, living, by Catholic standards of the time at least, in considerable prosperity.

That the Mangan fortunes subsequently underwent a serious decline is agreed by all sources, though its precise nature is so far impossible to establish. In both the autobiography and the letters to McGlashan, Mangan claims that this was due to his father's improvidence: "My father was a merchant of this city, and ruined himself by speculation. He had a princely soul but no prudence. It was when I was about fifteen years old that I awoke to a sense of the changes that had come over our household."[17] According to McCall, whom O'Donoghue follows (*Life*, pp. 4– 6), the grocery business prospered so well that the father decided to retire "with a competence" and began building speculations in the vicinity of the Bleeding Horse pub in Lower Camden Street.[18] A combination of failure here with his "habit of giving costly balls and parties" caused him to run rapidly through his "worldly effects" (McCall, p. 4). Concerning the first half of this story — the building speculation — no firmer documentary evidence has come to light than was available to O'Donoghue; concerning the account of the father's sociability, Mangan's own complaint of his "ardent and forward-bounding disposition" (*A*, p. 13) may bear it out. What is certain is that *Wilson's Dublin Directory* for the years 1806–1811 lists "Mangan, James" as grocer at 3 Fishamble St. and that from 1812 his name does not appear. From 1816, the same directory lists Patrick Smith as the proprietor of the premises, bearing out O'Donoghue's account that the latter, Catherine Smith's brother, was induced to come over from London to carry on the business till 1822 (see *Life*, p. 2). After this date, the premises cease to be listed under either name.[19]

None of the evidence thus available is conclusive concerning the Mangan family fortunes, though none of it contradicts the general outlines of the canonical accounts. The lack of hard information concerning the family, particularly during the period from 1825 until 1843, when the father died, constitutes the real "gulf" in Mangan's life. It is reasonable to accept that the Mangan family suffered a decline in fortunes during Mangan's youth, though to nothing like the extent that he suggests in the autobiography and in the letter to McGlashan. In all the auto-biographies Mangan constantly emphasizes the wretchedness of his childhood, not only through descriptions of his psychic condition, depressed as that was, but also through descriptions of his family home and environment that induce skepticism, at the least, in all of his biographers. Of the description of the "hovel" in Chancery Lane that inspired Meehan's footnote, O'Donoghue in turn remarks that "it is practically impossible that such a house (or part of a house) could have existed in that place at the time that Mangan lived in it" and, furthermore, that Chancery Lane was "a very 'respectable' place, indeed, in Mangan's early days" (*Life*, p. 12), a far cry from the doorless, windowless, stairless dens of the *Autobiography* (*A*, p. 19). O'Donoghue's research concerning the housing conditions in Chancery Lane at the time and McCall's statement that after the father's death the family "removed to more humble lodgings in Peter St., where they were still able to keep one servant" (McCall, p. 4) testify against so severe a collapse. Moreover, the impression, given by most of the biographies, of a semi-nomadic existence seems to have no substance. Before 1847–1848, the Mangan family are known to have used four addresses: 3 Fishamble St.; the house in Chancery Lane; Charlemont Street, where, according to T. D. Sullivan, Mangan's brother John died in May 1835; and 9 Peter St., whence Mangan addresses several letters to Duffy in 1846 (cf. NLI MS 138).[20] After this date, by all accounts, and perhaps after the death of his mother (which Sullivan gives as 1846 without a month), Mangan's life appears to have become more erratic, and his addresses more numerous.[21] His final address, where he was found before the illness that culminated in his death, was "an obscure house in Bride St." (*Poems* 1859, p. 19).

Furthermore, if McCall is correct in stating that the father died, "of a broken heart," shortly after his failure in trade (McCall,

p. 4), a considerable foreshortening of the period over which that
decline took place had occurred in his account, as in Mangan's
own. According to T. D. Sullivan, from information received
from a Mr. Coyle of the Catholic Cemeteries Company, the father
died at Peter Street in September 1843. A more protracted period
of successive declines might help to explain why, in the letter to
McGlashan, Mangan contradictorily states that it was at the age
of fifteen that he "awoke to a sense of the changes that had come
over our household" (a statement repeated in the autobiography,
A, p. 17) and that "this was in 1824," when he would in fact
have been twenty-one. As in 1823 the premises at 3 Fishamble St.
cease to be listed under either Mangan or Smith, it seems possible
that two separate crises are being conflated, one in 1818, the other
in 1823 or 1824. Certainly the decline in the family fortunes
coincides with a period of general economic depression in Ireland
whose impact on many middle-class Irish people was, as we will
see, one of the crucial factors in the rise of nationalism.[22]

Whether the family fortunes declined slowly over a long period, culminating in the father's death in 1843, or more abrupt-
ly, leaving a period of at least twenty-five years during which
nothing is known of the family bar Mangan's assertion that he
"toiled and toiled" on their behalf (Price, 22 September 1849),
there is little question that he began work as a scrivener's ap-
prentice in Kenrick's, 6 York St., in 1818, at the age of fifteen.
His own estimates with regard to the length of time he remained
there vary from three years according to the autobiography
(p. 19) to seven years according to the letter to McGlashan. The letter agrees with McCall's estimate (pp. 16–17), carefully calculated on the basis of Mangan's Almanack contributions and their
addresses, and from his friend and colleague James Tighe's
farewell poem to him (McCall, p. 17), that he ceased work there
in 1825. Independently of McCall, O'Donoghue confirms the
date of his termination of Kenrick's as 1825 (when the office in
fact closed) and adds that on the closure of Kenrick's Mangan
"moved to the office of a Mr. Franks in Merrion Square, and
thence proceeded to another office, kept by a Mr. Leland, in
Fitzwilliam Square . . . [where] he seems to have remained till
1836" (*Life*, p. 17).

Mangan appears, then, to have begun his career as a scrivener consequent on the decline of his father's fortunes. One inevitable and, for him, lamentable consequence was the premature cessation of his schooling, which had commenced at Michael Courtney's academy in Derby Square and continued, briefly, at William Brown's "classical and mercantile academy" at No. 14 Chancery Lane (McCall, p. 5). Enrollment at the latter institution indeed suggests that some such career as that of scrivener may not have been entirely unforeseen. Mangan claims, nonetheless, to have been appalled and traumatized by conditions in both workplaces, victimized and humiliated by his fellow clerks in the one, and even suffocated by chimney fumes in the other (*A*, pp. 18 and 26). Mangan asserts that he worked "from five in the morning (winter and summer) to eleven at night" (Price, 22 September 1849; *A*, p. 19), a claim irreconcilable with McCall's account of "many a convivial evening" at Bligh's bar on the North side of Dublin (McCall, p. 7). Suggestive though by no means conclusive evidence concerning this period is the letter from "D. C." to the *Nation*, 13 October 1849, which O'Donoghue cites. It asserts that the hours at which Mangan claims to have worked would have been impossible at that period in such an office, which would, moreover, have closed for four months during university vacations. Besides, on the basis of even the lowest recognized rate of pay, 9d. per hour, for such hours he would have been earning the "considerable amount per annum" — as O'Donoghue puts it — of £140.8 (*Life*, p. 16). Probably Price, an acquaintance of the Comet Club period of 1832 – 1833, is most accurate in estimating that his earnings with Leland "rarely amounted to 30s a week" (£40 per year) but "were still sufficient for his inexpensive and unpretending habits" (Price, 22 September 1849). This sum would certainly have been adequate, given that Emmet Larkin has calculated that the average per capita income of the Irish population was £6.7 in 1801, rising to £7.9 in 1851.[23]

The implication of the biographies that Mangan lived in virtually constant penury is thus scarcely borne out by what few facts can be established. In regular employment till 1836, he was thereafter writing constantly for the *Dublin University Magazine*, where the actual remuneration to Mangan is unknown but "was evidently sufficient to induce him to give up all work in attorney's offices" (*Life,* p. 78). Standard remuneration was reasonable at 16s. per sheet, though O'Donoghue claims Mangan did not receive this regularly, frequently selling himself short (*Life,* p. 78).

Apart from remuneration from various journals, Mangan found employment regularly (if not regular employment), first with the newly founded Ordnance Survey's topographical office from 1838 till its closure in 1841, and thereafter in Trinity Library till his dismissal in 1848. Both these jobs came through his friendships with the Irish scholars and antiquarians John O'Donovan and George Petrie. They had been joint editors of the *Dublin Penny Journal,* a journal aimed at disseminating knowledge of Irish antiquities, for which Mangan wrote in the early thirties, until its sale, due to its small circulation in Ireland, to a new, less scholarly owner in August 1833. On the founding of the Ordnance Survey, Petrie was put in charge of the topographical section, with O'Donovan as a field-worker, and found employment for Mangan as a copyist and transcriber of documents. Though Mangan's hours seem to have been erratic, he was regarded as "an admirable scribe" and was, moreover, in continual contact with the foremost scholars of his day.[24] This contact lasted till his death and obviously formed the basis for his excursions into Irish literature as well as giving him access to the major libraries of Dublin. J. H. Andrews, in his history of the Irish Ordnance Survey, states that the civil assistants to the Ordnance Survey were recruited at 2s. to 6s. per day in 1829, but by 1841 were considered better educated than the surveyors (who received 4s. daily in 1829) and were paid accordingly. Mangan presumably was considered one of the better educated, especially given his contacts, and would certainly have retained a salary at the £50-per-year level of his scrivenery days.[25] This is not to suggest that at any stage Mangan was particularly well off but, rather, that Duffy was probably correct to suggest that the familiar picture of the destitute Mangan is a shadow cast back from the last years of his life. Even the letters to James McGlashan and Charles Gavan Duffy which, due to their often obsequious tone, read at first like begging letters, are in fact mostly requests for payment due on work performed. Thus, for example, one letter to C. G. Duffy, dated 16 June 1846, refers to an Irish song of 36 lines and to 968 other lines of poetry sent since February and requests payment at the "usual rate" of 10s. per 50 lines (NLI MS 138, fol. 8). Another letter asks Duffy to obtain from James Duffy "£5 on account of work to be commenced on Saturday" (NLI MS 138, fol. 18); a further letter refers to £2 owed him by McGlashan (NLI MS 138, fol. 19; cf. fols. 9 – 10).

The difference between these letters of the period 1845 – 1847, to which he had already referred, writing to McGlashan, as "the darkest hour of my life" (Price, 3 November 1849), and the two to James Hardiman of December 1848 (RIA MS 12 N 20, fols. 138 – 39) is striking. The letters to Hardiman are written out of utter destitution, to a comparative stranger, begging the loan of a single pound to stave off eviction. Most significant of all is the remark in the first that there is "not a single soul in Dublin to whom I could make a similar application." By this date indeed, Mitchel had been transported, Duffy jailed, and the leaders of the 1848 uprising, all associates of the *Nation* and *United Irishman*, either jailed or transported. According to Duffy, the consequences of Mangan's involvement in the "political turmoil" were those "habits of irregularity and eccentricity, which, more than his revolutionary politics, brought his engagement with the College Library to an end,"[26] and it is from this period, with its resultant penury, stress, and apparently vagrant lifestyle, that the two main autobiographies date, only a few months before his death from starvation in the Meath Hospital on 20 June 1849.

MANGAN'S "SPIRITUAL EDUCATION"

The particularly intense expression of misery in Mangan's various autobiographical writings inspires most of his biographers to establish a set of actual events that might have formed the steps of his spiritual degradation. Consistently, Mangan's spiritual education (as Mitchel terms it, *Poems* 1859, p. 11) takes on a mythological or typological shape in the biographies. Once again, the factual bases of these myths are difficult to ascertain, and contradictory accounts abound even more than in the case of

Mangan's material circumstances. Here more than anywhere, one has the sense of a life and a figure being produced to conform to one or another myth of the poet through a quite considerable work of appropriation with regard to the facts.

For despite the insistence with which Mangan attributes the "springs" of his "moral insanity" to his childhood, attempts have constantly been made to fix the origins of his sense of wretchedness in later events. Mitchel, attempting to account for that "vacuum and obscure gulf which no eye hath fathomed or measured; into which he entered a bright-haired youth and emerged a withered and stricken man" (*Poems* 1859, p. 11), attributes it — and is the first major source to do so — to disappointed love. Mitchel's account, which he claims to have collected from those "who were [Mangan's] intimates many years," has become the locus classicus of the celebrated love affair:

> He was on terms of visiting in a house where were three sisters, one of them beautiful, *spirituelle,* and a coquette. The old story was here once more re-enacted in due order. Paradise opened before him: the imagination and passionate soul of a devoted boy bended in homage before an enchantress. She received it, was pleased with it, and even encouraged and stimulated it, by various arts known to that class of persons, until she was fully and proudly conscious of her absolute power over one other noble and gifted nature — until she knew that she was the centre of the whole orbit of his being, and the light of his life: — then with a cold surprise, as wondering that he could be guilty of such a foolish presumption, she exercised her undoubted prerogative, and whistled him down the wind. His air-paradise was suddenly a darkness and a chaos.
>
> (*Poems* 1859, p. 11)

The typical form of Mitchel's account is apparent, even without the adjoined comment that "it was a needful part of his education: if his Frances had not done him this service, some other as fair and cruel most undoubtedly would. She was but the accidental instrument and occasion of giving him that one fundamental lesson of a poet's life, *une grande passion*" (*Poems* 1859, pp. 11 – 12).

In his *Life* McCall follows Mitchel verbatim, and his assertion that the love affair made "a wreck of his too confiding heart" (p. 15) is equally unfounded. The evidence of a whole series of mentions of Mangan in the "Answers to Correspondents" column of the *Comet*,[27] along with Mangan's own assertion of a "moral insanity" dating from childhood, suggest that O'Donoghue is right to state that "the opinion which has been expressed by some that it was a love disappointment which changed a happy, contented, gentle Mangan into a wretched, hopeless outcast is an entirely erroneous one. His first poems are as much saturated with mournful feeling as his last" (*Life*, p. 17). Apart from these reservations, O'Donoghue's own account follows Mitchel's and only adds the supposition that "betrayal" by a friend was somewhere involved, an assumption again derived from Mangan's own writings. Mangan's version, in its most developed form, is as follows:

> From habits of prayer and fasting, and the Study of the Lives of the Saints, Mangan was at one period of his life drawn away, and enticed into the snare of Love and was even within an aim's ace of becoming a Benedict. But certain circumstances . . . interposed their ungallant proportions between the lady and him; and so he abode a Maledict, and Hymen despatched Cupid and Plutus to look for somebody else.
>
> (*IA*, p. 28)

The implication is clearly that Mangan himself felt the "love affair" to be the confirmation, not the origin, of his "malediction." In the meantime, we remain in ignorance of the exact nature of this event, and, not least, of the identity of the woman Mitchel names Frances.

It is interesting, nonetheless, that McCall's account sketches an undeveloped "involute" (in De Quincey's sense) around this affair and two earlier events in the poet's life. The first of these concerns a younger sister, who, according to McCall, "died in girlhood from the effects of a scald." Her death "so heavily preyed on his rather sensitive mind that he never afterwards ceased to regret the blue-eyed cherub, her image haunting him in his dreams" (McCall, p. 4). No other evidence exists for this tale, which he erroneously claims to have derived from the "impersonal autobiography" in the *Irishman*. Mitchel asserts that during the 1830s Mangan was "earning daily bread for himself and his mother and sister" (*Poems* 1859, p. 12), a suggestion he may derive from the letter to McGlashan in which Mangan states that he toiled "all for my parents, my sister, and my two brothers" (Price, 22 September 1849). No other account refers to the death of the sister, though the autobiography claims that his father led her "such a life that she was obliged to leave our house" (*A*, p. 14). Sullivan, in the *Weekly Nation* article, provides no date for a sister's death, which only adds to the doubts that this article raises as to the accuracy of McCall's data concerning Mangan's early life. Certainly all efforts to locate any record of the birth or death of the sister in the appropriate records have been fruitless.

The question of Mangan's sister thus remains as obscure as the love affair and is the more tantalizing insofar as it seems to intersect with the "ballad incident," an episode that McCall again expands out of the "impersonal autobiography's" account of a "hair-brained [*sic*] girl who lodged in [his] father's house" (*IA*, p. 27) into a full-blown childhood romance. The girl in question, McCall's "little girl of curling sunny locks, a couple of Summers his senior" (pp. 4 – 5), is supposed to have sent Mangan out in the rain to buy a ballad from a street singer, telling him the rain would only make him grow. The result of his wanderings in shy pursuit of the singer was a soaking that supposedly left him almost totally blind for eight years, from age five to thirteen. Pending further information concerning his sister and the love affair, the objective status of this involute remains unestablishable. Nevertheless, the discovery that Mangan indeed had an elder *brother* who must have died in infancy sheds another light on the matter, presenting at least a substantial basis for his often remarked obsession with the death of innocents. It is not impossible that Mangan, in conversation as in writing, may have converted his brother into a sister, as Joyce was later to do in deriving the Isabel of *Stephen Hero* from his real brother George.[28] Certainly it would seem that this death gets taken up into and becomes part of the generalized pattern of such poems as "On the Death of a Beloved Friend" (*Comet*, 10 February 1833, p. 334), written on the death of his German pupil, Catherine Hayes, to whom he had become very attached. Though the precise role played by these apparently linked events in a complex of betrayal, disappointment, and infant vulnerability remains tantalizingly obscure, that complex itself is crucial to the characteristic procedures of Mangan's writings, a phenomenon to be discussed more fully later in the context of the autobiographies.

Common to all the lives is the attempt to ascribe origins to Mangan's "constitutional" wretchedness. Constantly the symptom — the poet's shattered constitution made manifest in the form of events that appear to be significantly repetitive in structure — is identified as the anterior cause, in a process that the autobiography expresses quite acutely as "a woe within a woe, and 'within the lowest deep a lower deep[']" (*A*, p. 21). The last and in some ways the most important of these symptoms, given that for all the biographers it appears in one way or another as the nadir of his woes, is opium addiction or alcoholism, depending on which accounts are followed. Mangan alludes frequently to an addiction, particularly in his last years. One letter to McGlashan, having first ascribed his wretchedness to his working conditions, continues a little obscurely: "No, I am wrong — it was not even all these that destroyed me. In seeking to escape from all this misery I had laid the foundations of that evil habit which has since proved so ruinous to me" (Price, 22 September 1849). The poem "The Nameless One," published in the *Irishman* in 1849, in turn refers to "The gulf and grave of Maginn and Burns," that is, alcoholism. Price asserts in introducing the letter just quoted: "He first became an opium eater, and in seeking escape from the horrors of that dreadful drug, intemperance crept on him."

There would be no question as to whether or not Mangan was an habitual user of opium, at least during the 1830s, except that Mangan himself denies it in the "impersonal autobiography": "He never swallowed a grain of opium in his life, and only on one occasion took — and that as a medicine — laudanum" (*IA*, p. 27). This denial could well be discounted, knowing the lengths the opium addict will go to in order to conceal the habit, were it not for the evidence of Duffy (1908, p. 287) and Meehan (*PPM* 1884, p. x). Both are prepared to accept that Mangan was an alcoholic, and certain letters, in particular one addressed to Duffy (NLI MS 138, fol. 7), are in the form of pledges. Given the current successes of the temperance evangelist Father Mathew, Meehan would clearly be more inclined to ascribe Mangan's behavior to alcohol, an almost respectable and certainly accommodable addiction.[29] Meehan recounts how Mangan declined to take Father Mathew's pledge "simply because he doubted his ability to keep it," and he describes Mangan's struggles to avoid alcohol, all eventually undermined by the "waywardness" of this erring reprobate (*PPM* 1884, pp. xvi–xviii). Duffy asserts: "At our friendly *noctes* we never had any refreshment but tea, nor did he express the want or desire of any other, but I gathered from his confessions that in the 'days of his slavery,' as he used to call them, he had sometimes needed and found a more seductive stimulant" (Duffy 1908, p. 282). However, if it is assumed that Mangan was addicted to some seductive stimulant throughout his career (and certainly Mangan "relapsed," at least after the period of the friendly *noctes*), this statement would suggest, rather, the long duration of opium influence, which would have needed no renewal during their *noctes,* than the insistent cravings of alcoholism. Thus Price mentions a conversation one night "in the interval ere the instant of the necessity for the opium tranquilizer — for to a necessity it grew — had arrived" (Price, 11 October 1849). All Mangan's other biographers seem to accept that he was, at least during the 1830s, a frequent user of opium, but regard it as a palliative resorted to either in the scrivenery or in consequence of the love affair, or, even more generally, as an anesthetic (see *Poems* 1859, pp. 12–13; *Life,* pp. 56–59). Some of Mangan's own prose works suggest his interest in the drug, though due to the strong contemporary literary influence of De Quincey, one would be unwilling to infer too much from this alone.[30]

In fact the strongest evidence for the use of opium rather than alcohol lies neither in Mangan's own works, which allude frequently to both, nor in the testimony of friends liable to bias as well as clinical ignorance, but in the writer's behavioral patterns, which fit well, in that combination of unrealized intention and obsessive secrecy, with those described by De Quincey and evidenced in Coleridge.[31] In either case, it is clear that the process of addiction stands as the acutest image of the constant struggle against constitutional dissolution that Mangan and his biographers depict his life as having been. And again, it seems inevitable that any attempt to reach a stable ground for decision will remain suspended due to the support that either theory offers to the preferred myth of the respective biographer.

The slant of each myth varies according to the desire of the biographers, and though the broadest outlines of the accounts agree, the contradictions that arise at crucial points suggest the incommensurability of Mangan with the figure his biographers constantly seek to make of him. Meehan, Catholic priest and admirer of Father Mathew, seeks to project the moral lesson of Mangan's struggle against the "poppy of the west" (*PPM* 1884, p. x), while O'Donoghue and Louise Imogen Guiney, his American editor, seek, rather, to establish literary credentials for their subject and lay their emphasis on his opium addiction. Duffy, his nationalism considerably muted by 1880, projects an image of Mangan as "so purely a poet that he shrank from all other exercise of his intellect" and one who "cared nothing for political projects," while Mitchel, who in his *Jail Journal* represents himself similarly as an outcast and exile, portrays Mangan as ardently political and a rebel in every way against all that Britain signified.[32]

What all the biographies have in common, however, is the attempt to redeem the wretched and errant Mangan, reconstituting him as an ethical subject by identifying him with an aesthetic or political type. It remains to establish how that typology coheres with the aesthetics and politics of a nationalism that was emerging as the dominant ideological force of Mangan's time. Herein lies the canonical form to which the biographers seek to assimilate the writer, and against which Mangan's life and writings are so recalcitrant. Both the biographical elusiveness of the poet, which makes him impossible to identify in any sense, and the traits of his life — dependence, waywardness, inconsistency — frame a mode of writing that plays out a similar matrix of characteristics. His life appears resistant to a nationalist typology, and it frames a body of work that is equally inassimilable to a nationalist aesthetic. Yet in a sense Mangan's life embodies a virtual dialogue with the emergent nationalism of his time, particularly since, from the economic collapse of the family in the postwar depressions to his death during the Famine, he suffered individually from the very ills of Ireland that nationalism generally seeks to cure. The aesthetics and politics of nationalism take shape as the dominant intellectual and political response to those material conditions and impose quite specific demands on the individual writer and citizen. It is against these demands that the specific significance of Mangan's resistance comes to light.

2

The Spirit of the Nation

In his life of Mangan, John Mitchel sought to unify his image of the poet's apparently split and incoherent nature through a moment of passionate intensity in which the implicit identity of poet and nation is realized in the total identification of the poet with the national cause:

> In the continual movements of political associations, whether under O'Connell, or under the auspices of those immortal youngsters called the Young Ireland Party, Mangan never took any ostensible part; yet when he, in common with most other men, believed that a mortal struggle was approaching, and already imminent, he became vehemently excited. Whatever relic of manly vigor and force of character was still left living amid the wrecks and ruins of the man seemed to flame up; for his history and fate were indeed a type and shadow of the land he loved so well.
>
> (*Poems* 1859, p. 15)

The narrative evoked here, in which the integration of the individual subject is achieved through his integration with the nation itself, is fundamental to nationalist ideology.

It is thus no accident that such a pattern should structure Mitchel's account of Mangan. His own *Jail Journal*, composed during the period of his transportation for "felony," is the text that most clearly articulates the fixation of Irish nationalism on the question of individual and national *identity*. Mitchel's experience of the Famine, combined with the revelatory impact upon him of James Fintan Lalor's articles on the need for an Irish agrarian revolution, induced him in 1848 to break with Charles Gavan Duffy and the *Nation* in order to found his own more

uncompromising journal, the *United Irishman.*[1] Throughout
Mitchel's editorials in this journal, Ireland is constantly envisaged
as an individual body corrupted by foreign taints: "Our national
slavery is a constitutional taint pervading all the members and the
whole structure of our social body, deranging the functions and
poisoning the springs of our social life. The foreign taint is in all
our institutions, all our social arrangements. . . . We are a
property of England, body and soul."[2] The Irish nation, lacking
an internal constitution of its own, is a *property* both physically,
as a colony, and spiritually, insofar as its "properties" are
deformed or tainted by the foreign constitution that shapes it.

In his *Jail Journal,* Mitchel correspondingly portrays himself as
representative, in the fullest sense, of this Ireland, his actual exile
being the appropriate image of an Irish people alienated from its
rights of citizenship:

> So my moorings are cut. I am a banished man. And this is not mere
> *relegatio,* like Ovid's, at Tomi; it is utter *exsilium,* interdiction of
> fire and water; the loss of citizenship, if citizenship I had; the brand
> of whatsoever ignominy law can inflict, if law there be. Be it so; I
> am content. There are no citizens in Ireland; there is no citizenship
> — no law. I cannot lose what I never had; for no Irishman has any
> rights at present.[3]

Mitchel's legal "ignominy" constitutes a threat to his own
identity such as Ireland's slavery poses to its identity as a nation.
His response is to "take [his] personal identity to task" in a
process that uses the journal as a means to reconstitute his
subjective continuity: "This book will help to remind me of what
I was, and how I came hither, and so to preserve the continuity of
my thoughts, or *personal identity,* which, there is some reason to
fear, might slip away from me" (*JJ,* p. 71). Constantly falling
back on "memory and imagination" as his stays in exile and im-
prisonment (*JJ,* p. 133), Mitchel reconstitutes the *continuity* in
which his personal identity resides and thereby reenacts on the
individual level the practices of the nationalist who attempts to
discover the identity of his nation in its history.

The individual represents the nation on two levels. First, the
genesis of the individual is to be found in the history of his
country:

The general history of a nation may fitly preface the personal memoranda of a solitary captive; for it was strictly and logically a *consequence* of the dreary story here epitomized, that I came to be a prisoner, and to sit writing and musing so many months in a lonely cell. "The history of Ireland," said Meagher to his unjust judges at Clonmel, "explains my crime and justifies it."

(Preface to *JJ*, p. 20)

Second, the individual's positing of his identity as a *continuity* repeats the form that the nationalist gives the history of the nation, which he believes to be the source and guarantor of his own identity. Both Mitchel's suffering and his mission as an agent of social disorder are justified by his place in the creative whole: "No dis-organization in the world can be so complete but there will be a germ of new order in it"; Mitchel's wrongs are Ireland's, and justice for the one is justice for the other, "for the whole is greater than the part." Appropriately enough for the author of the biography that most emphasizes Mangan's doubleness, these words form the resolution of an extended dialogue between Mitchel and his "Doppelgänger," the figure of hesitation and doubt who accuses the "Ego" of seeking an arbitrary and personal vengeance for private wrongs rather than a truly impersonal political solution. Only as Mitchel absorbs his private wrongs in "Ireland's wrong" do he and his "Doppelgänger" finally "come to be of one mind."[4] In short, the integrity of Mitchel's position rests on his integration with the nation on which the continuity of his identity depends.

At several points in the *Jail Journal* this form of nationalist writing is posed against the writings of the Empire, which are seen as symptomatic of the hidden disintegration of its constitution, which belies Britain's apparent power. The products of the popular Family Libraries and Miscellanies are merely "dry skeletons of knowledge" that lack precisely that unifying *process* by which knowledge is got. They are, moreover, the result of a kind of superficial collage work, devoid of character and identity:

I complain of the universal system of compiling and scissors-editing, in that books under such treatment cease to be books — are no longer the utterances of individual men, but a composite gibberish. .... A book ought to be like a man or woman, with some individual character in its veins, and speculation in its eyes, and a way and will of its own.

(*JJ*, pp. 72–73)

Significantly, the books at which Mitchel's diatribe is aimed are primarily travel books comprising accounts of exotic lands that fall within the purview of imperial interests: such knowledge as they offer is, by virtue of its very expansiveness across the surface of the globe, superficial and antagonistic to the internal coherence of national and personal history.

Such meditations will eventually lead Mitchel to an almost dialectical reversal of the relationship between imperial power and the subjected nation that has come to be represented in the individual nationalist. For these books signally lack individual identity precisely insofar as they are commodities that trade the uniqueness of individual origin for interchangeability. In a quite literal sense, the products of the British popular presses *represent* commodities as well as *being* commodities, and the fascination that they display with superficial appearances divorced from the actual process of production, commerce, and expansion becomes for Mitchel the symptom of an unseen, internal disintegration:

> British wealth, commerce and civilization; statistics of cotton fabric — how many million yards of it are made by the year, and how many times this would go round the globe, marry, I believe the world's orbit — statistics of steel pens — how many tons of iron are snipped up into pens, — and yet how the quill trade (delightful to know) is not one feather the worse. What "literature" — what commerce there must be here! ... This is the character of all popular British "literature" which is *got up* in these late years "for the million" (poor million!). — Its look is wholly introverted: it can see or tell nothing in the world but the British empire and colonies. The true British spirit is now-a-days well content with itself — looks no longer without or above itself, but keeps gazing with stupid delight intently at its own navel. The symptom may be called *omphaloblepsy,* and is diagnostic of a very fatal national disease — a thorough break up, I trust, of the Constitution.
>
> (*JJ*, pp. 121–22)

The very process of composing the *Jail Journal* thus becomes Mitchel's riposte to imperial power. Whereas the rationale of his sacrifice had been to prove the absence of the Irish constitution, what his writing comes to plead is not only the soundness of the native constitution as he represents and reconstitutes it but, moreover, that it is the imperial constitution that is in the process of disintegration as the result of its own expansion. Significantly, the process by which Mitchel counters and overcomes the potentially deleterious effects of reading such superficial matter is of a piece with that by which, in the political domain, he had proposed that Ireland might free itself from the detrimental effects of imperialism. Confronted with the "stratified debris" of British popular literature, Mitchel's response is to turn inward, using his own resources of "imagination and memory" to engender another train of thought "far outside the intentions and conceptions of the writer, and even outside the subject of his writing" (*JJ*, pp. 122–23). Just so, the *de facto* "dissolution" of Irish society, which Lalor's articles had revealed to Mitchel shortly before his break with the *Nation,* is the condition for a rebirth of the Irish nation out of the "germ of order" that is contained in "social disorganization." This process, however, can and will take place only so long as, according to Mitchel's argument in the *United Irishman,* Ireland is compelled "to limit its wants and appetites to the resources of its own soil, and the industry of its own people."[5] Out of this vision of Ireland's necessity and Ireland's salvation arises Mitchel's utopic dream of a pre-capitalist rural society of independent yeoman farmers.

The title of Mitchel's article, "Poetic Politics," underlines the connection that is implicit between the nationalist project for unifying Ireland and the kind of literature through which it is to be achieved. Mitchel's anti-constitutional principles tend to make his writings more extreme and, occasionally, more far-seeing than those of his Young Ireland brethren. But the extremism of his writings, which was a late development and avowedly the product of unprecedented circumstances, only differentiates him in degree from Young Ireland as a whole while serving to throw into relief the fundamental forms of nationalist ideology. Even the virulently anti-capitalist solution that he — like many nationalists since — sought for Ireland derived from a reactionary response to the objective conditions out of which Young Ireland's nationalism emerged and from which it received its strongest impetus. It is to these conditions that we must now turn in order to trace the rationale for the *aesthetic* form taken by Irish nationalist thinking.

ORIGINS OF NATIONALISM

The primary ground for opposition to the Union of Great Britain and Ireland was economic. Criticisms of the effects of the Union on the Irish economy were widespread and by no means confined to nationalist or even O'Connellite writers.[6] The case for repeal of the Union, nonetheless, took some time to cohere. Of all the arguments used to persuade a largely reluctant Irish parliament to accept the Act of Union in the aftermath of the rebellion of 1798, the most strongly urged had been the political one. The assimilation of Ireland to the rest of Great Britain was to have ensured both the internal stability of the island and the security of the Empire as a whole, which had been severely tested by, respectively, the uprising of the peasantry and the threatened French invasion. But in these efforts to shore up an unstable outpost of the Empire an ulterior economic motive was before long discerned. Already in the eighteenth century, import duties had been imposed by England on Irish manufactures that might otherwise have undersold their English counterparts. By 1800, however, the position had reversed, and English industry had become vastly more productive than Irish competition, being technologically more advanced and consequently capable of producing more and cheaper goods. Under the Irish parliament of the 1780s and 1790s, nonetheless, Irish industry had not only survived but had expanded to an unprecedented degree due largely to the imposition of import duties on English goods.[7] It was no accident, therefore, that an economic clause that allowed for the gradual abolition of protective duties on English imports into Ireland was incorporated into the Act of Union. Neither the apparent evenhandedness of this measure, which equally abolished English duty on most Irish imports, nor the promises of increased markets for Irish goods in consequence were to the point: the superiority of English means of production made the one an anachronism and the other an irrelevance.

The effect of the Union on the Irish economy was, accordingly, to precipitate a prolonged period of industrial decline. The process of decline was to some extent mitigated by the Napoleonic Wars, during which Ireland was a major supplier of agricultural produce to British forces. But while the duration of the European wars saw some increase in the prosperity of farmers and graziers, both Catholic and Protestant, the depression of manufacturing industry was continual and severe. A succession of economic crises occurred, the first brought about by the slump in corn prices after the Napoleonic Wars in 1818, the second by the final abolition of import duties on English goods in the mid-1820s. The decline in manufacturing industries can be seen to have continued gradually but steadily in most of the country and in most industries until the end of the Famine. Two factors contributed to this decline. First, the flooding of the Irish market with cheaper English goods destroyed any possibility of Irish industry making headway against superior competition. Second, under the landholding system peculiar to Ireland (with the notable and significant exception of Ulster), tenants had no security of tenure and, with rare exceptions, paid their rent to absentee landlords. This meant not only that a vast amount of Irish capital was exported from the country but also that the quantities otherwise available for investment were minimal. What little capital remained seems largely to have been directed toward more profitable, agriculturally based enterprises, particularly grazing. Caught in a vicious spiral of decline, Ireland became increasingly a country whose economic activities were virtually circumscribed by the export of unworked raw materials, mostly agricultural, and the import of manufactured commodities from abroad.[8] In time, the disequilibrium between the depressed economy of a marginalized "internal colony"[9] and the imperial center comes to produce powerful metaphors for Ireland's condition that, as we have begun to see, are effective in structuring the political and cultural ideology of Irish nationalism.

As has already been remarked, the post-Union period in Ireland is marked by an unprecedented centralization of Irish society. Economic forces drove and accelerated this process, but if any consistent policy can be said to connect the various Dublin administrations, whether Whig or Tory by appointment, it is the unremitting desire to integrate Ireland politically with the Empire as a whole. This was already the avowed object of the Union, which dissolved the separate Irish parliament into the imperial parliament at Westminster. But the anomalous condition of Ireland within Great Britain, always evident in its poverty, Catholicism, different social structures, and so forth, led the administration in Dublin to measures of internal integration that involved a pattern of deliberate state interference which long preceded any comparable developments in other parts of the British Isles.[10] This development is signaled not only by the number of committees and commissions established to research Irish affairs, but by the establishment of a state-organized national school system, a national police force, and a military-inspired and -conducted Ordnance Survey which, until money ran short in 1841, was engaged in a systematic mapping of the whole island.[11] Paradoxically, while the integration of Ireland into the British market economy led to the depression and retardation of the Irish economy, its integration into the imperial political system necessitated the most developed and centralized bureaucratic system in the British Isles.

For some decades, the predominant tendency of Ascendancy conservatives was to resist and criticize such administrative interference in Irish society, primarily since the drive to integration involved the steady political emancipation of the Catholic population and the end of Ascendancy monopoly of political power. By the mid-1830s, however, faced with the fact of Catholic emancipation and the necessity of preserving what could be salvaged of Ascendancy political influence, conservative unionist thinking underwent a major transformation. Although criticism of specific administrative measures continued, the effect of this transformation was to bring Ascendancy ideology much more closely into line with the practical policies of the administration. Largely under the influence of Samuel Coleridge's *On the Constitution of Church and State,* unionist political theorists began to envisage a gradual evolutionary process by which Catholic Irish sentiments could be weaned from "primitive" loyalty to clan and faction and be attached instead to king and constitution. One means by which this political end was to be produced was cultural, involving the ideal rapprochement of Protestant and Catholic Irish on a common sense of cultural history; this argument is most lucidly articulated by Samuel Ferguson in a set of articles published in the *Dublin University Magazine* in the mid-1830s.[12] Another potential means was the extension of administrative intervention from political to economic domains. Sir Robert Kane, in *The Industrial Resources of Ireland* (1845), comments in a representative passage on "how slightly the true and only means of consolidating a people by giving them common habits of industry, of sobriety, of traffic, was thought about in this country." As his argument progresses, the identity of this economic argument with the cultural arguments of those such as Ferguson becomes clearer: "The idea of rendering fortifications useless, of erecting the bulwark of the state in the hearts of the inhabitants by fostering their industry, by encouraging their commerce and agriculture, and promoting their education, did not occur to the statesmen of that epoch."[13]

Yet despite persistent criticism of individual administrative policies, which was rarely unanimous among unionists, and despite the distaste of a landed, conservative aristocracy for the laissez-faire doctrines that governed the predominantly Whig administrations of these decades, unionist thinking constantly provides an ideological equivalent to the apparently pragmatic policies of an expanding bureaucracy. They have a common political end — the integration of a society marked by disintegration and clashing interests — and a common set of means — research designed to uncover the hidden ways of a still largely alien culture, education by which to assimilate that culture to the imperial mold. Inevitably, then, the unionist ideology, which initially purports to be anti-administrative, before long reveals its actual affinities with the expansive administration of the Empire. Given the ultimate dependence of an embattled minority of Protestant unionists on the coercive power of the legal apparatus of that administration, it is hard to see how it could have been otherwise.

The alternative to unionism, articulated first in the context of Daniel O'Connell's agitation for the repeal of the Union and more fully theorized by the Young Ireland group, which emerged from the Repeal Association in the mid-1840s, was to establish a separate and distinct center for Ireland, both politically and economically. The economic argument for Home Rule put forward by both the Repeal Association and Young Ireland was twofold. In the first place, it was argued, the right to self-government would permit the casting of laws appropriate to Ireland, including the imposition of protectionist duties on imports, which had little chance of ever being accepted by the English majority in the Imperial Parliament. In the second place, as a logical extension of home rule, the presence once again in Dublin of the major governing institutions would restore the city to its former economic and political centrality and attract home those absentee landlords whose residence outside the country imposed such a drain on Irish capital.[14]

With minor variations in detail, this was the broad economic argument espoused by O'Connellite repealers and Young Ireland nationalists alike. Initially, the leaders of the group that became known as Young Ireland — Charles Gavan Duffy, Thomas Osborne Davis, and John Blake Dillon — had founded their journal, the *Nation,* to assist O'Connell in the agitation for repeal. But their posing of nationality as the "first great object" and their emphasis on the *spiritual* nature of that nationality immediately differentiate the Young Irelanders from O'Connell. In all his political campaigns, whether for Catholic emancipation in the 1820s or for repeal in the 1840s, O'Connell's political methods had been singularized by their resolute pragmatism and his willingness to sacrifice principle for actual gain. This tactical pragmatism, which had proved remarkably successful in the building of mass movements among the Catholic peasantry, was of a piece with O'Connell's fundamentally utilitarian social philosophy, which left him more than willing to abandon Gaelic culture and language for the sake of material progress.[15] In this respect, as Young Irelanders were not slow to point out, the basic principles on which O'Connell's political thinking were based were also the ones he shared with the British administration: O'Connell's was an oppositional rather than a critical political philosophy.

Young Ireland was marked by a quite different class background and religious outlook. The majority of the group were drawn from the professional or mercantile middle classes, and the leaders of the group were concerned to emphasize not only the relatively high proportion of Protestant (i.e., Anglican) and Dissenting Irishmen in the movement, but also the anti-sectarian basis of their political tenets.[16] It is therefore unsurprising that the secession of Young Ireland from the Repeal Association in 1846, which was precipitated by a dispute over the principle of the right to resort to physical force, came as the culmination of a long series of debates over the proposal by the administration to establish nonsectarian University colleges throughout Ireland.

The narrowness of the class base of the Young Ireland group had immediate effect once they had seceded from O'Connell's Repeal Association, on which they had largely depended both for the wide circulation of the *Nation* and for their political influence in rural districts. Given the numerical weakness of the entrepreneurial middle class in Ireland and the country's primarily rural economy, it was virtually impossible that a political movement that drew its support largely from the professions, from minor officials in the administration, and from mercantile businessmen should have a widespread political base. This fact largely explains the abortiveness of the 1848 rebellion, but criticism of the Young Ireland movement for not realizing their own political isolation fails to grasp either the political goals or the ideological venture of the early Irish nationalists.[17]

In common with the majority of European nationalist movements of the early nineteenth century, Young Ireland was a movement of a relatively small intelligentsia in a country marked by a singularly uneven pattern of economic development and undergoing a process of modernization imposed by an imperial state.[18] Marginalized doubly, both in relation to a predominantly rural economy and in relation to the loci of government and economic power, this displaced and largely urban intelligentsia was driven to seek an alternative political center. It was in this context that the theory of the spiritual nation, transcending actual social and economic difference and offering a ground for unity that would integrate disparate interests into a coherent political force, gains its crucial importance for the first time in Ireland.[19] Culturally and politically, the concern of Young Ireland is precisely to articulate the "otherness" of Ireland around its *own* center, both geographically and politically, and in relation to the myth of a unified and coherent cultural past. This recentering of Irish politics is conceived as the necessary precondition to the reversal of the economic marginalization brought about by the Union. In consequence, priority is given to attainment of a cultural unity of the people in a domain specifically intended to transcend actual political and economic divisions.

THE POLITICAL IDEOLOGY OF NATIONALISM

According to Young Ireland doctrine, the struggle to revive a sense of the continuity of Irish cultural history with its obscured origins both prefigures and helps to produce the political integration that is actually lacking. The assertion of a distinct identity for the nation-state on the basis of a supposedly lost unity is an essential element of European nationalism in the early and mid-nineteenth century. Nationalism emerges as a political doctrine in this period to unify and legitimate the nation-state after the overthrow of arbitrary monarchic states, whose unity had been territorially defined and symbolized in the figure of the monarch.[20] Nationalism must accordingly be understood in relation to a nineteenth-century political theory that conceives the state itself to be the historical expression of the fundamental unity of any people, transcending the specific social conflicts that threaten to disintegrate civil society.[21]

In British political theory, which initially centers on the notion of the constitution rather than on that of the state, a development can be traced in which the largely static model of the constitution, conceived in the eighteenth century as a system of checks and balances, gives way to an evolutionary model, in which the reconciliation of opposing social forces produces an ever higher and more integrated realization of the essential spirit manifested in the English people. It is to this notion of the constitution that unionist ideologists appeal.[22] It is equally striking that in Young

Ireland writings, including even those of Mitchel, this model of
the British constitution is accepted as accurate and even admired,
although, for reasons that will be discussed, it must necessarily be
rejected as an option for Ireland. Beneath the superficial appearance of antagonism and incoherence on the part of England lies a
deeper coherence, a reconciliation of conflicting interests into
mutual necessity. Despite the antipathy to political economy that
is found everywhere in nationalist writings, it is clear that what
Young Ireland admires in the British constitution is the apparent
political coherence of a vigorous economy.[23]

The anomalous condition of Ireland, however, precludes the
kind of integration promised by either British political economy
or British political theory. Split between a rural subsistence
economy, which largely preexists both the use of money and the
exchange of commodities, and a maritime economy, whose
principal function is the mediation of the export of agricultural
produce and of capital in the form of the absentees' rent, Ireland
is marked by a literal and irreversible deterritorialization of all its
resources and a part of its people.[24] Among those who experience
this deterritorialization most acutely both in culture and in
economic and social position are the intelligentsia, whose class
position leaves them deracinated with regard to rural and Gaelic
Ireland and only awkwardly recentered with regard to the
Empire, on whose political power they are socially, economically,
and often culturally parasitic but from whose center they are
nonetheless excluded. Theoretically, the solution to Ireland's
economic predicament has already been given: to recenter that
economy within an Ireland that has regained the power to
regulate its own commercial laws and practices. In practice,
however, the strategy must be quite different and must effectively
reverse the political resolution of economic conflict provided for
in the British constitution. Recognizing their inevitable alienation
from the population as a whole, the nationalist intelligentsia seeks
to project the image of a spiritual Ireland that preexists its actual
economic destitution and political divisions, incorporating the
entire Irish people in the fundamental sameness of their identity
and the fundamental identity of their primary political interest,

that is, a self-governing Ireland. Political reconciliation here must precede economic revival.

Mitchel's abhorrence of the market economy and his countering of it by falling back on his personal resources as on Ireland's are thus entirely symptomatic of nationalist thinking. For the inundation of the Irish market with British-produced commodities stands throughout nationalist writings as the most vivid index of the dislocation of the Irish national identity, just as the depletion of its resources, capital and material, provides the most powerful index of its annihilation and incorporation by the Empire.[25] His constitution shattered by the unjust might of imperial law, Mitchel finds in the *Jail Journal* the means to reconstitute himself by locating a principle that precedes his apparent disintegration and dislocation: that of the continuity of his personal identity. At the same time, he opposes to the commodity economy, which threatens to engulf him and to make him one of its "properties," the utopian image of a rural economy that, based as it is on a pre-monetary economy and on the patriarchal possession and transmission of land from father to son, is defined by its unbroken continuity.

Though Mitchel's entirely rural, self-sustaining economy was not a vision shared by all nationalists, who were at least as concerned to stress Ireland's potential resourcefulness in all economic domains including the commercial, the pattern his writing evinces is fundamentally that of nationalism itself. The political coherence that will permit Ireland to fall back on its own resources as a self-governing entity derives from the continuity of *national* identity. Historical in its form, this continuity supplies the unity of spirit that underlies the apparent incoherence of contemporary Ireland. Such transcendental unity, in providing the principle of Ireland's political independence, equally grounds the demand that the Irish market be supplied with the products of Irish labor, that those artifacts, commodities, which are now the index of Ireland's deterritorialization by the Empire should come to be, like the people itself, regrounded in Irish soil.[26] As we will later see, the spiritual project of Irish nationalism transposes the economic form of the problems that inspire it: actual debt to the Empire is to be overcome by the assertion of originality, of indebtedness to no one. The appearances of dislocation or disintegration can be countered by reintegrating them in an obscured but common origin; the question is only how or where to locate that origin and its continuity or identity with the derived phenomena.

The necessity of commencing by affirming the ground for its own political and national identity differentiates Irish nationalism not only from British political thought but also from that of the revolutionary constitutional republics, France and America, which are to some extent its sources of inspiration. The revolutionary success of these nations defines in advance their political cohesion, which is only then enshrined in the constitution. Unlike them, Ireland seeks to define and constitute its nationhood precisely out of the actual or threatened loss of its identity. Despite frequent appeals to the example of the "giant nation" that "sprang from the waters of the Atlantic," Ireland's situation is more closely analogous to that of its European counterparts, Germany and Italy, and its version of nationalism is more closely related to theirs.[27]

Lacking as these "nations" do the *de facto* political identity forged by France and America in their military struggles against monarchy, their primary appeal is to a prior cultural unity on which basis the *right* to self-determination can be formulated. The distinguishing features of these nationalisms can be located in the fact that, as Eugene Kamenka neatly expresses it, "self-government requires a community that is to be the self."[28] The "self" of the nation is, in the first instance, discerned in the language that provides the objective basis for cultural unity. Mazzini, leader of the Young Italy movement after which the Young Irelanders were dubbed, puts the point unambiguously in terms that foreshadow the future expansionism of Italian nationalism: "Your country is one and indivisible. As the members of a family cannot rejoice if one of their number is far away, snatched from the affection of his brothers, so you should have no joy or repose as long as a portion of the territory upon which the language is spoken is separated from the Nation."[29] For Mazzini, language defines the "natural divisions" of the "Countries of the People," whose "innate spontaneous tendencies . . .

will replace the arbitrary divisions sanctioned by bad govern-
ments."[30]

The full complexity of an argument that relates the "innate
spontaneous tendencies" of a people to their language — thus
baldly stated by Mazzini — was initially developed by the German
post-Kantians, in particular by J. G. Fichte in his *Addresses to the
German Nation*.[31] These addresses, delivered in 1808 after the
defeat of the Prussians by the French, are concerned to provide the
basis for a German national resurgence by locating the constitutive principles of the German people beyond actual political
divisions. Fichte's argument opens with the idea that the defeat of
the Germans has come about as the inevitable consequence of
their spiritual contamination by French influences, which are, in
the fullest sense, foreign to the essence of the Germanic peoples. If
a large part of this argument is directed against the contamination
of the German language by the introduction of French vocabu-
lary, this is precisely because in the German language lies the
essence of the German nation:

> To begin with and before all things: the first, original, and truly
> natural boundaries of States are beyond doubt their internal
> boundaries. Those who speak the same language are joined to each
> other by a multitude of invisible bonds by nature herself, long
> before any human art begins; they understand each other and have
> the power of continuing to make themselves understood more and
> more clearly; they belong together and are by nature one and an
> inseparable whole.
>
> (Fichte, pp. 223 – 24)

The burden of Fichte's argument here is not simply that where a
language is *actually* spoken there exists a community with the
right to consider itself a nation. More important than that almost
contingent circumstance is the notion that the language of a
nation is a continuing and developing entity (Fichte, p. 55). The
defining characteristic of the German peoples, as opposed to the
French, according to Fichte, is that the former have continued to
use their original language and in so doing have remained in touch
with the living stream of an original language, whereas the latter
have exchanged their living Teutonic language for a dead Latin
one: "They get symbols which for them are neither immediately
clear nor able to stimulate life, but which must seem to them en-

tirely as arbitrary as the sensuous part of the language. For them this advent of history, and nothing but history, as expositor, makes the language dead and closed in respect of its whole sphere of imagery, and its continuous onward flow is broken off."[32] Ultimately, Fichte's argument leads him to distinguish "German" from non-German not on the sole basis of language and race, but on the basis of the acceptance or not of the will to secure "the eternal development of this spirituality by freedom" as opposed to "stagnation, retrogression, and the round dance" (Fichte, p. 127). It nevertheless supplies the rationale for a quite exclusive set of national discriminations.

Most important for Fichte is that the evolution of an original language is seen as reconcilable with its remaining "nature's one, same, living power of speech," developing, in a manner reminiscent of Coleridge's philosophical method, in "a continuous transition without a leap."[33] That reminiscence is no accident, for Fichte is concerned to demonstrate the continuity between philosophical concepts and the sensuous base of the language as a life-giving interchange between the sensuous designation and supersensuous "extended use of the sign," between perception and the conceptual metaphors that arise from and return on it through "another, direct, and living relation to his sensuous instrument" (Fichte, pp. 60–61). Fichte's insistence on the *living* nature of an original language is bound up in a reversible analogy between the "immediate" relations of body to spirit, perception to apperception, and those between the sensuous and supersensuous elements of the language.[34] The entry of the arbitrary into the language thus attaints the very life of the language. A similar analogy applies to the relation of the language to the nation, the former becoming the spirit, the latter the body. "Foreign" influence thus becomes an encroachment of death into the spirit, and the foreign qualities of the French nation are represented not only in the mechanical forms of their bureaucracy, but in the very fact of their dependence on a "dead" language and on the philosophy that arises therefrom, of "fixed forms" and "alienation from originality" (Fichte, p. 110).

The necessity of developing another unifying principle to replace the system of arbitrary monarchy thus involves the sense of a transition from a model of the state as an aggregate of members whose unity is centered on an *arbitrary* monarch (which Fichte would define as a "dead" form) to the model of a living, evolving body that contains within itself the principle of its own continuing unity just as the body contains a spirit that constantly shapes its "members" into a living unity. The "spirit of the nation" can be identified with its language, since that language, in the speech of the individual as in the continuous relations that bind together a linguistic community actually and historically, can be taken to represent ideally the medium through which those unifications are enacted. By the time that Mazzini was writing, in the 1840s and 1850s, it was almost axiomatic that, as Wilhelm von Humboldt had put it in 1822: "Language is the external manifestation, as it were, of the spirit of a nation. Its language is its spirit and its spirit is its language; one can hardly think of them as sufficiently identical."[35]

The fundamental problem that an identification of the "spirit of the nation" with the national language would present for Irish Romantic nationalism is quite apparent. Not only were there already two language communities in Ireland, the Irish and the English, but the former of these, in which it would have been most consistent to locate the defining spirit of the Irish nation, had already ceased by 1800 to be the dominant language of culture or even, for that matter, the principal language of the majority.[36] Thomas Davis, one of the principal members of the Young Ireland group, registered in an article in the *Nation* of 1843 the fact that only "about half of the people west of a line drawn from Derry to Waterford speak Irish habitually," though it was still common "in some of the mountain tracts east of that line."[37] The loss that the decline of Irish involves was expressed by Davis in terms that at once suggest the parallels between Irish and German nationalistic theories and the necessary differences:

> The language, which grows up with a people, is conformed to their organs, descriptive of their climate, constitution, and manners, mingled inseparably with their history and their soil, fitted beyond any other language to express their prevalent thoughts in the most natural and efficient way.
>
> To impose another language on such a people is to send their history adrift among the accidents of translation — 'tis to tear their

identity from all places — 'tis to substitute arbitrary signs for picturesque and suggestive names — 'tis to cut off the entail of feeling, and separate the people from their forefathers by a deep gulf — 'tis to corrupt their very organs, and abridge their power of expression.[38]

The burden of Davis's article is an exhortation to the middle classes in particular (for whom, he claims, it was "a sign of vulgarity to learn Irish") to relearn their native language. What German nationalists feared in prospect — the increasing contamination of their national language by that of a politically and commercially more powerful nation — had in Ireland already occurred, virtually irreversibly. The power of Davis's rhetoric at this juncture registers the multiple deterritorializations that, he is aware, afflict the nationalist intellectual all the more consciously than the middle-class merchant who willingly abandons the Gaelic language for the commercially more functional English. Already by virtue of class and education, the nationalist is contaminated by the English language and culture. He is triply dislocated in his own nation: his language is no longer fitted to the land to which his identity would be bound; the signs that he receives in place of the fitting names are arbitrary, devoid, like the commodities which flood the economy, of any natural relation to Irish ground; and in consequence, he is cut off from any lived relation to the history and traditions of the nation. Perhaps most significantly, given the political aims of nationalism, he is deprived of voice at the same moment that he ceases to be "representative" of the Irish people: his "power of expression" is "abridged." Whether "set adrift among the accidents of translation" or occupied in the business of relearning a lost, or, as in many cases, never-possessed tongue, the Irish nationalist is in the position of Fichte's "foreigner," dependent on the dead letter of history rather than that continuous correspondence with the past which the "living stream" of an original language provides.

The loss of the national language is one aspect of, and may stand as symbolic of, a whole set of discontinuities that cut the Irish people off from the "entail of feeling." The actual disunity of the nation, which permits England to oppress it, is replicated in the ignorance of the Irish concerning their own past as well as their present: "For centuries the Irish were paupers and serfs, because they were ignorant and divided."[39] Faced with ignorance and division and with the necessity of looking to history for the establishment of his identity, the Irish nationalist — in a move that replicates that of the conservative on the opposite wing — has deliberate recourse to history and to research to furnish both the image and the very process of unification. Where the German nationalist's identity is guaranteed by his language, revitalized by the philological tracing of the sensuous origins of his supersensuous ideas, the Irish nationalist revitalizes a relation to history that might have represented only death and division, finding in it both the lesson and the promise of unity. Charles Gavan Duffy summed the case up retrospectively: "Rightly understood, the history of Ireland abounded in noble lessons, and had the unity and purpose of an epic poem. . . . The true lesson they [the national annals] taught was that Irishmen were enslaved because they were divided."[40]

The notion of a continuity that has only to be sought to become live underlies Duffy's conception of history as a mere lifting of the veil from the past. The counterpart to that assertion of the continuity which research restores is an education through which the people are to be restored to their past. The slogan that formed the banner above the *Nation*'s leaders each week perfectly encapsulated the complex of ideas that the organic metaphor is able to hold together: "To create and foster public opinion in Ireland and make it racy of the soil." The concept of the Irish *race* is thus to be grafted to its *roots* in sensuous contact with the land, through which it imbibes the particular *taste* of its spirit. And if the ambition of the nationalist is to create nationalist opinion, he will achieve it as a re-creation, fostering the seed that is an *a priori* presence in the soil of Ireland.

This belief in the possibility of forging through research of whatever kind the unity of the nation, historically and politically, points to the curious formal coherence between nationalist and unionist thinking. The reasons for that coherence are perhaps already apparent: quite as much as the unionists, the middle-class Young Irelanders lacked, in consequence of the historical conditions of their existence, any "organic" connections (to borrow Gramsci's formulation) with the people in whose name they claimed to speak. In consequence, both parties invoke an alternative concept of organicism that rewrites actual discontinuity as merely a moment in the continuously evolving narrative of the Empire or the nation. Ironically, their mutual preoccupation with historical research aims to transcend the effects of that history, and their politics becomes in turn most ideologically effective where it seeks to belie actual political differences. Such a move was required if either party were to claim to speak in the name of an integrated Ireland, since the very existence of each was in effect the product of the social and cultural fragmentation induced by imperialism. The subsequent course of Irish history leaves little doubt that their thinking was instrumental in forging a modern Irish "national consciousness." What remains to be seen, however, is the extent to which, necessarily, that consciousness was *ethically* and *aesthetically* constituted at the expense of historical political consciousness and at the cost of denying the full subjective and cultural dislocations undergone by a colonized people.

THE ETHICS AND AESTHETICS
OF NATIONALISM

Despite all the *Nation's* efforts to "create and foster" popular unity in Ireland in the 1840s, the rebellion of 1848 was abortive, which only demonstrated once again the total lack of unity in Ireland and the total failure of the Young Irelanders to achieve popular support. But contemporary and modern criticisms of this failure and of the general ignorance of the Young Irelanders of the Irish language, which is intimately bound up in that failure, themselves fail to observe that it is precisely on a sense of separation that nationalism is founded.[41] The isolation of the Young Irelanders with regard to the Irish people repeats the discontinuities in Irish history and political life that bring about the constitutive drive of nationalism toward the production of images of unity. The instinctive distaste of the bourgeois for the civil disorder represented by the sporadic and loosely organized tactics of the Ribbonmen terrorist groups — "the most important underlying fact of Irish internal history up to the days of the

Fenians and the Land League," according to at least one historian[42]—finds its ideological rationale in the double meaning of the notion of principle which supports the ideal of union. If on the one hand the notion can be defined in terms of the first and formative principles of Romantic epistemology, it has on the other hand a set of ethical implications, which tend in the end to ossify into "fixed moral principles." The appeal to the concept of growth as opposed to cultivation in the moral sphere is an apt indication of the intimate linking of moral and formative notions of principle at the heart of nationalist thinking, a linking which becomes more important the further the nationalist is perceived to be isolated in his society. For that linking of the two senses of principle enables an account of the relation of the individual to society that can be theorized in terms of union rather than antagonism:

> Dis-union was the fixed character of their [Gaelic] nationality, made up of a cluster of clans. It is the evil which appertains to all localism, like a cholera house beyond the gates of a city. Centralization in great crises, is more favourable to union than localism; but union in its keeping degenerates into uniformity, and thence to slavery. It is the problem of the human race to reconcile individual liberty and association; a problem which all nations think they have solved at some period of their history, our own among the rest.[43]

Morality thus enters the nationalist ideology as an ethical injunction where it is conceived that the freedom and full identity of the individual are achieved only when he is immersed in the greater life that is the nation. The problem of democratic nationalism is, as Mazzini argued in terms reminiscent of the *Nation* writer just quoted, "to find a centre for all the many interests" and "to prevent the clash of individualities." Its exponents are accordingly "driven to the sphere of *principles,*"[44] to an education that will cultivate in the individual those moral principles that are the repetition in the finite individual of the eternal principles of the divine essence of life, or, on yet another level, a repetition in the individual of the national spirit, which in himself he represents. The whole man, the man of integrity, becomes thus the man who is integrated with and reproduces the spirit of his nation.

Robert Emmet's famous appeal for the suspension of his epitaph until his country "takes her place among the nations of the earth" stands as the classic statement of the Romantic Irish nationalist insofar as the question of the individual's true meaning is bound up with the nation's assumption of its own identity and both are cast in the future tense.[45] It is exactly in becoming — in the strictly Coleridgean sense of the term — a *symbol*, which "while it enunciates the whole, abides itself as a living part of the Unity, of which it is the representative,"[46] that the martyr is transformed simultaneously into a "confessor": by his absolute identity with the fullness of meaning that the spiritual nation embodies he invokes the realization of that identity by the members of a nation that is yet to be. If such a demand necessarily involves what is in political terms a potentially disastrous process of "ironing out the contradictions and inconsistencies for which the present tense would furnish all too much evidence,"[47] such a sacrificing of the real in the name of the ideal is exactly what characterizes the ideology of nationalism, seeking in its past the original principles for the form of the nation's future evolution.

In such a manner the self-appointed martyrs of nationalism participate in that process by which "the future shall realize the promise of the past," their actual present becoming a mere parenthesis whose meaning is given and assimilated by the origin and goal of the nation. Through his association in the continual labor of creating the nation to which he is bound and called, the nationalist transcends the potentially divisive effects of his presence as an individual subject and reenters the continuous stream which, we have seen, provides Romantic thought with the analogy by which it can produce a method that is unifying in effect at all its stages. History accordingly ceases to be political insofar as it ceases to register struggle and conflict and becomes a process that produces a unity that transcends actual division. The spirit of the nation, hypostatized against the alienation of a middle-class intelligentsia, theoretically encompasses all classes insofar as it is always identical to itself. Anti-progressive in its ethical and economic prescriptions for Ireland as it perhaps had to be, Young Ireland's ideology appears even more profoundly conservative when compared with the quite similar postulates of racial identity issuing from its unionist contemporaries. That conservatism is prescribed by the aestheticization of history and politics, which rapidly comes to supply the pivot of nationalist thinking. Culture comes to represent the site of unity elsewhere denied by historical facts.

The figure of the martyr, his identity totally immersed in the spirit of the nation, forms the ideal paradigm of the individual's relation to the nation. But what the martyrs provide are only the moments of intensity, the "burning symbols," to use Pearse's expression, in which the national spirit is most clearly manifested. In the absence of a constitutional incarnation of that spirit, the continuity that links those moments must be supplied from elsewhere. Literature in the broadest sense is already devoted to rememoration as the medium through which a knowledge of the past of the nation is conveyed and preserved for future restoration. More than that, its instrumental function as the medium of the spiritual nation comes to establish literature as the very form of the national constitution:

> One of the grand social bonds which England — in fact, every other nation but ours — possesses, is the existence of some *institution* or *idea* towards the completion of which all have toiled in common, which comprehends all, and renders them respectable in each other's eyes. Thus her *history* knits together all ranks and sects in England. . . . Each has erected a story of the constitution. They value each other, and acknowledge a connection. There are bright spots in our history; but of how few is the story common! and the contemplation of it, *as a whole,* does not tend to harmony, unless the conviction of past error produces wisdom for the future. We have no institution or idea that has been produced by all. We must look to the present or future for the foundation of concord and nationality. We must set ourselves to erect some such institution or idea. A national literature is in its very essence amalgamating, and may eventually become the great temple of concord.[48]

In this sense "literature is practical . . . and the writer is a man of action,"[49] participating in the construction of the nation within which he will be "comprehended." The mutual inter- dependence of writer and nation in nationalist theory was succinctly expressed by the *Nation* critic D. F. McCarthy: "A great literature . . . was either the creation or the creator of a great people."[50] The ambivalence of that formulation indicates exactly the problem with which the Irish nationalist is confronted when appealing to literature as a national institution. If the function of literature is to form and unite a people not yet in existence, how will a writer of sufficient stature arise, given that it is from the people he must arise if he is to express the spirit of the nation?

The problem is one that has in various ways confronted all nation-states on their assumption of a distinct identity and that has been resolved theoretically in equally various ways. The most apposite parallel to the Irish context would be the deliberate attempts in Germany to construct a literary language through the combined efforts of translation from other languages and research into medieval Germanic poetry in a tradition that stretches from Luther's translation of the Bible to the researches of scholars such as Karl Simrock and the brothers Grimm in the nineteenth century.[51] Allusion to the German tradition, however, reminds one forcibly of the "anomaly" of the Irish situation, in which the virtual loss of the Irish language causes a twofold break in the continuity of that process. In the first place, simple ignorance of Gaelic tradition permitted the assumption — rooted in centuries of indifference on the part of the English-speaking community — that that tradition could not itself constitute a national literature, that it was too primitive and unsophisticated to do so. "There are," remarks Thomas Davis with something of the tone of a mason assessing the monumental work to be performed, "great gaps in Irish song to be filled up," gaps which he attributes to "ignorance, disorder, and every kind of oppression."[52] In the second place, even the use of the rubble of Gaelic tradition for the foundations of the institution of national literature will have to be permitted by research and translation. Unlike the German nationalist, who can conceive translation of foreign material to be assimilation and research to be revivifying, the Irish nationalist's work of research and translation is determined by a gap and is involved in an assimilation of the native to the foreign, Irish into English, thus incurring the risk of being "set adrift among the accidents of translation."

The theoretical resolution of these difficulties entails an almost exact repetition of the forms of the nationalist recourse to history, elaborated this time in the idea of the "ballad." If the national literature is to be "the very flowering of the soul" of the nation,[53] rather than an institution arbitrarily imposed upon it, it will, like the nationalist himself, need to be made "racy of the soil" and absorb the spirit of the people. That spirit is to be found in the ballad. By the time D. F. McCarthy had assembled his *Book of Irish Ballads* in 1846, the idea that ballads represented the original and primitive poetry of a people was a critical commonplace. McCarthy's introduction to the anthology, however, recasts this notion in order to appropriate it to specifically Irish concerns. His belief that "Hesiod and Homer built their beautiful and majestic structures on the original ballads that were probably floating among the people" leads him to a formulation of the need for a ballad poetry in Ireland to form the basis of a literature that, deriving from such ballads, will be equally filled with the "distinct character and peculiar charm" of Irish genius.[54] What is of most importance to McCarthy is the belief that contact with the Irish spirit, which a knowledge of ballads provides, will give back a distinctive character to an Irish literature which must perforce be written in English:

> To those among us, and to the generations who are yet to be among us, whose mother tongue is, and of necessity must be, the English and not the Irish, the establishing of this fact is of the utmost importance, and of the greatest consolation: — that we can be thoroughly Irish in our writings without ceasing to be English; that we can be faithful to the land of our birth without being unfaithful to that literature which has been "the nursing mother of our minds", that we can develop the intellectual resources of our country, and establish for ourselves a distinct and separate existence in the world of letters, without depriving ourselves of the widely-diffused and genius-consecrated language of England, are facts that I conceive cannot be too widely disseminated.[55]

Thus through a thorough knowledge of the *spirit* of the Irish ballad, translation in the widest sense becomes assimilation, and the language which might have been the badge of conquest is reinfused as a national as well as an individual "mother tongue."

A parallel argument in an anonymous *Nation* article on Barrett Browning and Tennyson clarifies even further the historical principles involved and the kind of demands made on the Irish writer by the nationalist. Lamenting the fact that "the healthy growth of an Irish literature" has been "thwarted and impeded" by English domination, the writer continues with a sketch of the ideal evolution of a literature:

> The different stages of social development have their distinct characters written in the development of mind. First there is the ballad, simple, direct, and unadorned; then lyric poetry, the epic, the drama, history, philosophy, each growing naturally out of the other. So are all great national literatures built; . . so must it be here, if we are ever to have a literature of our own.[56]

This being the natural course of development, the very fact that English literature is "the nursing mother of our minds" constitutes an impediment to a healthy growth, introducing the refinements of a fully developed national literature to force the growth of a plant whose first shoots are scarcely apparent. The remedy is already familiar:

> The philosophical tone of a high civilization does not suit us; we have our history to make, and our writings must help us make it. We want strength, earnestness, passion, the song and ballad, all that fires and nerves the minds of men. Perfection in this is to be attained, not by studying English co[n]temporary poets, but by becoming saturated as it were with Irish feeling, by learning the Irish language, sympathising in every beat of an Irish peasant's pulse, by being filled with knowledge of Ireland's past and of boundless hope in her future.[57]

Once again the nationalist is called to identify totally with the nation, evacuating himself of the subjectivism of an English civilization in order to be "saturated" and "filled" with the Irish spirit, his present only part of an unbroken arc stretching from past to future. That spiritual identification serves to conceal — or to suture, as one's point of view may be — the gap that drives one artificially to "make" a history, whether national or literary.

The demand made by *Nation* writers such as Davis and McCarthy for the full-scale production of ballad poetry is not, then, simply a call to the work of propaganda through direct statement and appeal, a kind of "poster art," as Padraic Fallon has suggested. This aim might have been most effectively attained through precisely the sort of street ballad that the *Nation* writers despised as an Anglo-Gaelic hybrid.[58] Far more important than the present for the nationalist is the future, and in calling the Irish to the labor of ballad writing, the Young Irelander is looking to lay the foundations of a national literature that is yet to be. The lack of individuality in the ballads published in the nationalist journals, and reprinted in the enormously successful anthology entitled deliberately *The Spirit of the Nation,* is thus a part of the program rather than a failing.[59] Total immersion of the writer's identity in that of the nation was seen as the first condition of a process that sought to fabricate a foreshortened literary history in which the development that had hitherto been thwarted might speedily be made up. For if, in the first stage of that missed development, the ballad would have been the anonymous voice of the people, in the attempt to forge the trace of a never-existent literary history an *impersonal* balladry becomes the necessary first step. The spirit of the nation may thus manifest itself uncontaminated by a subjectivism which would be the mark of English civilization and be kept pure for future emergence in a fuller growth of the literary tradition. And, implicitly, the more intense the production of ballads, the more rapidly can the gaps be filled in and this primitive or "minor" stage be transcended.

Accordingly, the program of Young Ireland comes to replicate the very aesthetic history that legitimates the subordination of the Celtic races. The absence of a "fully formed" literature becomes the index of a low level of historical development in both the political and the cultural sphere, while the production of a literature that will mediate the image of transcendental Irish unity becomes the remedy for the political divisions consequent on underdevelopment. That literature, which projects a transcendent space of quite literal reconciliation, is envisaged as attaining mediating power by its capacity to replicate the original identity of the Irish race. In turn, that capacity depends upon insisting that the nationalist writer be totally identified, as an individual, with the spirit of the nation, which lacks any other form of representation. Thus what is, for a nation with a political state constituted independently of its cultural identity, merely a means to legitimation becomes in the context of nationalism an instrument of political action. In consequence, the political instrumentality of the aesthetic sphere, which is dissembled by its major theorists, is highlighted by a nationalism that otherwise accepts the logic of the forms of thought that legitimate domination. It is the failing of Irish nationalism never to have questioned the idealism of identity thinking, which, even in its resistance to imperialism, links it closely to imperialist ideology. If an explanation for this phenomenon is required, it may be found in the fact that Irish nationalism, in its early theory as in its later practices, has always sought to be an instrument of bourgeois hegemony.

Both the failures and the intents of Irish nationalism were manifested with great clarity in Mitchel's *Jail Journal*. Similarly, the demands made on the writer by the nationalist are evidenced in Mitchel's life of Mangan. But, as we have seen, Mangan's inconsistent and wayward life is inassimilable to that typology: the ethical portrait of the nationalist poet is imposed on a figure who largely exceeds its categorical frame. This biographical resistance to assimilation will in the following chapter be seen to be written into those poems of Mangan's that have traditionally been taken to be representative of his nationalist commitments and, more significantly, the implications of his peculiar modes of translation will be seen to suggest the problematic nature of nationalist theories of translation as a mode of assimilating the Gaelic to the English. Mangan's biographical elusiveness and the refractoriness of his idiosyncratic translations will become the guiding metaphors for an understanding of the effects of a minor practice, in its refusal of assimilation or identification, and of the political orientation of an aesthetic of major writing.

3

Great Gaps in Irish Song

THE RHETORIC OF SINGULARITY

Mitchel's introduction to his edition of the *Poems* inaugurated the still conventional view that Mangan's earlier poetic career was a preparation for the fullest expression of his poetic gifts under the influence of the Young Ireland movement in the 1840s.[1] His association with this movement began in 1842 with his ditty "The *Nation*'s First Number" and lay dormant until his most productive years from 1845 to his death in 1849, during which he wrote regularly for that and other nationalist journals. During these years he encountered much newly researched Gaelic material and experienced the full horror of Ireland's economic and political condition during the Famine. But, given the aptness of this configuration of factors to the formation of a committed nationalist poetry, what is most striking when Young Irelanders write about Mangan is the extent to which they register the poet's refractoriness, his reluctance to commit himself fully to the nationalist cause. Mitchel's account, written ten years after his transportation, gives the nationalist myth of the writer as martyr integrated and explained in the moment of his engagement in the cause, and representative of the general fate of his nation. Charles Gavan Duffy's account of Mangan's relation to the Young Ireland movement is more sober and fits more closely with the pattern of the poet's life insofar as we can establish it:

> I thought the gifted and gallant young men associated in the enterprise, who were afterwards known as "Young Irelanders", would bring him companions for his mind and heart for the first time and that his slumbering nationality would be awakened by their design to raise up their country anew and place a sceptre in her hands. But his habit of isolation had hardened, he shuddered at the idea of social intercourse.[2]

Duffy anticipates in the individual poet a latent "spirit of the nation," which might be revived in association with the collective labor of the nationalist movements. What he encounters instead is not merely indifference to nationalism as such but a "habit of isolation" that refuses any association whatsoever. An earlier account, the obituary for Mangan published in the new series of the *Nation* in September 1849, makes some attempt, in a more overtly religious rhetoric, to reconcile the conflicting images of Mangan as writer and as man:

> Melancholy in anyone, most tragic in a man of genius is it to see the separation between the speculative and active powers, the curse of the fall, become an utter divorce, and the will lie prostrate and impotent beneath the feet of tyrannic habit — to see fancy, imagination, poetic susceptibility still subsisting, and at a breath giving forth music to delight and benefit mankind, while the Man, the lord of these, is drifting hopeless and powerless to ruin and death.[3]

Reconciliation falls short in separation, his fall remaining unredeemed by the ethical act of reintegration with the nation. In an essay that has maintained that "in Mangan the very Gaelic heart seems poured out," it becomes essential to separate the spirit of the writing from the figure of the writer, the latter isolated, drifting, unethical, mortal, the former immortal and ethical in its effects. As with Ireland itself, the actual outer form belies the transcendent spirit it conceals.

Many attempts were made to persuade Mangan to produce nationalist literature more than sporadically, and to conform to the nationalist ideal of writing.[4] But even the ballads and poems that are most frequently read as the evidence of Mangan's nationalist tendencies are marked internally by the disintegration that nationalist-oriented accounts of his writings seek in one way or another to overcome. The fissure that the *Nation* article imposes between man and writing or Mitchel depicts as being resolved by political commitment is in fact intrinsic to the structure of those writings. Comparing passages from such poems with examples selected almost at random from *The Spirit of the Nation*, or even from the prose of Mitchel's own exhortatory editorials, one is struck at first by the rhetorical similarities:

> Know, then, your true lot,
>   Ye faithful, though few!
>   Understand your position,
>   Remember your mission,
> And vacillate not,
>   Whatsoever ensue!
> Alter not! Falter not!
>   Palter not with your own living souls!
>   (Mangan)
>
> Stand together, brothers all!
>   Close together, close together!
> Be Ireland's might a brazen wall —
>   Close together, tight together!
> Peace! no noise! — but, hand in hand,
> Let calm resolve pervade your band. . . .
>   ("Theta")

Yes! with our fellow-citizens rests now the fate of Ireland. If they quail, or shrink, vacillate, pause, postpone, or exhibit the slightest weakness — if they balk the hopes of a single Irishman, or give one enemy another chance to scoff, 'twere better they had remained slaves, contented in their slavery, or, being discontented, had hanged themselves.

>   (Mitchel)[5]

Viewed in the context of Mangan's poem as a whole, however, a tension can be seen to subsist between an imperative voice that mimes the nationalist projection of unification into the future, and a present tense in which an accumulation of substantives mimes the situation that evokes that projection, the perpetual *imminence,* that is, of the realization of the *immanent* idea of the nation. The nationalist's present is depicted as a perpetual labor in perpetual suspension. For each generation of readers of "The Warning Voice," the suspension is to be repeated:

> To *this* generation
> The sore tribulation,
> The stormy commotion,
> And foam of the Popular Ocean,
>   The struggle of class against class;
> The Dearth and the Sadness,
>   The Sword and the War-vest;
> To the *next,* the Repose and the Gladness,
>   "The Sea of clear Glass,"
> And the rich Golden Harvest![6]

If, as at the end of the "Irish National Hymn," Mangan continually assumes the privilege of "one whom some have called a
Seer,"[7] he is most typically a prophet who intimates but does not
see, stressing the gap that persists between expectation and event:

> And I heard, as I guessed,
>   The far-echoing sound
> Of a trumpet, with tones,
>   And lightnings and thunders,
> As ye read of in John's
>   Revelation of Wonders.
> What meant they? I trow not.
> What next might befal?
> And how ended All?
> This, too, friends, I know not —
> For here were my cords
>   Of Sleep suddenly broken
>   The bell booming Three;
> But there seemed in mine ears,
>   As I started up, woken,
> A noise like fierce cheers,
>   Blent with the clashing of swords,
>   And the roar of the sea![8]

Exactly at the point where the significance of the vision — final
defeat or final victory, hell or apocalyptic prelude to a new
earth — seems about to be grasped and controlled, the vision is
interrupted. With that refusal to endow his "vision" with its
expected meaning, Mangan introduces a disarming, distancing
irony, one compacted by the ambivalence of "as I guessed,"
"seemed in mine ears," "a noise like." The poem's dream is
described as "a Stream / That in vain seeks the light," and that
"mocks our control" (stanza 1).

Constantly opposed to nationalist projections, which come
gradually to appear as misrecognized alienation from the plenitude they pursue, is the figure of the poet who stresses his
irredeemable alienation. "A Voice of Encouragement" begins
expressly with the assertion that the speaker is "a man unworthy
to rank in your number," "his music and diction / Rather . . .
fitted, alas! to lull to, than startle from, slumber." The uneven
faltering "numbers" of Mangan's nationalist poems reflect that
act of self-subtraction from the nationalist vision — which

depends, after all, on the "cords / Of Sleep." In the fuller context of the nationalist ballads, this self-subtraction, which operates precisely through emphasis on the singularity of the writer, functions simultaneously as a critique of nationalist politics and aesthetics.

"Self-subtraction" in this context becomes a parodic version of the ethical self-effacement called for by the nationalist literary program. Rather than project perfect integration, Mangan insists on the ineradicable residue of a self-conscious and alienated selfhood which cannot be assimilated to "the spirit of the nation." And his failure to integrate aesthetic representation with ethical action, "To live [his] poetry — to act [his] rhyme," is what most troubles his nationalist contemporaries. Nor is their unease unwarranted: Mangan's writing, in its recalcitrant insistence on the inassimilable remainder, intimates that their utopia of identity will only be achieved over the poet's dead body and suspends the issue of nationalist politics in protracted speculation.

THE GAELIC TRANSLATIONS

The nationalist recourse to the ballad form as one in which the individual is effaced in order to permit the reproduction of a national spirit is largely determined by the need to overcome the break in continuity that the loss of Gaelic as a national language entails. From the outset there exists an intimate connection between the composition of "original" ballads and the transla-tion of those Gaelic poems on which the former are supposedly modeled. That connection goes beyond the relation of model to imitation, however, insofar as the demand made of the translator repeats that made of the balladeer — that he should become the transparent medium for the spirit of the nation. An article in the *Nation* praises both Mangan and Ferguson for exactly that quality, noting only how one arrives there through study, the other simply through identifying with his nation:

> Whether in translation or original, they seem almost alone in the art of reproducing for us the inner heart and outward vesture of the bygone ages of Ireland, that lie so obscure for us. Yet between them there is a large difference — Ferguson seems to have rendered himself, by zealous study, as familiar with old Irish ways as Walter

Scott with those of the middle ages. Mangan, on the other hand, seems rather to penetrate without study, and by the instinct of the poet and his own Irish sympathies, into the feelings and sorrows of those too sorrowing times.[9]

This contemporary judgment is almost entirely reversed by a recent critic writing on Mangan and Ferguson:

> So that when Ferguson turns to versifying a selection of poems from Hardiman's collection, his intention is in no way that of Mangan, who always wished to make his originals as expressive of himself as possible. . . . Ferguson had that kind of personality which expresses itself in impersonality, in a kind of self-effacement, so that he makes an excellent translator, remaining absolutely true in as many particulars as possible, to the spirit, tone and rhythm of his originals, and to their curious, if at times chaotic image sequences.
>
> We get, in the appendix affixed to the four Hardiman articles, twenty translations which are as faithful to their Irish originals as it is possible to get in English versions. Here, the act of the imagination is one of transparency, of self-denial, curiously analogous in its self-surrender to that "negative capability" of which Mangan was incapable.[10]

The difference between the two assessments pivots at least in part on a difference of opinion as to the nature of Mangan's self: to the nationalists, Mangan's true self is that in him which can be identified with Ireland, while to Welch it is that which intrudes uncomfortably to obscure the "transparency" of the ideal translation. But in that notion of "transparency," the opposed evaluations meet around a common expectation.

Welch is of course right to locate an ideal of transparency at the center of Ferguson's theory of translation. What is not so clear in his account of Ferguson is the close bond between the ideal of the translations and the political theory of the articles to which they form a practical appendix. The "Hardiman articles" which Welch mentions were a series of articles published in the *Dublin University Magazine* as a review of the Irish antiquarian James Hardiman's collection of Gaelic poetry, *Irish Minstrelsy*. Hardiman's aim was, quite explicitly, to vindicate the Irish poets "against the ignorance and prejudice by which they have been assailed, particularly during the last century."[11] Accordingly, he published the originals in parallel text, facing English versions by a team of translators who versified the Gaelic in a mode that uneasily combines the conventions of late Augustan descriptive verse with those of Romantic meditative and ballad poetry. The Gaelic is thus thoroughly "anglicized," but Hardiman's political sentiments are revealed time and again in the extended notes he appends to the text.

Ferguson's articles on the *Irish Minstrelsy* seek accordingly to depose Hardiman as authority, displacing his "spirit of petty anti-Anglicism" and his poetry's "scheme of dissension" with "the reconciling strength of an honest literature."[12] Ferguson's aim was to present a theory of the gradual development of the native Irish loyalties from the immediate clan to the idea of a constitutional monarchy, obliging a transition from investment in the sensuous to investment in the supersensuous.[13] Knowledge thus becomes unifying rather than — as with Hardiman — divisive and sectarian. The ideal of transparent translation repeats this theory at two levels. In the first place it ensures a continuous transition into which no arbitrariness enters, rather than furnishing a perpetual reminder of the nation's separation from its past. In the second place, the ideal of transparency allows for the undistorted reproduction in English of the essential quality of the Gael, which, for Ferguson, as for Arnold some thirty years later, is "sentimentality." That being the case, the ascertaining of that quality, in which translation plays a fundamental role, is a crucial stage in the process of cultivating its growth in the right direction. If Ferguson finds that "their sentiment is pathetic" and that "desire is the essence of that pathos,"[14] his mission will be to direct that "desire" away from a lost past and toward the idea of unity.

Providing, in the first Hardiman article, prose translations of Irish poems that represent "the words, and unmutilated thoughts, and turn, and expression of the original," Ferguson is obliged to observe that "the idiomatic differences of the two languages give to the translation an uncouth and difficult hesitation, which in the original did not affect the Irishman."[15] But by the time Ferguson comes to write his verse translation, the "uncouthness" of the prose translation has become an essential part of the verse in rhythm and idiom, reflecting exactly Ferguson's idea of the primitive but powerful sentiments of the

Irish race. Hardiman's edition is criticized for failing to communicate this: "All the versifiers seem to have been actuated by a morbid desire, neither healthy not honest, to elevate the tone of the original to a pitch of refined poetic art altogether foreign from the whole genius and *rationale* of its composition."[16] In opposition to that "foreign," "morbid desire," Ferguson's style is a clear medium through which the *living* genius of the Irish race can express itself, "unrefined" and, ultimately, as raw material to be worked on in the service of a political end.

Is it then the case that Mangan, contrariwise, allows his personality to intrude upon his translations, which would indeed repeat the procedure we have analyzed in his political writings? Any reading of Mangan's Gaelic translation is immediately vexed by the question as to whether he actually knew Gaelic. There is some small evidence that Mangan began to study Irish seriously in the late 1840s, having already toyed with it earlier in the 1830s, but it seems that his understanding of the language even then must have been rudimentary and faulty at best.[17] Certain it is, however, that on a number of occasions Mangan availed himself of the versions he found in Ferguson's Hardiman articles, in order to produce his own poems. These versions, taken from Ferguson and written in reaction to his manner, are among the most frequently cited of Mangan's Irish translations, and generally regarded as his most "successful." Given the representative nature of Ferguson's practice as a translator, a detailed comparison of the versions is instructive with regard to the distinctiveness of Mangan's practice.

Perhaps the most celebrated of Mangan's translations from the Gaelic is "Dark Rosaleen." In addition to the best-known version, which was published with that title in the *Nation* of 30 May 1846, Mangan wrote two other versions entitled "Roisin Dubh" (Dark-Haired Rose), published in the *Poets and Poetry of Munster,* but according to O'Donoghue representing earlier versions of the poem. Mitchel in his introduction to the *Poems* collates these two versions "to illustrate his method of translating" but does not elaborate on what he intends to illustrate.[18] No single original of the poem can be established, but the various versions form part of a tradition of similar personifications of

Ireland, cognate with the better-known "Kathleen ni Houli-han." Ferguson provides only a prose version of this poem, but the ordering of its seven stanzas and their thematic concerns suggest that this—perhaps with the Irish text given in Hardiman—may have been Mangan's primary source.[19] Ferguson's translation involves him in an attempt to refute Hardiman's assertion that the poem is an allegorical political ballad concluding "with a bold declaration of the dreadful struggle which would be made before the country should be surrendered to the embraces of our hero's hated and implacable rival":[20]

> This, says Mr. Hardiman, is an allegorical political ballad—it seems to us to be the song of a priest in love, of a priest in love, too, who had broken his vow, of a priest in love who was expecting a dispensation for his paramour, of a priest in love who was willing to turn ploughman for his love's sake—nay to practice the very calling of a priest to support her.[21]

Ferguson's insistence begins eventually to trip over itself, and remains a little unconvincing, if only because, whatever the original intention, Hardiman's "allegory" will inevitably be read into "Roisin Dubh." Ironically, Ferguson may even have helped that reading, given that, for obvious reasons, he translated fairly literally as "Your pardon will come from the pope [*sic*] and from Rome in the East" (stanza 1), the Gaelic "Tiocfaidh do phádún ó'n b-Pápa, a's ó'n Ró'imh an-oir," which Hardiman's translator Furlong had blurred into the lines: "For the friends that come eastward shall see thee at last; / They bring blessings — they bring favours which the past never knew."[22]

Mangan's celebrated version takes up Hardiman's reading of the poem, a point which Mangan makes quite explicit in a prose introduction, where he even stresses obliquely what is, in fact, supplementary allegorical allusion: "The true character of and meaning of the figurative allusions with which it abounds, and to two only of which I need refer here—the 'Roman wine' and 'Spanish ale' mentioned in the first stanza—the intelligent reader will, of course, find no difficulty in understanding."[23] The singular density of this version is perhaps attributable to his synthesizing of the two views of the poem, as love song or allegory, which Ferguson and Hardiman opposed to each other. It is in these opposite directions that his other versions respectively tend. One stresses the element of the love relationship that Ferguson perceived:

> I dashed through Erne: — the world may learn the cause from
> Love;
> For light or sun shone on me none, but *Roisin Dubh!*

The other stresses the personification of the land as Roisin, and the apotheosis this involves:

> O never mourn as one forlorn, but bide your hour;
> Your friends ere long, combined and strong, will prove their
> power.
> From distant Spain will sail a train to change the scene
> That makes you sad, for one more glad, my Dark *Roisin!*
> (*PPM* 1849, p. 263)

From the synthesis of the two interpretations emerges a poem in which the heavily stressed internal rhyme scheme of the other versions, which tends to break each line into segments, modulates into a series of tonal variations on the vowels of the first lines, which contain its thematic statement:

> O my Dark Rosaleen,
> Do not sigh, do not weep
> (stanza 1)
> 'Tis you shall reign, shall reign alone,
>   My Dark Rosaleen!
>   My own Rosaleen!
> (stanza 4)
> And gun-peal, and slogan cry,
>   Wake many a glen serene,
> Ere you shall fade, ere you shall die,
>   My Dark Rosaleen!
>   My own Rosaleen!
> (stanza 7)

The tonal pattern of "Dark Rosaleen" repeats formally the suspension of the speaker's desire around the apotheosized woman in whom "life, love and saint of saints" (stanza 3) are condensed, a suspension which is echoed in the verbal dominance of futures which are almost conditionals. In this respect, Mangan's poem becomes the great nationalist ballad it has been taken to be: not as an exhortation, but as a representation of the asymptomatic progress of the nationalist project toward an idealized land whose domain is always in the future. The perception of the stasis or suspension at the core of this process is peculiarly Mangan's.[24]

That quality of suspension is, and has often been noted to be, the dominant quality of the most highly regarded of Mangan's Gaelic translations. Padraic Colum has noted the "architectural" qualities of "Dark Rosaleen" and of the "Lament for the Princes of Tyrone and Tyrconnell." Welch also, in the course of a very fine analysis of the rhythmic scheme of the latter poem, remarks that its success derives from the fact that it is "static." And, as Chuto has remarked, in this poem, as in "Dark Rosaleen," it is to the conditional mood that Mangan turns.[25] The dominant trait of Mangan's writing in the Irish translations, which incline constantly toward elegiac models, is indeed this quality of suspension, the speaking voice caught between a lost ideal past and an apotheosized future, neither of which is approachable except in the conditional mood. But to understand the recurrence of this pattern in Mangan's work as the manifestation of a peculiar disposition, which precedes as a source the utterance that is the poem, is to draw on a theory of writing that is particularly questionable in the area of translations. Not only must the vexed question as to the relation of a source poem to its translation or to the translator be thrown open, but the probable *function* of specific deviations, inevitable as these are in any translation, has to be foregrounded before they can legitimately be identified with the expressive drives of the writer.

This problem of the identification of the writer with his object is one of the primary concerns of another poem based on Ferguson and Hardiman, Mangan's "Lament over the Ruins of the Abbey of Teach Molaga."[26] The possibility of subjecting this poem to widely differing readings is already apparent in the gulf between Hardiman's and Ferguson's commentaries. For Hardiman, it is predominantly a lament for one of the "appalling monuments of the ravages committed by the first protestant reformers."[27] Ferguson grants Hardiman's account of the poem, but once again appropriates his original to exemplify the loyal attachment of the Irish to their inherited beliefs. The poem becomes, for all its anti-Protestant sentiments, a kind of "neutral ground," as Protestant meets Catholic on the basis of shared feeling: "we would be men without hearts if we could not appreciate such a melancholy and touching complaint as this sweet elegy."[28] The parallel, established by Hardiman in his note, between the destruction of the abbey and the dispossession of the Irish poet Collins's family by a "ruthless band of privileged marauders," the "Act of Settlement Men,"[29] is not mentioned in Ferguson's commentary. Rather, Collins's decline is generalized in both versions of his translation.

The parallel between abbey and poet, however, is much more insistently established *formally* in both of Ferguson's versions than in that of Hardiman's translator, Thomas Furlong. The latter, indeed, provides a fine illustration of the tension that subsists between the tenor of Hardiman's commentaries and the "refined," Englished style of the versifications. A considerable instability of diction is apparent throughout Furlong's version. On the one hand, a Romantic convention of the solitary mourner finds its appropriate descriptive diction and rhythms:

> The wind with silent wing went slowly by,
>   As though some secret on its path it bore:
> All, all was calm — tree, flower, and shrub stood still,
> And the soft moonlight slept on valley and on hill —
>   (stanza 2)

On the other, the soliloquy is reminiscent of eighteenth-century moral verse in its vestigial antithetical forms and circumlocutory diction:

> Where far from crowds, from courts and courtly crimes,
> The sons of virtue dwelt, the boast of better times.
>   (stanza 3)
> The hissing weasel lurks apart unseen,
> And slimy reptiles crawl where holy heads have been.
>   (stanza 9)

Where the uneasy relationship between two modes leaves the parallel between Furlong's poet and the ruined abbey to be rather insecurely tacked on at the end of the poem, Ferguson's version repeats and reorganizes a parallelism that has been available throughout the poem, between the present and former states of the abbey. The speaker's dead friends and children, "powerless and corrupting" in the abbey, leave him as soulless and cut off from continuity as the ruin itself, its "abbot, rule, and order" reduced to "a heap of clayey bones" (stanzas 19 and 16). His heart, his capacity for feeling, shrunk to the dimensions of a nut, only "Death's deliverance were welcome," allowing him to merge finally with the abbey which is his image (stanza 20). Effectively, Ferguson depoliticizes the poem by universalizing the condition of decay and converting abbey and poet into each other's reflection: victims alike of an ineluctable natural process, the specific cause of the decay of each — British imperialism — is elided.

Turning to Mangan's version, we may observe that the differences to be traced there from Furlong's and Ferguson's versions go far beyond his much stronger stress on Catholic rite and the responsibility of "brutal England's power" for the ruination of the abbey (stanzas 8, 9, 17). Already in the first stanza, Ferguson's "Meditating and reflecting" is replaced by a speaker whose "soul and strength lay prone." The "proneness" of the subjected soul to color its objects with its own emotions is hinted in the fifth stanza:

> The memory of the men who slept
> Under those desolate walls — the solitude — the hour —
> Mine own lorn mood of mind — all joined to o'erpower
> My spirit — and I wept!

The overpowered spirit subsequently envisions a quasi-paradisal former state of the abbey, "yonder Goshen," where "unity of Work and Will / Blent hundreds into one" (stanzas 6–10). The vision is, however, already suspect, "yonder Goshen" having been the place of refuge that turned to slavery for the children of Israel.[30] Not only is this merely the *thought* of the speaker; it is, furthermore, anxiously "burdened" with the swift passage of time: "With Charity and the blessed spirit of Prayer / Was each fleet moment *fraught*." An ambiguity of mood — indicative or subjunctive — attaches to this Paradise's triumph over misfortune, which is, after all, dependent on the "fortunate stars": "their fortunate stars / *Had* triumphed o'er all ill!" These ambiguities issue in the change that is the concern of the subsequent stanzas (11 – 15).

The deviation from Ferguson's version is equally striking: in place of the parallel established in the latter between the two *states,* and maintained within and between the stanzas of the poem, Mangan's change appears as a *process.* The ruined abbey, already perceived in the fourth stanza as "crumbling to slow decay, the remnant of that pile," becomes involved in a continuing process of degradation which is mimed in the sequence of the speaker's perceptions of it. Hardiman, deriving his information from a pair of guidebooks, had stressed in his note that "the building, though unroofed, is entire" and offered a lengthy description of its continuing magnificence.[31] Ferguson's version of the poem mentions successively all the elements of the building as still standing, though ruined. Mangan's speaker's attention, however, shifts progressively from "its mouldering walls" and "pillars low," overgrown by grass and gowan, to the "unsightly stones" choking its wells and the completion of the building's razing by the elements:

> Tempest and Time — the drifting sands —
> The lightning and the rains — the seas that sweep around
> These hills in winter nights, have awfully crowned
> The work of impious hands!
>
> (stanza 13)

The source poems, including Collins's, had all posed the abbey's survival of natural forces against its destruction by the impious. Here, finally, the "monumental shapes" have "vanished all," and the poet is left contemplating the "whitening bones" of its former inhabitants.

If the poet's feelings find vent briefly in a furious cry against the English tyranny (stanzas 16 – 17), that outcry is immediately perceived to be misplaced, the change being within the poet even more than without:

> Alas! I rave! . . . if Change is here,
> Is it not o'er the land? Is it not too in me?
> Yes! I am changed even more than what I see.
> Now is my last goal near!

The dimness that had been attributed to the ruin (stanza 4) is now on the speaker's eyes (stanza 19), and Mangan gives an ironic turn to an inconsistency that had passed unobserved by the other translators: the abbey is the vision of a *blind* man ("Gone is the use of eye and ear," Ferguson, stanza 19, rhymed version). In the final stanza of Mangan's version, which has no equivalent in the Irish or in any other version, a suspension is introduced that arrests the speaker's suicidal wish:

> I turned away, as toward my grave,
> And all my dark way homeward by the Atlantic's verge,
> Resounded in mine ears like to a dirge
> The roaring of the wave.
>
> (stanza 20)

Death is suspended as a mere simile, "as toward my grave," the poet's return being only "homeward." And if the blind poet, on his "dark way," still insists on a natural correlative for his feelings, it mocks his hopes as another semblance, "like to a dirge," its "*re*sounding" only an echo of the heavily appropriated "dreary, shingly, billow-beaten shore" of the opening stanza.

In its first publication in the *Nation,* the absence that underlies the poet's appropriation of the ruin is nicely confirmed and repeated in a footnote that provides an ironic contrast to Hardiman's recourse to guidebooks: "Literally 'The House of (St.) Molaga,' and now called Timoleague. Our readers will find its position on the Map of Munster."[32] At this point Mangan's ironic play becomes particularly intricate. Where the other translators of the poem had simply adopted the anglicized form of the name, Mangan here reverts to the Gaelic name, only to find himself obliged to retranslate it. Since the place-name is metonymically derived from that of the abbey itself, the full title of Mangan's poem becomes implicitly absurd, given that it only makes sense so long as the anglicized transliteration disguises the meaning that full translation foregrounds. Similar gestures are found throughout the ballads of the *Nation,* with the difference that nationalist balladeers tend to be content merely to revert to a superficial rewriting of the anglicized name in Gaelic orthography.[33] Retained or restored in this form, the Gaelic name becomes a picturesque index of Irishness, appearing to localize and reroot an English writing while actually seeking to master the otherness of Gaelic speech and culture and assimilate it to an English literary culture. The peculiar vacillation that results, between an ineradicable alienation and a process of familiarization, produces a significant index of the contradictions that trouble the nationalist project for a representative Irish literature.

Mangan's referral of his reader to the Ordnance Survey Map of Munster provides a further twist. Davis, recognizing implicitly the probable ignorance of *Nation* writers with regard to the rural countryside of Ireland, had advised nationalist ballad writers to have recourse to the new Ordnance Survey maps in order to gain a sense of the topography of the areas about which they were writing and to find the proper form of Irish place-names.[34] Mangan, of course, had worked for the survey, primarily under John O'Donovan, one of whose responsibilities had been the establishment of standard English forms for Gaelic place-names. Mangan would, therefore, have been familiar not only with the considerable practical difficulties associated with this task but, moreover, with the vagaries and arbitrariness of transliteration and translation.[35] Where translation might render at once a meaning and a history, while nonetheless assimilating the foreign into the dominant language, transliteration obscures both meaning and history under the superficialities of phonetic approximations.

Thus when Mangan, with a characteristically more acute sense of irony than Davis possessed, refers his readers to the "Map of Munster" for the location of the abbey of Timoleague or, rather, Teach Molaga, he points up the distortion on which the nationalists' project is founded, their identity "torn from all places," their history set "adrift among the accidents of translation," their "picturesque and suggestive names" displaced by "arbitrary signs." At the same time, he focuses on the nature of the theoretical detour by which their project sought to reterritorialize an Irish consciousness in English: they are referred, not to an intimate knowledge of the location, which Collins presumably possessed and which Davis regarded as the necessary supplement to maps, nor even, like Hardiman, to guidebooks, but to a map produced by the British military establishment. It is consequently merely one more twist to this irony that, contrary to what the various versions imply, the map will show that Timoleague is not on the edge of the sea. Mangan's "Teach Molaga" thus mobilizes an intricate conjunction of reflections on Irish political life. The poem is a translation, thus already an approximation of Gaelic in English, a fact highlighted by its relationship to two previous, politically oriented appropriations of the same poem. As a translation it proceeds to thematize the very nature of such appropriations, incorporating into itself the process of decay that afflicts the abbey, as the speaker seeks to cast it in his own image. In turn, the nature of that speaker, at once blind and therefore alienated from the object he purports to see, and inwardly more changed than the external world which has been destroyed by British power, reflects upon the readers of the poem. Printed in a journal that is published in Dublin and written in English and is distributed in rural districts where it effectively disseminates English culture and language, the poem both participates in this process and reflects upon it in its scholarly apparatus. Just as the nationalist medium, an English-language journal, depends for circulation on the deterritorialization of the reading public which it seeks to "make racy of the soil," depends, that is, on a detour by which Irish identity is returned to the people by way of its eradication, so the very map to which the reader is referred is an index of the process of administrative homogenization, territorial and linguistic, against which nationalism struggles but on which it depends for its emergence and dissemination.

Translation itself, then, embodies a duplicity which can stand as the approximate index of a contradiction that, in varying degrees, afflicts all nationalisms. Devoted to the unification of a people by the revitalization of a hypothetical past unity, cultural or political, nationalism depends nonetheless on exactly those forces that tend to deracinate a people and that, by instigating an uneven process of modernization, fragment those social structures which come to appear in retrospect as the expression of a coherent and unified national consciousness.[36] Translation, envisaged in both nationalist and unionist cultural thought as an unrefractive medium that restores continuity with the past and transmits the national spirit untransformed, involves for all that an assimilation of alien material in a process of cultural homogenization that is utterly foreign to the older culture. Invoked as a mode of return and reintegration, translation, even by virtue of those very terms, enacts and accentuates the dislocation out of which the dream of unification arises. In the specific context of Ireland, the common assumptions that underlie the cultural theories of both unionist and nationalist politics serve to illuminate their mutual ideological dependence on an expansive administration, without whose instrumental drive to integrate Ireland into the Empire neither the means nor the recipients for the dissemination of alternative ideologies of integration would have existed.

THE ESTRANGEMENT OF THE POET

The vast majority of Mangan's writings are translations in one form or another or are about translation, a fact which will lead us to further consideration of the particular theory of translation that is implicit in his work. But before turning to a discussion of the *University Magazine* articles that contain most of this work, a reading of a couple of poems which are classified by D. J. O'Donoghue as "Original Poems Relating to Ireland" and which were originally published in the *Nation* will help to indicate the extent to which Mangan's writing, in whatever mode, continually returns to ironic reflection on the ideal of transparent mediation which is central to nationalist aesthetics. This reflection is not confined to the theory and practice of translation but in some instances extends to the consideration of other arts. Once again, it is on the disturbing, refractive interference of the artist in the representation that Mangan's poems pivot.

In an early issue of the *Nation*, Thomas Davis had elaborated a nationalist program for painting in an essay entitled "National Art," which is more or less a companion piece to his "Ballad History of Ireland." The essay laments the absence of a school or tradition of painting in Ireland that could represent her history and her landscape. The sort of historical and landscape painting that Davis clearly had in mind correlates to ballad poetry at its most transparent. And, as in the ballad, the inevitable otherness of the represented is overcome by "self-consistency" in the domain of the ideal, which also becomes Davis's rationale for the imitation by Irish artists of great masters of other lands:

> The artist pays the most minute attention to truth in his drawing, shading, and colouring, and by imitating the force of nature in his composition, all the clouds that ever floated by him, "the light of other days", and the forms of the dead, or the stranger, hover over him.
>
> But Art in its higher stage is more than this. It is a creator. . . . The ideal has resources beyond the actual. . . . It is creation, it is representing beings and things different from our nature, but true to their own. In this self-consistency is the only nature requisite in works purely imaginative.[37]

In that "imitating the force of nature" and in the ideal of "self-consistency," one is again dwelling in the ideal world of principle which overcomes discontinuity and forges identity by going "beyond the actual."

It is this deactualization of the landscape that Mangan addresses in a poem published later in the *Nation,* "The Lovely Land," which is based on an unspecified landscape by Daniel Maclise, a painter whom Davis mentions in the course of his essay and who was indeed working in London, in part for *Fraser's Magazine,* in part producing very un-Irish historical and epic paintings.[38] The first stanza of the poem, addressed to the painting, already signals its deceptiveness as Mangan correlates the fanciful work with illusory objects of solace:

> Glorious birth of Mind and Colour!
> Gazing on thy radiant face
> The most lorn of Adam's race
> Might forget all dolour!

Just as part of Davis's plan for National Art was the purchase of foreign casts for imitation, so Mangan fails to recognize in this deceptive painting the contours of an Irish landscape, seeing in it, rather, the work of one or another foreign painter, representing foreign or mythical lands:

> Rich Italia's wild birds warble
> In the foliage of those trees

> I can trace thee, Veronese,
> In these rocks of marble.
> Yet no! Mark I not where quiver
> The sun's rays on yonder stream?
> Only a Poussin's self could dream
> Such a sun and river!

Not only is the Irish version of its own landscape mediated through a foreign tradition, but that foreign painting itself is *dreamt*, the actual further removed from the representation. Moreover, Mangan pursues the concealed identity of the artist rather than the objective "truth" of an immediately presented landscape.[39] In the course of the poem the landscape finally transforms into a magical location for fancy, beyond both art and the actual:

> This is some rare clime so olden,
> Peopled not by men but fays:
> Some lone land of genii days,
> Storyful and golden!

With the projection of Mangan's desire "for magic power to wander / One bright year through such a land," a re-vision of his perception locates the landscape in Ireland, collapsing the vision of the golden land. The subsequent move of the poem nevertheless retains Mangan's ambivalence with regard to the "coloring" process embedded in representation. While condemning himself for not recognizing Ireland through the painting, he is equally ashamed of having to see Ireland first through the painter's mediation:

> Shame on me, my own, my sire-land,
> Not to know thy soil and skies!
> Shame that through Maclise's eyes
> I first see thee, Ireland!

The painting conceals the actual at the very moment it represents it, mediated images being all we can ever attain to. Appropriately, then, the landscape is finally returned into another form of representation as the means to "love" for it. A particular ambivalence attaches to the word "so": therefore, or in just the same way? "So shall I, from this day forth, / Ever sing and love thee!"

Appropriate also is it that Mangan's recognition of Maclise's object centers on an artifact, and one whose identity had itself become questionable in recent times, the Irish pillar tower. Padraic Colum has remarked on the frequency with which he finds this image returning in Mangan's writings, as the only object that gives him "the sense of homeland."[40] Mangan was not alone in articulating a "sense of homeland" based on this particular feature of ancient Irish architecture:

> For the pagan origin of the towers has become a sort of creed among the middle classes, who seem to feel a vague national pride in having monuments of an indefinite antiquity, and greedily accept any suggestion, however impossible, that will help to refer them to that dimly-glorious period when our ports were better known to merchants than those of Britain, and fleets from Tyre and Sidon floated round the favoured seats of Druidic learning.[41]

D. F. McCarthy's poem "The Pillar Towers of Ireland" is a typical example of such uses of the apparently remote past of these towers as a metaphor for the continuity of Ireland's history: "There may it stand forever, while this symbol doth impart / To the mind one glorious vision."[42] The article just quoted, however, is a review of George Petrie's *Ecclesiastical Architecture*, whose painstaking research had apparently "demythologized" the round tower by proving its origin to be monastic and Christian rather than lost in the remote distance of pagan times.

The previous week Mangan had published in the *Nation* a poem that linked architectural and artistic motifs with the insubstantial fabric of Irish dreams of past cultural magnificence. The poem, "A Dream of Connaught in the Thirteenth Century," is not a translation, but once again its "sources" are multiple and open up a range of ironic perspectives. The poem is preceded by an epigraph that refers, once again, to Poussin, but to which Mangan gives a doubly deflected translation: "'Et moi, j'ai été aussi en Arcadie.' — And I, I too have been a dreamer. — Inscription on a painting by Poussin."[43] The original painting depicts Arcadian shepherds discovering a tomb on which are engraved the Latin words *Et in Arcadia ego*, normally understood to suggest that even in an earthly paradise, death is present. Mangan's double translation, first into French, then into English, diffracts the Latin text in such a way that an identity is suggested between the presence of death and the presence of the dreamer in paradise. This identification becomes the burden of the poem, a fact which is emphasized when the actual burden, "But it was the time / 'Twas in the reign / Of Cáthal Mór of the Wine-red Hand," is discovered to be an echo of the refrain of Tennyson's poem of 1842, "Recollections of the Arabian Nights": "For it was in the golden prime / Of good Haroun Alraschid." In Tennyson's poem, the innocence or naïveté of the boy reader allows him to penetrate the magical world of the *Arabian Nights,* only to end with a rather awkward and unresolved suspension of the vision.

In place of the innocence that permitted access to the land of fancy in the latter poem, Mangan poses the passive relation of an entranced dreamer to a landscape whose fanciful, magical features are once again linked to the superficial effects of light:

> I walked *entranced*
> Through a land of Morn;
> The sun, *with wondrous excess of light,*
> Shone down and *glanced*
> Over seas of corn
> And *lustrous* gardens aleft and right.
> (stanza 1, emphasis added)

The passive relation of the dreamer to his vision is maintained throughout the stanzas immediately following:

> Anon stood nigh
> By my side a man. . . .
> Then I saw thrones
> And circling fires,
> And *a Dome rose near me, as by a spell,*
> Whence flowed the tones
> Of silver lyres,
> And many voices in wreathèd swell,
> And their thrilling chime
> *Fell on my ears.* . . .
> (stanzas 2 – 3, emphasis added)

The motifs of music and of the "silver lyre" or harp, emanating from a stately building, and the paradisal setting indicate the substantial source of the poem to be Hardiman's introduction to his *Irish Minstrelsy.* In an extended passage affirming the antiquity of Irish culture Hardiman speaks of the music of ancient Ireland precisely in relation to a cultural harmony: "such peace and concord reigned among them, that no music could delight them more than the sound of each others [sic] voice: *Temur* (*Tarah*) was so called from its celebrity for melody, above the palaces of the world. *Tea* or *Te,* signifying melody or sweet music, and *mur* a wall. *Te-mur,* the wall of music." Hardiman continues to relate "a youthful dream or vision of Cahiremore, monarch of Ireland," which represents the harmonious state of the nation under his sovereignty in the form of a melodious tree.[44] Almost certainly this "Cahiremore" is one of the sources for Mangan's "Cáhal Mór," and the "musical walls" that of his musical dome. But whereas the dream of the Irish king, sovereign "over all the nation," is interpreted to betoken harmony, Mangan's dreamer brings about the collapse of the dream as he willfully intrudes upon it:

> I sought the hall,
>   And, behold! — a change
> From light to darkness, from joy to woe!
>   (stanza 4)

The penetration of the vision by the dreamer, his attempt to identify with it and appropriate it, produces only estrangement, both of vision and dreamer: he "walks forth" in the final stanza into a transformed, denaturalized landscape, marked by the figure of death:

> I again walked forth;
>   But lo! the sky
> Showed flecked with blood, and an alien sun
>   Glared from the north,
>   And there stood on high,
> Amid his shorn beams, a skeleton!

Integral to the alienation of the dreamer from his dream, the dream from the dreamer, is the final framing of the poem as one dreamed "in the Teuton's land," which prevents the naturalizing of the transformed landscape, as if it simply represented the actual famine-stricken condition of Ireland which the poet on awakening will pose against his quasi-allegorical dream of past glories. Both this assumption of the German mask, and the Oriental references—to Tennyson's poem in the refrain, the use of "Khan" for the Irish *Ceann* (chief), and the dome of the visionary landscape—mark the entirety of the poet's estrangement both from his representations and from the landscape they represent. That willed estrangement challenges quite directly the ideals of continuity and integration that sustain nationalist demands on art and poetry, and will direct attention to Mangan's Oriental and Germanic writings, in which the groundwork for an alternative conception of the nature of writing is sketched.

4

Veils of Sais

Translation as Refraction and Parody

THE PROBLEMATICS OF EQUIVALENCE

On the basis of poems such as those discussed in the previous chapter, Mangan has been represented as an early poet of nationalism and as a founding father, however flawed, of that cultural nationalism which from the 1830s to the present has sought to root Irish art in Irish soil. An attentive reading of the material, however, shows that this representation depends on the simplification of his writings or the obscuring of the specific characteristics that differentiate them from the texts and context to which they respond. Recent accounts have seen the writing as flawed in itself but refer the flaws to an ambivalence that lies within the poet. The poems become examples of failed self-expression and the failure, in turn, becomes symptomatic of the predicament of a subjective poet drawn reluctantly into the political arena, or of the minor poet who is unable to find a coherent personal voice.

Though these two representations of Mangan appear at first to be radically at odds, they both depend on a privileging of an anterior moment, historical or biographical, as the validating origin of national or personal authenticity. The production of subjective consciousness through literature, like the production of national consciousness through history or the historical ballad, appropriates an original moment of unmediated experience and strives to render its transmission immediate, unrefracted by the admission of the alien or inauthentic. Hence those critics who valorize self-expression appreciate equally a mode of translation that appears, on the contrary, to be self-effacement: the translator here reproduces, on the model of self-expression, the original whose authenticity must be preserved. That this understanding of translation accords perfectly with that of nationalist theory scarcely needs to be stressed. In foregrounding the mediative function of writing, Mangan's poems on Irish matters thus suggest the outlines of a critique both of nationalist theories of writing and of those that would privilege lyric self-expression as the mark of the most achieved literature. Nor is it accidental that the mode through which this critique takes place is primarily translation, in which, to be sure, the questions of the relation of an origin to its derived product, of the represented to the representation, of the authentic to the secondary, of the alien to the familiar, are critical.

The vast majority of Mangan's writings go under the name of translation. It has also long been known that Mangan, as he himself put it, "perpetrated a great many literary sins, which [. . .] would appear to be 'the antithesis of plagiarism' " (*IA*, p. 28). The number of evidently fraudulent translations among his "Oriental" writings led Mitchel to classify them as "Apocrypha," and O'Donoghue as "Oriental Versions and Perversions," while Mangan's German translations are seeded with "anti-plagiarisms" attributed to the pseudonymic poets "Selber" (self) and "Drechsler" (turner, or, more appropriately, elaborator). An equally uneasy relationship subsists between Mangan's versions and those source poems that can be attributed to existent authors. The versions range from recognizably faithful translations to total transformations based, it seems, on no more than the slightest verbal or thematic hints in the original poem. On other occasions, sources for versions that are attributed to existent writers have not been traced, which may mean only that they are so thoroughly adapted as to be unrecognizable.

One is faced here with the problem, familiar enough in the study of translations, of demarcating borderlines in the continuum between original poems and "perversions," and between "perversions" and "faithful translations." A further, even more vexed problem in the study of translations is the definition of a "faithful translation": is one to define it in terms of prima facie verbal accuracy, or of the transmission of the intention or "spirit" of the poem? Throughout the history of Mangan criticism these problems have been implicit, but rarely, if ever, stated. In practice, they have often been obscured by impressionistic readings of the source texts in pursuit of rough formal and verbal equivalents to the translation, the degree of visible deviation becoming the scale of originality. Alternatively, it is asserted that Mangan's versions bear a relationship to the originals in which, even where most deviant, they remain true to the intention and spirit of their source, sometimes becoming, paradoxically, truer.[1]

The ideal that the translated text should in some sense or other be the "equivalent" of the source text governs all these evaluations of Mangan's translations. The notion of "equivalence" is crucial to a theory of translation for which the central issue is the primacy of the original and the conservation of its authenticity in the secondary text which is its translation.[2] The evaluation of the translation thus takes place in hermetic relation to the original, which it must transmit "without loss of value," and largely ignores the question as to the function of the translation itself, its relation to the target culture and its ideologies. It is, of course, only an aspect of the latent idealism of equivalence theories of translation that it need never be assumed that the perfect equivalent can actually be obtained: that ideal is merely the concept that governs the evaluation of the relative merits of specific translations. Such idealism, however, retains the trace of precisely what is at stake in translation generally speaking, that is, the fundamental opacity of one language to another, or their basic incommensurability. If two languages, let alone two cultures, are irreconcilably different, on what ground is one to measure the equivalence of translation to original? What common measure could begin to assess the value of the derived product in relation to the original to which it is supposed to be equivalent?

The provisional resolution of these problems is posited in the period predominantly by reference, once again, to the *process* rather than to the product of translation. Through the seventeenth and eighteenth centuries, the question of equivalence as outlined here was peripheral: the conception of literature in relation to modes of imitation easily accommodated a variety of modes of translation and legitimized, as for Dryden and Pope, the transformation of originals such as Homer or Chaucer to conform to Augustan modes. For Johnson, indeed, verse that was so idiosyncratic as to be insusceptible of translation was scarcely verse at all.[3] It is only when those specificities of language that render it radically *untranslatable* come to be recognized as representative of the unique spirit of any culture or national language that the problem of equivalence comes to the fore. In this context, equivalence theories of translation partake of that dialectic of originality, individuation, and identification which we have seen to structure nationalist ideology. In the tradition of thought on the origin of language that runs from Herder through von Humboldt, to emerge in Matthew Arnold later in the nineteenth century, each individual language is differentiated out of the original mode of human perception that underlies language in general. The ground for equivalence is accordingly located in the original pre-linguistic experience, which the process of translation seeks to repeat in order to establish, as it were, a common origin for source and target texts.

Once again, it is within the German tradition that the most illuminating analogies with the Irish situation are to be found. The conscious project of forging a German literature that would rival those of France and England motivated an unprecedented labor of translation in Germany during the late eighteenth and early nineteenth centuries and a corresponding production of theoretical discourse concerning translation itself. As in Ireland a half-century later, the goal was twofold: on the one hand, it was hoped that the assimilation of foreign texts, particularly those of ancient Greece and Rome, would contribute to the forging of an independent German literature; on the other, the virtues of German as a language into which to translate, its apparent ability to accommodate other languages and structures of thought with minimal distortion, came to be an index of the "originality" of the German language itself, proving it to be more in touch with the roots of human perception than, for example, the hypercultivated French language. Within a general theory of translation resting on "the postulate of the unity of languages,"[4] the individual translation becomes assimilative precisely by being a re-creation of the original text through repeating the moment of origination that preceded it.

At this point the series of problems that attend equivalence theories of translation becomes manifest. In the first place, to seek to recreate as from the original text merely causes the problem of the authenticity of any reproduction of the original to recede one degree farther. The consequences of this recession are twofold: first, poetic creation itself becomes already a process of translation, and translation merely its repetition, which saves translation only by problematizing the very concept of original poetry; second, rather than stabilizing the ideal of the single and perfect equivalent, the idea of re-creative translation produces the possibility of a potentially infinite set of equally valid and authentic translations.[5] In the second place, the ideal of an authentic reproduction of the original in translation highlights precisely the assumptions concerning the organic relationship of the individual to his native language that invalidate the ideal of equivalence from the outset.

In his essay "Über die verschiedenen Methoden des Übersetzens" (1813), which is both representative and summary of German thinking on translation in this period, Friedrich Schleiermacher outlines the apparent alternatives only to encounter a virtual aporia. One method proposed is to attempt the re-creation of the original work as if it had been composed initially in the target language. One seeks accordingly to repeat the original author's primary experience and to reproduce it authentically. But, as Schleiermacher points out at length, to do so is precisely to destroy the authenticity of the original, which is entirely informed by its mother tongue:

> Indeed it might be said that the aim of translating in such a way as the author would have originally written in the language of the translation is not only out of reach, but also null and void in itself, for whoever acknowledges the shaping power of language, as it is one with the peculiar character of a nation, must concede that every most excellent human being has acquired his knowledge, as well as the possibility of expressing it, in and through language, and that no one therefore adheres to his language mechanically, as if he were strapped into it, to use a superficial simile, and

that no one could change languages in his thinking as he pleases, the way one can easily change a span of horses and replace it with another; rather everyone produces original work in his mother tongue only, so that the question cannot even be raised of how he would have written his works in another language.[6]

The alternative suggested by Schleiermacher is that of "bringing the reader to the original." This process is modeled on another kind of reproduction of an original experience, namely, the reading of a foreign text in its original language, which, even for the most proficient linguist, always retains a degree of strangeness. The translation will accordingly take on something of the quality of the original text and, moreover, of its language, but at the risk of corrupting the translator's language. The result is, first, a tendency to produce translations that, like Schleiermacher's own, are alien both to the source and to the target language, and second, once again, a multiplicity of versions, each of which will bear a different relationship to the original text and render a different aspect of its foreignness. Paradoxically, the attempt to totalize the impression of the original begins to partake of that cumulative process which Schleiermacher finds so inadequate in imitation, "which is composed of parts obviously different from the parts of the original, but which would yet in its effects come as close to the whole as the difference in material allows."[7]

Indeed, in the course of Schleiermacher's argument, the products of translation come to appear increasingly similar even to those other modes of transmission from which he had intended to distinguish translations proper, that is, paraphrase and interpretation. The translator, unwilling to contaminate the spirit of his own language with the spirit of an alien one, is driven either to paraphrase the original or to "transpose his author's entire knowledge and wisdom into the conceptual system of another language," with the result that "the wildest arbitrariness" becomes possible.[8] Subject to the arbitrary caprice of a method of "transposition" in which equivalents are again sought *between* languages rather than by way of re-creation from the root, translation partakes once more of a proliferation of appearances detached from their origins, and as in paraphrase, "neither the spirit of the language transformed nor that of the original are given the opportunity to reveal themselves." The products of translation become like those superficial "conversations of the market-place," divorced from "the deep root of a particular language" and referred to the domain of the interpreter.[9] The logic established by the concept of an ideal equivalent thus renders its ideal impracticable, demonstrating that the grounding of equivalence in a return to the original moment founders exactly insofar as it is the authenticity of the origin that is to be reproduced. Theoretical emphasis on the *process* of translation, by which the equivalence of the product to the original is to be regulated, produces in the end the possibility of an infinite proliferation of translations, all equally valid, precisely because the theory formally reduces the uniqueness of the original to the repetitions of an originating moment that is always the same and in which the same is always reproduced.

Schleiermacher's own remark that "the market-place is every-where" may serve to remind us that, while he seeks to deni-grate interpretation as belonging with commerce and diplomacy, the marketplace is nonetheless active in his own theory, as gen-erally in theories of translation based in the concept of equiv-alence. Indeed, insofar as interpretation remains the primitive mode of translation, bound to the immediate presence of the ob-jects of the interpreted discourse, translation is necessarily dom-inated by an economy of relative values in which equivalents are detached from their original context and are, moreover, de-fined by that detachment. If, in seeking to ground equivalence of meaning in the labor of recreating the original, the theorist of translation repeats the work of the political economist who seeks to reduce the proliferation of equivalents to unity, it is with the similar result of reducing that labor to an abstract and formal repetition. Referred back to the original for the standard of value, the translator finds either that the original must stand outside that economy and cannot be used as a measure, or that it is itself a product of an identical labor of creation and can provide only a relative measure formally identical with that of any translation. The concept of a mode of human creativity that is essentially identical and reproducible undermines the very specificity that it was drawn upon to preserve in transmission.

Equivalence theories of translation thus meet the same kind of problematic as do nationalist attempts to preserve a hypothetical continuity beneath cultural transmissions in general. Resort to the concept of originality as the ground from which to reduce multiplicity to unity concludes by losing the singular origin itself in the totalizing homogeneity that alone can guarantee continuity with the origin: the individuation of nation, individual, or even artwork appears to subside into the anterior identity of the universal human, the race, or human creativity, in a model of integration derived in fact from the economic need for an integrated marketplace. In Germany, theories of the origin of language derive their impetus initially from resistance to the homogenization of cultures under French economic power, but conclude by offering philosophical legitimation to an imperial ideology of the evolution of superior races out of the one human form. In Ireland, as we have seen, nationalism requires the revival of the original racial "genius" as a precondition to resisting British economic and political power, only to depend on that same power for its own dissemination. The English base of Irish nationalism is, of course, exactly what the nationalists seek to disguise in having recourse, even more unambivalently than their German counterparts, to an ideal of translation in which the original can always shine translucently through its representations.

Accordingly, when Mangan practices a mode of translation that reflects upon the distortive, appropriative effects of translation, it is necessary for the critic, in order to grasp the complexities of his approach, to have recourse to a theory of translation that does not rely on the concept of equivalence. Theoretical access of this kind is offered by the concept of "refraction," introduced by André Lefevere in order to describe the effects of intercultural transmissions in general, including translation strictly speaking.[10] Part of Lefevere's contention is that it is impossible to consider the process of refraction or the specific function of the refracted text (whether at the level of what motivates the choice of text or at that of the particular transformation it undergoes) apart from the set of ideological constraints that produces the cultural system in question. In the present field, Ferguson's Gaelic translations are a classic case of the refraction of texts, especially given the ideological constraints that motivate their reception as adequate equivalents of their originals.

REFRACTIVE TRANSLATION AND PARODY

Reading among the *University Magazine* articles that contain the greater part of Mangan's translations, one becomes increasingly conscious of how aware, and how explicit, he was prepared to be about the "refractive" nature of his work. This is particularly the case in the series of "Literae Orientales," his translations from Persian, Arabic, and Turkish poetry in the *Dublin University Magazine*. In the prose articles that frame the translations, Mangan time and again refers to the problems posed by the attempt to carry over the artifacts of so alien a culture into English. Thus, in the fourth article of the series, he remarks:

> Our conclusion is a matured one: we state, and we challenge the entire world of linguists and littérateurs to refute the statement, that Oriental Poetry is not fairly readable in an English translation, — that there is no practicability of idiomatically translating it with effect into our language — perhaps into any of our languages. We do not question the qualifications of the translator for his office . . . all that we mean to aver is that Oriental Poetry apparelled in western dress becomes essentially unrecognizable, forfeits its identity, ceases to be an intelligible object of apprehension to the understanding. It must be read in the original, and, *ce qui est plus et pire*, it must be studied in it; for the bare reading will not answer.[11]

At the opening of this article, Mangan claims to have made a similar statement two years previously, qualifying "a high encomium" on Oriental poetry "by something tantamount to a declaration that that Poetry could not be translated with effect into English" (*LO* 4, p. 377). This comment is for those "intelligent and tasteful few who take an interest in the subject of the papers contributed by us to this Magazine," for only those readers with sufficient interest to look up the comments will be able to catch his ironic drift, either here or a little further on where he challenges them to ask for the explanation as to why his translations, successful as they seem, bear out his assertion (*LO* 4, p. 377). For, on looking up the second article, one finds that not only does Mangan *not* offer a "high encomium" and, rather, at the end of the article states his intense dislike of Oriental poetry,[12] but further, that his comments on the possibility of translation are directly opposed to those of April 1840:

> The languages of all civilized nations, philosophically considered . . . are unquestionably upon a common level as far as regards the vocabularies of genuine thought and feeling. No one of these languages can be richer than another, because no one of them comprehends an ampler stock of ideas than another. . . . For all legitimate purposes of conception and expression we believe that the English language, the German language, and the Turkish language are upon a perfect equality with one another. We believe that that which is good poetry in any one of these languages may be made to appear equally as good poetry in any other of them, if the translator be possessed of skill enough to make it appear so, and that translators may be possessed of such skill there can be no doubt.
>
> (*LO* 2, p. 293)

Mangan's ironic play with this dissembled contradiction allows that there may in fact be no essential contradiction between the two statements. So much is signaled by the word "appear" in the latter citation. The "wide gulf by which we of Europe are severed from the Eastern nations" (*LO* 4, p. 377) is traversed by the "appearance" of translation, and in a certain sense it is the gulf between languages that provides the infinite possibilities of the translator's art. One has only to remember that what this involves (and Mangan is deliberately encouraging his readers of April 1840 to reflect upon this) is not the transparency of the translator but his active "skill" in producing appearances that are an appropriation rather than a transmission of Oriental poems.

Mangan in fact offers two possibilities for translating Oriental poetry, which seem to recapitulate Schleiermacher's categories: either it must become "essentially unrecognizable," forfeiting its identity when "apparelled in western dress," or the translator must himself forfeit his identity. The latter option, however, does not imply the process of "negative capability" that a selective reading of Mangan's commentary in pursuit of "self-expression" might suggest. A reading of his comments in context permits one to follow the undermining irony that runs through a passage that is ostensibly a program for "self-effacement" and introduces the discussion of the absolute differences between Western and Oriental habits of mind that we have just cited:

> He [the translator] must for a season renounce his country, divest himself of his educational prejudices, forego his individuality, and become, like Alfred Tennyson, "a Mussulman true and sworn". Over the wide gulf by which we of Europe are severed from Eastern nations in religious worship, modes of thoughts and habits of feeling, and in the governments, customs and social systems that spring out of these and react upon them sans intermission, no bridge is thrown — the enthusiast must plunge into its depths and scale the opposite steep, or abandon his purpose for ever. If he would appreciate Oriental Poetry, if he would even make any approach to understanding it, he must first disencumber himself of all the old rags of his Europeanism and scatter them to the winds. He must act in the spirit of Goethe's maxim —
>
> > Wer den Dichter will verstehen
> > Muss in Dichterslande gehen.
>
> He must be satisfied to accept sounds for symbols, influences for ideas, and dreams for tangibilities.
>
> (LO 4, p. 377)

On tracing Mangan's own "influences" in this passage, one discovers that he is not suggesting that the superficial resemblance of his poems to the apparent features of Oriental poetry is the product of the kind of self-effacement that he here seems to advocate. The fuller context implied by his two quotations undermines that supposition. The reference to Tennyson directs one once again to the poem "Recollections of the Arabian Nights" in which the "True Mussulman . . . and sworn" is the infant whose privileged access to "the golden prime / Of good Haroun Alraschid" is gained not by divesting himself of his educational prejudices or plunging into the gulf of separation, but by the innocence which, preceding both prejudice and separation, permits one to sail backward down the "forward-flowing tide of time."[13] The maxim of Goethe's, on the other hand, is taken from the quatrain that forms the epigraph to the "Noten und Abhandlung" which Goethe found a necessary adjunct "zu besserem Verständnis des West-östlichen Divans" and which occupy more space than the poems themselves in that volume.[14] In these notes to the *West-östlichen Divan* is included a section, "Über-setzungen," that outlines what Goethe terms the three epochs or stages of translation.[15] The first of these represents our initial encounter with the foreign text and its appropriation into our own terms: "[sie] macht uns in unserm eigenen Sinne mit dem Auslande bekannt." It is comparable to Schleiermacher's "paraphrase." The third, and highest, represents that in which "man die Übersetzung dem Original identisch machen möchte": one tries, as in Schleiermacher, to make the translation identical to the original. These two epochs might be represented respectively by Eugene O'Curry's or John O'Donovan's prose renderings of the Gaelic and Ferguson's verse translations of the same. But it is the second epoch, which bears some relation to the concept of "refraction," that is most relevant to Mangan's practices as a translator. Here, "man sich in die Zustände des Auslanders zwar zu versetzen, aber eigentlich nur fremden Sinn anzueignen und mit eigenem Sinne wieder darzustellen bemüht ist": one tries to put oneself into the situation of the foreigner, but really one only appropriates and reproduces the foreign in one's own sense. This is exactly what Mangan is driving at in his description of the problems of translating Oriental poetry and, so long as we recognize that the appropriation is one of which his articles and "translations" would have us be aware, it may serve as a description of his own practices.

The application of Goethe's description of the second epoch of translation to Mangan's own procedures as translator gains peculiar validity when it is observed that Goethe wishes to term that epoch "parodic, in the purest sense of the word" ("Solche Zeit möchte ich im reinsten Wortverstand die parodistische nennen"). Goethe's conjunction of parody and translation is singularly apposite, despite the ambivalence of his use of the term *parodistische* in its purest sense. Discussions of parody have constantly emphasized precisely the ambiguity of the word's meaning rather than its "pure" sense. The original Greek *parodia* can mean equally a song *dependent* on another or a song sung in *opposition* to another, a distinction caught neatly in the German terms *Beigesang* and *Gegengesang*.[16] This ambivalence attaches equally to translations of the kind to which Goethe here refers. In the first and most obvious sense, all translations are *Beigesänge*, dependent from the outset on the original material to which they refer. An element of imitation is as inseparable from the activity of translation as it is from parody, however much a translator may seek, as Schleiermacher does or as Goethe does in his third epoch, to transcend the status of mere superficial imitation. But, much as the function of parody is the mockery and displacement of the targeted text from its authoritative position, so in translations, and especially in those of the sort that Goethe here intends, the relationship of dependence on the original modulates into one of displacement. The translation supplants its original in both a literal and a metaphorical sense.

In the first place, the translation, as readable version, takes the place of the original text in the target culture, a phenomenon utterly familiar in the case of the Bible or Homer. This process, without which successful translation is inconceivable, is in the second place reflected in a more subtle displacement through which translation approximates even more closely to parody understood as *Gegengesang*. The supplanting of the original is a more radical effect of translation than a mere exchange of language: the very possibility of translating, of rendering a text other to itself while still claiming the essential identity of the two versions, begins to open the question as to the authority that the original holds by virtue of its originality. Not only is the original obliged to appear as itself a kind of translation, a movement which we saw to be intrinsic to German Romantic translation theory, but in a quite real sense it also becomes a secondary text, referred to as a kind of commentary on the translation that has supplanted it. So much is made manifest in the production of parallel texts, or in the notes which remain as a residue or trace of the alien in the margins of a translation. But what this remainder insists upon is that parodic texts, and this is perhaps even clearer in the case of translations than in that of parody proper, operate precisely by the continuing oscillation between dependence and opposition. The parodic text is marked by its refusal ever to supplant entirely the text on which it depends, so that no complete supersession of the original text takes place such as would finally reconstitute the parody or translation as itself an original. While the aim of parody in the simplest sense is the destruction of the targeted text by means of the mimicry and mockery of its style or structure, the parodic text continues to presuppose "a reference to the subject which is parodied, and a necessary dependence on it."[17] Similarly, even where the ideal of translation is to achieve an equivalence with the original so perfect, indeed, as to efface it, the inevitable failure to attain that ideal and to overcome cultural differences holds open the oscillation between likeness and strangeness that defines the peculiar aura of the parallel text. It is, of course, precisely insofar as they maintain the play of differences by emphasizing the persistence of a dependent relationship to an anterior text that parodic texts succeed in foregrounding reflection on the refractory and appropriative nature of all texts.

Both Mangan's "original" and his translated texts can thus be seen as parodic "im reinsten Wortverstand." As we have already seen, a text like "Lament for the Ruins of the Abbey of Teach Molaga" can only be read fully in relation to the texts that precede it; so read it becomes, in a very direct sense, parodic translation. What it refuses to do is to supersede the anterior texts on which it depends, a relationship which is itself parodied in the note that refers the reader to the Ordnance Survey maps. By holding open that relationship, the parodic text invokes reflection upon the appropriative or refractory nature of translation precisely by refusing to exonerate itself from the same processes. Again, exactly because the poem is a translation and will therefore be assumed to reproduce the characteristics of the original with minimum distortion, it can incorporate a reflection upon the extent to which appropriation and refraction are fundamental elements of all writing: the "pathetic fallacy" of the blind man's vision is ascribed in the first place to the original, not to the translation.

Like the parodic translations of Goethe's second epoch, but with a greater self-reflexivity, Mangan's parodic writings continually emphasize not just the assimilation of the original to the foreign but, further, the inauthenticity of the writing that is the product of that process. The appearance of translation is matched and framed by a writing that is not what it appears, a point which is of course lost when the Oriental poems, for example, are extracted from their prose contexts and made to appear as samples of Mangan's somewhat perverse genius. Neither the distorting effects of selection or citation nor the understanding of that process as "per-version" in the strict sense was unfamiliar to Mangan. The refractive effect of disjunctive citation is, indeed, one of the classic parodic strategies he employs in order to undermine faith in the appearance. Thus, for example, in the passage cited above, the citation from Tennyson, which appears to be grammatically and argumentatively entirely assimilated, turns out when traced back to its source either to be perverted from its original meaning or to pervert the argument into which it has been incorporated. It works similarly against the second citation, from Goethe, through which a whole scholarly apparatus is brought into play in the attempt to overcome the gulf that separates the like from the unlike, only to conclude with a meditation upon translation that ultimately in none of its stages allows a more than apparent equilibrium between the two poles. Wrenched from context, neither citation renders its fullest implications without a supplementary labor of interpretation, which involves a further regression into the anterior text.

This procedure is not of course one that provides access to the true meaning ironically concealed beneath the appearance: rather, citation, like translation, problematizes the relation of any text to whatever, text or "experience," is anterior to it. Goethe's lyrics in the *West-östlichen Divan* are already imitations through which "authentic self-expression" is mediated, and produce as a supplement the labor of authentication that is contained in the "Noten und Abhandlungen" which are, in fact, the trace of a work of study that is *prior* to their ostensible occasion. Tennyson's innocent, oneiric entrance to the world of the Arabian Nights is not only a *Recollection,* it is crucially a reverie preceded by reading. Mangan's own text is, as we have seen, complicated not only by citation, but by citation of his own previous articles which have concerned themselves with the impossibility of representative translation, the citing of another culture. What is perverse about the refractory text — citation, translation, or parody — is not that it refracts its source but, importantly, that it seeks to trouble the very order of priority by which the transmission of texts and cultures is to be governed. By another logic than that which governs the continuous assimilation and reproduction of the origin in the derived, the text that cites is prior to that which is cited. Recollection precedes reverie and the reverie precedes the reading that inspires it. The citations, which are supposed to support the text that depends upon them, fail to do so precisely because they have ceased to be anterior to it and have in turn become dependent on it for transmission. Recessiveness, which is a constant effect of parody, particularly insofar as all parody is in the broadest sense citational, partakes of that same interplay of dependence and supersession that is the most general quality of parody.[18] Accordingly, unlike Romantic irony, it does not even imply the possibility that the process of return toward the origin, however unattainable that origin may be, may reproduce formally the identity of the derived and the original. If, in metafictional parody, it is the function of parodic treatments of fictional mediations to criticize the modes in which the antecedent real is appropriated, in the kind of parodic text with which we are here concerned it is the very status of anteriority and originality that comes to be called into question.

PARODIES OF PARADISE

Throughout the "Literae Orientales" Mangan employs a variety of parodic modes which, in varying degrees, address the status of sources and origins. The simplest of these is, of course, the question of the immediate sources of the material that he uses in the articles. Jacques Chuto has shown in his article "The Sources of James Clarence Mangan's Oriental Writings" that much of Mangan's source material can be traced in Joseph von Hammer-Purgstall's *Geschichte der osmanischen Dichtkunst,* which he criticizes and openly translates from in the second of the "Literae Orientales."[19] Throughout that series Mangan extracts scholarly passages from von Hammer, distorts them or appropriates them — with varying degrees of disguise — as his own, and frequently sets up blind trails through false or inaccurate references. A similar process can be found in his use of Barthelémy D'Herbelot's *Bibliothèque orientale.*[20] Furthermore, even when one has followed up such sources, one finds that more often than not the stated sources of the poems themselves — of which von Hammer's four-volume work contains thousands — are either nonexistent, misattributed, or when existent, have, as Mangan quite honestly says, completely forfeited their identity. Many of the poems are Mangan's own invention, as is, for example, "The Time of the Barmecides."[21]

The scholarly apparatus of Mangan's "Literae Orientales," seeded with references that lead to nothing or to indirections, parodies the scholarly pursuit of a truth that his appropriations constantly apparel in Western garb. Similarly, his notes are an ironic subversion of the illusion, promoted by poems such as Tennyson's "Recollections of the Arabian Nights," that there is an easy and innocent access to be gained to the world of the Orient through imaginative identification. Such notes, of course, form part of the pleasure of another style of "Oriental" poem, adding a superstructure of erudite exoticism to the verse. The most relevant example in the context of Mangan's writing is probably Thomas Moore's *Lalla Rookh*, a long "Oriental" romance in verse and prose published in 1817, which was deliberately composed to exploit the fashion for Oriental romances initiated by Lord Byron and Samuel Rogers. The plethora of notes in Moore's work gives an indication of how the sensuous exoticism of the verse is supported by the exoticism of the intellect, with the intention, not in the end so unlike Tennyson's, of allowing the reader to feel carried more effectively into an authentic Orient. Turning, on the other hand, to Mangan's "The Hundred-leafèd Rose" (which is, Chuto points out, a condensation of a poem of one hundred couplets by Lamii translated in von Hammer), one perceives how many of his references merely "unveil" pieces of common knowledge disguised in the text by the "Oriental" nomenclature — "Al-Khalill" is more familiar as Abraham, "Jose" as Joseph of the many-colored coat, "Issa" as Jesus, "Balkis" as the Queen of Sheba — or even raise further obscurities, as with the confusion that surrounds the identity of "Manszur."[22]

The difference between Moore's notes and Mangan's lies in their opposed functions. Moore's provide a set of sources that substantiate the authenticity of the Oriental scenario. To read among them is, almost literally, to be enriched and reassured of containing and possessing the Orient. In Mangan's case, the notes perform quite the opposite role, actually undermining one's sense of mastery of a certain field; while accumulating a vast capital of ostensibly authenticating sources, they turn the reader's investment of labor into a depletion of his resources. Both the poems and the articles absorb their readers in a quest for origins which, since those origins are perpetually falsified, becomes unendingly protracted. At times, Mangan's play reaches the point of deliberate *self*-parody, as where he rewrites the apparently conventional "Time of the Roses" (*LO* 1, pp. 290–92) as "The Days of Nouroz'iz" (*LO* 4, pp. 380–81). Even in the few poems scattered among the "Literae Orientales" where a burlesque intent is not made evident, the recessive quality characteristic of parodistic texts is already so deeply inscribed as to belie the conventional reading, furthered by their anthologization out of context, which understands them as lyrical expressions of a Mangan lurking beneath an Oriental persona.

Perhaps the classic instance of an Oriental persona who has suffered this dubious identificaiton with Mangan as the suffering, nostalgic poet is the speaker of "The Caramanian Exile," kidnapped as a youth to become a Spahi or soldier of the tyrant against his own people.[23] No Oriental source has been traced for this poem, and Mangan strongly hints in the prose text both before and after the poem that it is one of his own productions. Suggesting that Doctor Wilde, the Irish antiquarian, might think of writing a history of the Caramanian struggle against the Ottoman Empire, Mangan claims that "we shall be ready, at a day's notice, to deposit in his hands a dozen or so of such poems as the following" (*LO* 5, p. 536); at the end of the poem he remarks that "one is not often electrified by such outbursts of passion and feeling in Ottoman poetry" (*LO* 5, p. 538). One would, however, be too quick in assuming that the poem is therefore an elegy expressing Mangan's own sense of alienation. A probable "source" of the poem's refrain — "Karaman! O, Karaman!" — can be traced in the second of the "Literae Orientales" articles. Here the reading of a brief relic of the exiled Caramanian poet Yusuf Scheiki to Al Shemseddin, a general engaged in the conquest of Constantinople, "caused a light like that of the sun to illumine his features as he sat one day in his tent, and he shrieked aloud, O, Kermian! O, Kermian!" (*LO* 2, p. 302). Around that shriek, in a variant spelling, Mangan seems later to have built his poem, rather as Poe constructed "The Raven" almost mathematically around the word "Nevermore."[24]

The "Karaman" of the poem is again spelt differently, as if to indicate the problems raised for the translator by the renaming of places, problems similar to those that the Irish Ordnance Survey and the nationalists were constantly confronting. Once one is exiled or alienated from the home and language of one's forebears, is not the renaming of places in the "original" language a further alienation, in which they become at best a reminder of loss, or at worst exotic misfits finding an uncomfortable place in another language, demanding a footnote to elucidate them? Transliteration, with its attendant "accidents," becomes a virtual parody of "literal translation." This orthographical uncertainty — excised from all editions of Mangan's poems — forms an external frame for the uncertainty attaching to "Karaman" within the poem, which appears only in dream, and even there only as semblance:

> I see thee ever in my dreams,
>   Karaman!
> Thy hundred hills, thy thousand streams,
>   Karaman! O, Karaman!
> As when thy goldbright Morning gleams,
> As when the deepening sunset seams
> With lines of light thy hills and streams,
>   Karaman!
> So thou loomest on my dreams,
>   Karaman!

"Karaman" looms as a dream out of the loss, which the constant repetition of the word can name but never reattain. The speaker oscillates between this dream and another semblance, of present reality, whose subjective seeming is caught up in the rhyme chain "dreams-seams-seem":

> The hot bright plains, the sun, the skies,
>   Karaman!
> Seem deathblack marble to mine eyes,

> Karaman! O, Karaman!
> I turn from Summer's blooms and dyes;
> Yet in my dreams Thou dost arise
> In welcome glory on my eyes,
> Karaman!
> In thee my life of life yet lies,
> Karaman!

Caught up in the perception only of semblances, where no reality inheres in either "deathblack marble" or "Summer's blooms and dyes," Mangan's exile invests his life in yet another semblance, the dream of a home from which he has been dragged as a child. The progressive intensification of the rift between the present and former selves of the speaker through the following stanzas leads his thought into a double movement of retrospection and foreboding characteristic of Mangan's writing:

> Of late my thoughts rove more among
> Thy fields; — foreshadowing fancies throng
> My mind, and texts of bodeful song.
>
> (stanza 7)

Once again, however, the meaning of these "bodeful texts," which, as in the elegy on "Teach Molaga," should be death, is held in suspense while the foe invades the last stanza. At this point, Mangan the scholar reenters to cast doubt on the authenticity of the poem and to parody its dilemma in the burlesque "Wail and Warning of the Three Khalenders," which follows it. The suspension of the speaker's attempt to return to and identify with his origins is doubled in the contextual problematizing of the poem's own relation to the putative source that might have endowed it, in turn, with an authentic identity.

Mangan's parodic obscurantism with regard to the tracing and reproduction of origins is not merely playful virtuosity but has a quite specific relevance both to British cultural ideology and to the reflective forms of resistance to it that are current in the early formation of Irish cultural nationalism. The studies of Orientalists and philologists of the fifty years preceding Mangan's articles had done much to give a scientific orientation and therefore credibility to the tradition that placed the Eden of human origins in the Middle East. In keeping with that political tradition in

German linguistic thought which sought to identify German as an "original" language, German philologists such as Alexander von Humboldt, Franz Bopp, and the brothers Grimm, as well as more speculative philosophers such as A. W. Schlegel, had begun to trace the origins of European languages from Indo-Aryan roots, while Oriental scholarship had begun to trace the migration of Eastern peoples westward.[25] In the British context, where Oriental scholarship had a more material base in the actual possession of colonies in the Middle and Far East, a founding figure is Sir William Jones. As early as 1789, in his *Sixth Anniversary Discourse* to the Asiatic Society, Jones felt able to state categorically that Iran was the single true origin of the Indo-Aryan peoples.[26]

As the close affinities among the various products of Western European research into the Orient might suggest, the ascription of "originality" to the Oriental peoples is quite ambivalent in its intent. The assertion that the Eastern races represent an earlier stage of human history than the Western races transforms easily into the assertion that they are accordingly more "primitive" and, therefore, given an evolutionary model of human history that is at once racial, linguistic, and political, that they are susceptible of cultivation and development by Western powers. The apparently disinterested research of the Asiatic Society is thus intimately linked with the requirements of British commerce and colonial administration on two levels, that of furnishing cultural and material information to guide imperial exploitation and control, and that of ideologically legitimating colonial intervention. "Knowledge," as Mangan himself put it, "is not Power, but knowledge readily suggests a mode for the acquisition of Power."[27] In Jones's writings this function of scholarship is made quite explicit, and his attitude to the Orient is entirely proprietorial: on first seeing the coast of Asia, he says, he was unable to help remarking upon "how important and extensive a field was yet unexplored, and how many solid advantages unimproved."[28] In his "Second Discourse" he goes on to show how the linked studies of the history, geography, and mineralogy of "*these inestimable provinces*" were "momentous objects of research to an *imperial*, but, which is a character of equal dignity, a *commercial* people."²⁹ The metaphor of "concealment" is recurrently used of the as yet unexplored resources of Asia, and research into sources and resources comes to be perceived as a kind of unveiling or mining, metaphors which in turn aptly encapsulate the interrelation of imperial activities in bringing concealed material into the light of day. It is precisely this model of truth as a progressive excavation and assimilation of the concealed and primitive and its instrumental function in validating imperial appropriation that Mangan's Oriental articles appear to undermine, being themselves minefields for the unwary reader in search of origins.

The metaphors that justified Britain's colonialism in the East clearly have parallels in the discourse on the "internal colony" of Ireland, just as the engagement of British scholars in Orientalist research shares the assimilative function of projects such as the Ordnance Survey, administrative research, or Ferguson's translations. It is, of course, a further index of the reflexive relation of nationalism to imperialism that Irish scholars concerned even before the full emergence of nationalism to vindicate Ireland's "originality" had had recourse to argumentation quite similar to that used by Jones to vindicate the superiority of Indo-Europeans to the Oriental races. Proof of the venerable nature of the Irish race was furnished by a large body of scholarly opinion that had been able to trace in the Irish language the signs of an Oriental origin. The foremost of these scholars, whose methodology consisted largely of an impressionistic etymology based on the phonetic resemblances of words, was Charles Vallancey, to whose researches Mangan alludes when he remarks in the fourth of the Oriental articles that "according to Vallancey every Irishman is an Arab" (*LO* 4, p. 393).³⁰

Theories that link the Irish with the remote origins of mankind, which are the extreme fringe of the drive to vindicate and unify Ireland through research, have a popular equivalent that is exemplified by *Lalla Rookh,* in the parallel fashions of Orientalism and Celticism.³¹ The exoticism of both, which is sustained in the popular imagination by the comparative remoteness of their location from the centers of Empire, is involved in the notion of an "original people" in the sense of one that is less removed from untamed natural origins than the civilized European. If this implies a certain barbarism, it is a barbarism that is the result of the natural, uncontrolled expression of passion and sentiment, a notion whose ambivalent status is again evident in the more sophisticated uses made of it later by Ferguson and the Young Irelanders, in their different ways. The "originality" of the Oriental poet — or of the Celtic — lies in his closeness to the "origins" of humankind and human feeling, an etymological play whose paradoxes are, as James Stam has argued, at the heart of those Romantic aesthetic theories for which the original genius is he who returns to and repeats the original moments of human perception, stripped of the veils of inherited customs and rules.[32]

Mangan's response to such theories, particularly with regard to Oriental poetry, is simply to deny and even invert the premises on which they are based. The first article of the "Literae Orientales" stands as an introduction to the problems of origins, in both senses, that his Oriental series will raise. On the historical level, we are obliged to follow a learned disquisition whose real bearing is a demonstration of how little the Orientalists in fact know about the history of our supposed Eastern origins. But before we embark on this disquisition, Mangan has made his most lucid statement of the way in which, even if we acknowledge that the mind's human sympathies are with the East, we are actually speaking of "its conceptions of the East." "The mind," he says, "is without a home on the earth"; it is "a vagrant whose barren tracts are by no means confined to the space between Dan and Beersheba" (*LO* 1, p. 274). Its fascination with the East becomes, then, a fascination with the shadow of its own nostalgia and projections. The passage in which this argument is developed is long and intricate, but the multiple ironic shifts contained within it demand that it be read as fully as possible:

> That shadowy species of affinity which the mind in its complacent moods delights to assume as subsisting between the Orient and its own images of Genii-land possesses rich and irresistible charms for human contemplation. Imagination feels averse to surrender the paramount jewel in the diadem of its prerogatives — a faith, to wit, in the practicability of at some time or another realizing the Unreal. If the East is already accessible, so may be at last — the reverse who dares prophesy? — "the unreached paradise of our despair;" and

so long as the Wonderful Lamp, the dazzler of our boyhood, can be dreamed of as still lying *perdu* in some corner of the Land of Wonders, so long must we continue captives to the hope that a lovelier light than any now diffused over the dusky pathway of our existence will yet be borne to us across the blue Mediterranean. Alas! wanting that which we have not, cannot have, never shall have, we mould that which we really have into an ill-defined counterfeit of that which we want; and then, casting a veil over it, we contemplate the creature of our own fancy with the same sort of emotion that may be supposed to have dilated the breast of Mareses, the artist of Sais, when he first surveyed the outlines of the gigantic statue himself had curtained from human view. Yet it is on the whole fortunate that Speculation can fall back on such resources. Slender and shifting as they are, they serve as barriers against Insanity.

(LO 1, pp. 274–75)

The statue of Sais to which Mangan here refers is a topos familiar from the German Romantic tradition with which he was profoundly engaged: some years later he was himself to translate Schiller's "Das verschleierte Bild zu Sais."[33] The veiled statue at Sais is the image of the truth; in Schiller's version the student who rashly raises its veil in the Temple of Isis is driven mad and never communicates what he has seen. In Novalis's version, in his fragmentary novella "Die Lehrlinge zu Sais," two representations of the statue emerge: in the body of the tale, the pilgrim discovers on raising the veil that the statue represents his first love, to whom he has unwittingly returned in the course of his wanderings; in a brief note among the sketches for continuing the novella the image that the pilgrim sees on raising the veil is that of himself.[34] Novalis's two representations are, of course, linked in their common indication that the perception of the truth depends on a prior return to the sources of perception. What is singular in Mangan's version is that the image concealed beneath the veil, and, indeed, "surveyed" even by the artist only when *already* veiled, is not truth but, rather, "an ill-defined counterfeit of that which we want," a "creature of our own fancy." The origin that underlies the appearance of concealment is already the projection of our own desire to attain the origin, an origin that is itself already falsely figured in a heavily appropriated Orient. The role of art in this process, as Mangan's stress — absent from both

Novalis and Schiller—on the prior productive work of the "artist of Sais" suggests, is not that of demystification but, rather, that of counterfeiting and veiling. Our relationship to the work of art corresponds precisely to our relationship to the ideal origin, which distracts the mind in its irredeemable alienation from a paradise that is the projection of its own despair. The mind remains, accordingly, in the domain of "shadows," in a never-ending play of speculation which is represented in the logic of Mangan's argument as being not merely the index of perpetual alienation but, furthermore, the inevitable product of the effort to transcend it. The products of original genius and the original paradise of Genesis are displaced onto the fanciful land of the Genii, mythical beings who, as Mangan would have known if only from his readings of D'Herbelot, once occupied but were dispossessed of the pre-Adamic world.[35]

The Oriental "translations" that are prefaced by this passage protract the speculation on origins that is Mangan's explicit concern. There is, as we have seen, a quite superficial play with the counterfeit work constantly in process and perpetually complicated by the fact that we can never be consistently sure whether or not a source really is available: the counterfeit itself may always be only an appearance of forgery. One field of Oriental poetry to which Mangan constantly returns, Ottoman (or "Osmanlee") poetry, allows him to complicate the issue further and to engage with the quite fundamental differences between Western and Oriental poetry. Taking his cue from von Hammer's preface to the *Geschichte der osmanischen Dichtkunst,* Mangan stresses once again, in the introductory article to the series, that Ottoman poetry is not to be qualified by originality: "Nobody ever dreamed of claiming originality for the poetry in question: nor need we care whether it be original or not" (*LO* 1, pp. 274–75). Von Hammer, in an extensive justification of his choice of the word *Dichtkunst* rather than *Poesie* to characterize Ottoman poetry, explains that Turkish poets base their works "on the slavish imitation of Persian and Arabic poetry, or genres and forms produced by them." The resultant quality of artificiality and unnaturalness thus differentiates such poetry from *Poesie,* defined by Goethe in the *West-östlichen Divan* as being "neither speech nor art" but, rather, based entirely on nature and the "true expression of an excited and elevated spirit."[36] Ottoman poetry is thus for von Hammer the contrary of *Poesie* in the strict sense, being defined precisely by imitation rather than originality. Thus as Mangan exploits this series of definitions, he is elaborating upon the fact that the numerous poems that he derives in one sense or another from the Ottoman will be themselves imitations of imitations, writings doubly removed from an "originality" already shown to be suspect as a concept.

By the fourth article in the series, Goethe's emphasis on *expression* as the defining characteristic of poetry in general is taken up by Mangan to furnish the basis for differentiating Oriental poetry as a whole (and not just Ottoman poetry) from Western poetry. His discussion emphasizes once again the incommensurability of Occidental and Oriental cultures, the beauties of Oriental poetry being "of a nature to be but imperfectly tested by any of those standards that we commonly apply to the merits of poetical composition among ourselves." As poetry for Goethe is "always the true expression of an excited and elevated spirit," Mangan stresses the validity of an Oriental poetry in which, on the contrary, *impression* dominates:

> Indeed if we were succinctly to describe the difference between this poetry and our own we should say that the latter depends upon *Expression,* but the former chiefly upon *Impression.* It is true that Expression always proposes Impression as its end, and that Impression is producible only by the agency of Expression, but what we mean to assert is that whereas in the West strict attention to the modes and accidents of Expression is indispensable to the production of Impression, in the East it seems almost wholly superfluous.
>
> (*LO* 4, p. 378)

Thus where Western poetry is evaluated in relation to the spirit that precedes and informs it or to the "unifying soul of Thought" which is "the great irradiating light of Imagination," we are but rarely able to overcome that prejudice which characterizes an Oriental poetry that has no interest in expression as "misty currents of fancy" or as "a lawless, unfixable, ghostlike thing, irreducible to rule, unamenable to criticism, and in its constituent elements as little to be trusted for permanence as the colors of the chameleon or the tableaux of the kaleidoscope" (*LO* 4, p. 378).

Oriental poetry is thus referred to the superficial play of colors and appearances, envisaged as a product of fancy rather than of an imagination whose vivifying and informing power is based precisely on the repetition of the original moment of creation. The import of Mangan's irony is especially ambivalent throughout the passage, particularly where he uses Hamlet's remark about "a god kissing carrion" to typify *Oriental* tropes, with the result that it becomes virtually impossible to establish how Oriental poetry is to be evaluated in relation to Western poetry. The point is precisely that the ground for equivalence has been removed insofar as the preconditions for poetry in each culture are entirely different: the abstract form of a universal human creative labor is lacking. The gulf can accordingly be bridged only by the *appearance* of translation, since any translation that sought to reproduce its original by way of returning to the original mode and moment of creation would doubly misrepresent an Oriental poetry that is to be characterized as profoundly unoriginal in any Western sense of the term. Hence it is more or less indifferent whether the poems translated have, like "The Hundred-leafèd Rose," an actual source or are, like "The Time of the Roses," "original" poems. But exactly because the uncertainty with regard to sources casts suspicion on the authenticity of these apparent translations, we are not hereby presented with a virtual equivalent of an authentic Oriental experience of poetry. The closest we reach to what Mangan represents as the habitual attitude of the Oriental reader is the direct contrary of the latter's readiness "to trust both *in* and *against* appearances" (*LO* 4, p. 379). The veils that his "perverted" translations cast around their object are lifted only to reveal counterfeit images that induce in the interested few an irreversible disposition to suspicion *of* rather than trust *in* appearances and the illusion that they are subtended by "that which we want." The consequent multiplication of ungrounded appearances becomes the stimulus to an assiduous cultivation of suspicion with regard to the formative (*bildend*) power of originality and authenticity.

5

Oversettings from the German
Dissembling the Sublime

TRANSLATION AS ANAMORPHOSIS

Mangan's translations from and articles on German literature of the late eighteenth and early nineteenth centuries constitute the greater part of his literary output. Most of this work appeared in the *Anthologia Germanica,* a series of articles that were published in the *Dublin University Magazine* from the mid-thirties to the mid-forties and were supplemented by further anthologies, such as those entitled "Stray Leaflets from the German Oak." Throughout the 1840s, German material by Mangan also appeared in a variety of other journals, including the *Nation* and the *Irish Penny Journal.* The material he translated is remarkably various, ranging from the work of major figures such as Goethe, Schiller, Jean Paul, Novalis, and Heine to lesser-known writers including Justinus Kerner, Christoph Tiedge, and Friedrich De La Motte Fouqué.

Certainly the most prolific period of Mangan's writing career was that of the German and Oriental writings, and it coincided with a period in which the fashion for German literature and thought had reached its height in Dublin. The modishness of German thought and writing should, however, be read as the index of an underlying shift in public attitudes, as both a symptom of and an influence on related transformations in the political and aesthetic orientations of the reading public. The history of the reception of German literature in Ireland is closely analogous to that of Orientalism and Celticism, and it reveals a similar transformation in the understanding of the relation of aesthetic cultivation to ethical and political concerns. Both Celtic and

Oriental literatures initially represented the wild and uncultivated margins of civilized sensibility but came gradually to represent not so much a threat to the rational organization of civil society as evidence of the susceptibility of the primitive to cultivation. Similarly, German literature of the *Sturm und Drang* and of the early Romantics was initially understood in the context of the French Revolution, as symptomatic of emotional Jacobinism and excess. The enormous popularity of German plays in Dublin at the turn of the century was quite explicitly seen to relate to the spirit of the United Irishmen of 1798 and of 1803.

The subsequent fashion for German literature, in the 1830s and 1840s, coincided equally with a period of social upheaval, yet the attitude to German writing then reflected a shift in understanding that was not solely concerned with the internal developments of that literature itself. Early issues of the *Dublin University Magazine* already included articles on German writers, commencing with an account of Professor Zander's public lectures on the history of German poetry in the third number, and the *Magazine* continued to publish a considerable quantity of translations from and articles on German literature by Mangan and other writers. The sanction that this journal, conservative as its leanings were, came to accord to German thought and writings was based primarily on the extent to which that literature was seen to advocate the cultivation of emotional disorder into an evolving order: it provides accordingly the perfect model for the cultivation of the Irish people away from emotional Jacobinism and toward constitutional order by means of that cultural education which the *University Magazine* hoped to promote. On the nationalist wing, and somewhat later, a similar appreciation of the Germans was based, as we have seen, on admiration for the role played by literary culture in forging, out of disunity and deprivation, both a German literary tradition and a national consciousness. In the context of a more general shift in cultural and political thinking, the incoherence which German literature had initially represented came to supply the ground for a higher political or ethical unity, within the state and within the individual respectively.[1]

It is in large part the failure to grasp this transformation in the reception of German literature that has determined the lack of serious attention given to the specific nature of Mangan's translations. As with his Orientalist works, it has generally been assumed that in his translations of the German *Sturm und Drang* poets Mangan found oblique outlet for his own emotions and betrayed translation by indulging in self-expression. Despite the long-acknowledged inclusion in Mangan's *Anthologia Germanica* of evidently false translations of poems by "Drechsler" and "Selber" (the former of which combines the figurative sense of overelaboration with the suspicion, in the wake of Carlyle's *Sartor Resartus*, of excrement or rubbish), despite the fact that some of these translations are parodic in the primary and obvious sense, and, moreover, despite Mangan's own unsystematic but repeated criticisms of the Germanic tendency, the habit of identifying Mangan with emotional dispositions expressed in the poetry has persisted since Mitchel's introduction to the *Poems*. Mitchel writes thus:

> No reader who considers the man Mangan, and his sad, strange death-in-life, will wonder to find that in his selection of poems for translation, he has been irresistibly drawn to so many whose burden is dreary retrospection, or a longing for the peace of the grave. There is also another class of ballads, in which German excels all others, and which never did, and never will find so fitting an interpreter as Clarence Mangan: — those poems, namely, which strive to utter that vague, yearning aspiration towards somewhat nobler and grander than the world can give us, — that passionate stretching forth of hands to reach the ever-flying Ideal, which must be to us all as the fair Cloud Juno was to Ixion. It is the mysterious Longing which Schiller calls *Sehnsucht*.
>
> (*Poems* 1859, p. 29)

Mitchel's version of Mangan's relationship to the German poets he chose to translate has become canonical at the expense of ignoring Mangan's own criticisms of the material he is transmitting. In the first place, Mangan is entirely aware of the unevenness of the material he includes in his articles, making it quite explicit whenever he is translating from school anthologies such as those compiled by Wilhelm Klauer-Klattowski or Dr. O. L. B. Wolff, and which, in Mangan's words, consist of repertories of "incredible quantities of middling poetry."[2] Given the enormous vogue for German literature, the anthological nature of Mangan's work is directed toward providing a survey of German writing rather than exhibiting the translator's own elective affinities with any particular set of writers.

When, therefore, in the midst of an anthology of minor German poets Mangan stops momentarily to criticize German poetry in general, it is precisely because these poets represent the lowest common denominator of a tendency equally to be found among the major writers of that tradition. His criticism, moreover, is directly opposed to the interpretation that Mitchel put on Mangan's writings. Mangan is clearly concerned to focus both characterization and critique on the *delusions* of *Sehnsucht*:

> If we were asked what it is that constitutes the leading character-istics of German Poetry, we should be disposed to answer — Too adventurous an attempt to assimilate the creations of the ideal with the forms of the natural world. Throughout that poetry we can trace a remarkable effort to render vivid and tangible and permanent those phantasmagoria of the mind which by the statutes of our nature are condemned to exhibit an aspect of perpetual vagueness and fluctuation.[3]

It is apparent that the nature of Mangan's critique of German poetry is analogous to that of the extended commentary on the Orientalist impulse cited in the previous chapter. As he continues to characterize the poetry, his description again plays with the opposition between the superficial impression and the illusion of interiority, and with the paradox of the discovery of convention-ality where what is expected is originality. Far from the outward expression of an inner impulse to original creation, what Mangan discloses is precisely the conventionality and superficiality of what he is translating:

> Wearing the outward mask and semblance of that which it professes to be, it stands exposed, when stripped of those, as a revelation of incongruities and absurdities — a picture, the group-ing of which presents us with but a mass of blots and shadows, an anomaly with which the heart cannot sympathize — which the understanding is powerless to grapple with. It is, after all, beautiful, but conventionally beautiful, not intrinsically.
>
> (*AG* 4, p. 405)

The only perceptible difference between this poetry and that of the Ottomans is that whereas the latter has no pretensions to being original, instead elevating imitation to a high art, German poetry, precisely by laying claim to expressive originality, produces a false semblance that belies the absence of the interiority it claims to contain.

Paradoxically, then, translation becomes in Mangan's writings not simply the deformation of the original that Schleiermacher feared but, rather, a means of demystification that takes place by way of what his contemporaries constantly referred to as "mystification." Parodic translation strips away the "outward mask and semblance" of poetry precisely by emphasizing the radical disjunction between the surface and the interior which, supposedly, it masks in order to reveal. So radical is that disjunction, indeed, that what is found when the original is unmasked is the absence of substance, the subsistence of "incongruity" and "anomaly" rather than the subjective integrity of the original poet. Accordingly the very models of interior and exterior, of the origin and its derivation, collapse in anomaly: stripping away a false surface, we find beneath it merely another mode of superficiality, "blots and shadows," "a picture" in place of the represented.

Translation thus becomes a mode of criticism rather than representation. Its demystifying function operates by drawing attention to the refractive effects of transmission and by reflecting in turn on the deformations already at work in the "original" itself. "Mystification" in turn becomes a means to ironize the reader who accepts at face value the duplication of the original in the translation, and a way of provoking that reader into suspicious confrontation with translations. Frequently enough, Mangan insists on the need for the reader *not* to accept his translations but to use his own judgment by making exactly the collations that will reveal the disjunctive effect of his work. As in the following passage, Mangan is constantly implying that the refractive nature of his translations is not "for nothing":

> The rudeness of our versions generally is a fair presumption for their faithfulness. We know that we have been charged with paraphrasing and even travestying our originals; and the charge

may be true or false; we neither admit it nor deny; but good-natured judges will perhaps be inclined to consider that we are as literal as the difference between the structure of English and the structure of German will allow us to be. In reality there is no reason that we should perpetuate paraphrases. Translations are considerably easier. To give the words of an author as he has given them himself is obviously less of a task than to be at the trouble of inventing for him words that he never intended to give. The *dolce far niente* of literal rendering must in any case be preferable to the supererogatory fatigue of circumlocutory wantonness. Moreover, a paraphrase, palmed on the public as a translation, is an imposture, and the palmer is an impostor; and the character of an impostor is one that no man assumes for nothing.

The privilege of individual opinion, however, we have always respected; and on that account we decline to offer any formal exculpation of our Anthologies. Were we to pledge our word of honour that we have not deceived the public they would be in a manner coerced into the adoption of a particular belief with regard to the question at issue. We deem it more eligible to leave them the unshackled exercise of their proper judgement.[4]

The intricate network of underminings in this passage, which is generally characteristic of Mangan's prose, indicates the real "duplicity" in which Mangan's translations and articles are involved. Far from the *dolce far niente* of literal translation, Mangan is constantly exercising the right of judgment and asking the reader to do the same. To offer an "exculpation" would merely be to allow the reader to relapse into the security of believing himself to be reading either "originals" in a transparent, literal translation, or else paraphrases which stand themselves as "original creations" and need not to be referred to their sources.[5]

This is not to say, however, that Mangan should be regarded as an "original poet" whose matter simply happens to be another poem in another language. Mangan's response to the problem of the difference between the structures of two languages, and, indeed, between cultural systems, is not to suggest, as did a contemporary translator from the German, J. H. Merivale, that where deviation results in the translator's "surpassing" the original, "he is, in strictness of speech, no longer a translator, being himself an original poet."[6] He is equally far from the method of another contemporary German translator, John

Anster, who in his translation of Goethe's *Faust* attempted to work back through each passage to "the creative spirit of the same living imagination felt alike through all." Such a method eschews the attempt to provide literal equivalents by pursuing the original creative moment that lies behind the superficies of expression. A similar method, of which Anster is suspicious even where he himself avails of it, is that of "looking for the thought rather in the etymology of the words which the author employs, than in the meaning which they have acquired in their practical application."[7] This is clearly to displace the concept of originaity from the poet to the language itself.

Generally speaking, Mangan's method, if one can elaborate a consistent method out of statements whose meaning is intimately bound to the articles that form their context, is the juxtaposition of linguistic surfaces. In German as in "Oriental" poetry, what interests him is the production of surfaces that are more or less delusive, as in the case of Ludwig Tieck's poetry: "There is something on the surface of it that mocks our penetration; so that when we try to look at it stedfastly (*sic*) we feel as if our eyes were filmed over with scales. It appears to us at once bright and dark, like polished ebony."[8] To this surface, nonetheless, Mangan directs his attention. "We are," he says in his article on Goethe's *Faust*, "sticklers for adherence to the apparent and superficial signification of all that comes before us in the guise of Language."[9] Elsewhere, he criticizes Schiller's epigram, translated as "The Art of Style," in which it is claimed that in the deep thinker more is concealed than developed: "But nobody knows what he conceals, or whether he conceals anything or not, and so nobody can give him credit for his concealments. If a man writes anything he must write something, and the something that he does write is *prima facie* the unabridged and perfect exposition of his thoughts."[10] This insistence on the surface of expression, rather than the concealed thought that produces it, issues in the theory and practice of Mangan's translation in the form not of metamorphoses which maintain a continuity of spirit between one language and another despite formal changes, but of *anamorphoses* which distort the appearance of the poem to various degrees in translating it from the surface of one language to that of another. The process of distortion is the significant aspect of the work of translation, and that process can work to highlight or gloss aspects of *either* poem. Consequently, the source poem in a certain sense ceases to be an original, given that it becomes, in the comparison, as secondary to the translation as the translation is to it. Abandoning the striving after an ideal equivalent permits instead the treatment of *all* works as each other's equivalents, undoing the subordination of the secondary to the primary.

If Mangan's translations consequently manifest a considerable degree of falsity, this is not without provoking reflection on the element of falsity that enters into artwork of whatever kind. The parodic falsification of the original unmasks the prior falseness of its claims to reproduce a primary origin, to render the substance beneath the shadow or the identity beneath the disguise. Similarly, the poetry of *Sehnsucht* provides, as an object of translation, a particularly apt domain for the study of a mode of translation that abandons the striving after the unattainable ideal of the absolute equivalent. Any mode of translation that invoked such an ideal would theoretically repeat and confirm the yearning of its original to identify with an absolute. Parodic translation accordingly becomes doubly disjunctive in rejecting that ideal both formally and thematically. Insofar as the poetry of yearning may be regarded as the lyrical expression of canonical aesthetics, predicating a domain of perpetual transcendence as the proper locus of the human subject's freedom, a study of Mangan's translations in this genre assists in illuminating not only the anti-aesthetic function of parody but also the manner in which his writing falls outside the categories that define a "major" writing.

TRANSLATION, REPETITION, AND *SEHNSUCHT*

Nowhere is poetry read univocally as self-expression more clearly subordinated to the biographical myth of "poor Mangan" than in the use made of his translation "And Then No More," a version of Friedrich Rückert's "Und dann nicht mehr."[11] Mitchel chose in his introduction to see in this poem the quintessential expression of Mangan's "master misery," that hopeless love whose typological function has already been discussed. His reading has become canonical, persisting virtually unquestioned to recent times.[12] But though Mitchel noted that the translation embodies certain "interpolations," he did not interrogate them further, content to see in them a means to covert self-expression. Mangan's own presentation, however, stresses not the lyrical pathos of the poem but, rather, its peculiar status as a translation of a translation. Rückert was best known, like his friend von Hammer-Purgstall, as a translator from Oriental languages, and Mangan presents the poem as representative of Rückert's work. The brief lyric elaborates a unique, quasi-visionary glimpse of a young girl through a succession of moments that repeat and transform the original figurative flash of perception. In the logic of the poem, its successive moments plot out the gradual "unveiling" and subordination of the girl, a process which culminates in her premature death:

> Ich sah sie nur ein einzig Mal und dann nicht mehr;
> Da sah ich einen Himmelstrahl, und dann nicht mehr.
> Ich sah umspielt vom Morgenhauch durch's Thal sie geh'n;
> Da war der Frühling in dem Thal, und dann nicht mehr.
> Im Saal des Festes sah ich sie entschleiern sich;
> Da war das Paradies im Saal, und dann nicht mehr.
> Sie war die Schenkin, Lust im Kreis kredenzte sie;
> Sie bot mir lächelnd eine Schal': und dann nicht mehr.
>
> . . . .
>
> Ein einz'ges Mal, als sie erblich, war herb die Lust
> Des Lebens, süss des Todes Qual, und dann nicht mehr.
> Ich sah die Rose Braut im Flor verschliessen in
> Die dunkle Kammer eng und schmal, und dann nicht mehr.
> Ich will um's Rosenbrautgemach im Mondenglanz
> Noch weinen meiner Thränen Zahl, und dann nicht mehr.

The insistent refrain of transience — "Und dann nicht mehr" — is counterpointed by a succession of internal rhymes that transform the uniqueness of "ein einzig Mal" into a series of points along a curve that maps a double vector, the reduction of the girl from a *Himmelstrahl* to the absent object of the poet's grief, and the shift of the poem's focus from the girl to the poet: *Mal, Himmelstrahl, Thal, Saal, Schal', fahl, stahl, Qual, schmal, Zahl.* In the course of elegiac celebration, the repetition of the unique transforms the unique itself into an occasion for mere enumeration, and the occasion into a pretext for the poet's transcendence of his original occasion. The inevitability with which the two curves of the poem's logical structure conjoin suggest an ulterior function in the lament for the transience of the unique. The mastery of the writer over the object onto which his own mortality is displaced leaves the actuality of that object — girl, rose, or bride — formally indifferent. The *process* of transcendence, which is the poem's thematic subject, is also its raison d'être.

It is the *process* by which the poetic "pretext" is appropriated and transformed, and the formal indifference of the unique object to that process, that Mangan's translation addresses. The unique and transient moment of vision merely structures the repetitions of the fixated mind which progressively mythologizes or derealizes its object. The relative circumstantiality that attaches to the several occasions of Rückert's poem is strikingly absent from Mangan's version, where the visionary woman, picked out from "amid the throng," is otherwise undifferentiated: "But whence she came, which way she went, what garb she wore, / I noted not; I gazed awhile, and then no more!" That very generality is the condition by which the unique moment is elevated into "the unreached Paradise of our despair." It is also, the structure of Mangan's poem seems to suggest, the condition of our failure to reach that paradise. Where Rückert has figured the girl initially as a *Himmelstrahl* or as "das Paradies im Saal," in Mangan's version a reverse development of perception into an ever-increasing unreality is organized around a progressive shift from "Eden's light on Earth," through "Paradise on Earth awhile," to "Earth looked like Heaven a little while," culminating in its complete derealization in "The earth was Peri-land [fairyland] awhile" in the final stanza. A similar movement can be traced in the reperception of the vision, from the relatively distinct "Amid the throng she passed along," through "She shone before mine eyes," to "Her presence thrilled and lighted," while in the final stanza comes only the wish to see her "shape" again. The death that is expected as the result of that second vision is the culmination of the poet's rather than the girl's decline, while that decline counterpoints the progressive derealization of the vision:

"The shallop of my peace is wrecked . . . ," "My desert breast . . . ," "Death would soon heal my griefs."

If in Rückert's poem the emotional curves finally conjoin at the point of the poet's elegiac transcendence of an object whose aesthetic rationale lies in its being lost, in Mangan's version it is, rather, that two opposed curves move progressively apart. The repetitions of the original moment, in each of which it remains formally identical — "I saw her once, one little while, and then no more" — are purely ideal, unlike Rückert's, and enact a kind of recession of the lost object into unreality. That recession is counterpointed by the failure of the poet to employ fixation and repetition as means to transcendence. He is instead left in suspension, longing for an unattainable moment in which repetition and self-annihilation would coincide. The thematic concerns of the version are thus duplicated in its generic determination as a translation that, in repeating its original, implies the desire to transcend it or to re-present it so identically as to escape the relationship of dependence. Yet the version instead establishes a process in which the progressive deviation from the original negates the possibility of identical repetition by which alone such transcendence could be achieved.

The failure to achieve identical repetition is the condition that structures the poetics of *Sehnsucht,* just as the impossibility of identification with the object of knowledge determines the structure of Romantic philosophical method. In both cases, however, the endeavor to overcome that fundamental scission is given value not in terms of the object, which is in any case proposed as a priori unattainable, but in terms of the ethical effects of the process itself, insofar as it perpetually reestablishes the moral transcendence and autonomy of the subject. Hence the apparent contradiction of an aesthetic whose mode is desire but whose ethic is predicated on the refusal to possess what is desired. Where it rests on the theoretical ground of ideal equivalence, translation not only conforms to a Romantic aesthetic but reproduces in its intention the very form of a *Sehnsucht* for the ideal. Parodic translation, on the other hand, emphasizes the dependent status of the translation and, in stressing its falsifying resemblance to its object, focuses on the productive and refractive nature of the work rather than its disinterestedness. In a sense, parodic translation knows itself as both subject and object, predicated on an original yet in turn mediating that original, which is its subject. Accordingly, the subjective longing to transcend both object and occasion can in parodic translation issue only in a suspension formally overdetermined by the generic condition of dependence which defines the parodic text.

The effect of the poetics of *Sehnsucht* is always to produce a residue of selfhood as the remainder left by the irremediably divisive process of striving for unity or totalization. That striving is, ultimately, directed toward the increased potency of the subject: "it confers the ability to integrate ever more experience into a meaningful totality."[13] Such is the function of *Sehnsucht* in the writings of Ludwig Tieck, one of the principal figures among the German *Frühromantiker,* whose work has been aptly characterized as the constant pursuit of a "truly subjective expression of the forlorn melancholy of the transitory."[14] The conditions of "longing" are addressed in Ludwig Tieck's poem "Sehnsucht," which Mangan translated under the title "Life Is the Desert and the Solitude."[15] As its title implies, the poem both dramatizes this pursuit and interrogates the origins of yearning:

> Warum Schmachten?
> Warum Sehnen?
> Alle Thränen
> Ach! sie trachten
> Weit nach Ferne,
> Wo sie wähnen
> Schönre Sterne.

Since the "fremdes Land" which is the object of longing is no more than the product of fancy (*Wähnen*), its nominal contents are cursorily catalogued ("Leise Lüfte / Wehen linde, / Durch die Klüfte / Blumendüfte"), only to give way to the core of the poem, which elaborates the tension between subjective longing and the resistance to its fulfillment that is posed by the objective, physical aspect of the subject, represented as a mode of abstract power. The product is an endless effort at approximation, since every movement of the subject toward the "undiscovered far land" ("unentdeckte ferne Land") is frustrated by the stern bonds ("ernste Bande") that restrain him: "Schnell muss alles untersinken, / Rückwärts hält mich die Gewalt." The formal nature of the process is indicated in the exact repetition of the opening lines which forms a coda to the poem. The cycle of languishing and longing recommences as the absolute subject, indifferent to content and drawn only to the abstract category of distance which motivates his *Sehnsucht,* negates every object as a supererogatory restraint on his autonomy.

Mangan borrowed the title "Life Is the Desert and the Solitude" from Edward Young's version of *Othello, The Revenge,* apparently alluding to the fate that Hegel saw to be that of such "negative ironists" as Tieck.[16] But where Tieck's poem implied that the tension between subjective longing and objective restraint was the source of the cycle of *Sehnsucht,* Mangan's version insists rather more strongly that both visionary fancy and its destruction lie on the side of the subject. While his opening lines appear to repeat quite exactly the opening of Tieck's own poem — "Whence this fever? / Whence this burning / Love and Longing?" — the following lines transform the original along a line that exaggerates the formal quality of Tieck's yearning and, as in the translation from Rückert, introduces a sense that repetition redoubles unreality. Though Mangan removes the solecism by which tears supposedly "strive" ("Thränen . . . trachten"), that striving itself is transformed into a "roaming" after stars that, rather than providing fixed marks, "wander" in their own bliss. Even the rather archaic poetic expression used by Tieck, "für und für" ("for ever and ever"), provides material for a transformation that suggests that the object of "Love and Longing" is merely its own repetition, turn after turn:

> Ah! for ever,
> Ever turning.
> Ever thronging
> Tow'rds the Distance,
> Roams each fonder
> Yearning yonder,
> There where wander
> Golden stars in blest existence!

The features of his far land which Tieck nominally catalogues are in turn softened into "fragrant Airs" and "rich vagrant Music." And if in turn the far land begins to take on the appearance of an Oriental "Peri-land" once again, equipped with "fairy Bowers and palace Gardens," this Oriental aura may prepare us for a deft transformation of Tieck's "unentdeckte ferne Land" into an "undeveloped Land." Mangan's phrase neatly condenses the sense of a domain that is at once vague or veiled and available for "development" by the subject who wishes to penetrate its concealment and, "wanting what we do not have, cannot have," appropriates it for his own projections. Mangan clearly associated the kind of subjective domination that characterizes Tieck's poetry with its counterpart in the economic domain, remarking in his essay on Tieck's poetry that "Every emotion that tenants his heart must pay a rack-rent or the income of his happiness is so far deficient."[17]

Since any "undeveloped land" is — spiritually as well as economically — available for such exploitation only so long as it is produced by the dominant subject, there is, in Mangan's version, no tension between subjective longing and objective restraint. Since the "absolute ego" constitutes its own objects, the power which is finally appealed to to "rive" the dreamer's chain is already a projected figure within landscapes which "gleam but by the *spectral* sky / That lights *my* shifting dreams" (emphasis added). Accordingly, the moment at which the dreamer attempts to occupy the "undeveloped land," to gravitate toward identification with his own projected object and "render vivid and tangible and permanent those phantasmagoria of the mind," is the very moment in which the vision collapses. Mangan's coda, as if miming the gesture of a syllogistic proof, does not repeat the opening exactly but answers its initial "Whence?" with a "Hence." This constitutes neither closure nor perpetual repetition, however, but leaves open the question as to whether *Sehnsucht* is the product of a genuinely realizable ideal or merely of the inevitably frustrated effort of the subject to grasp objects which its very desire for mastery negates.

MANGAN'S ANTI-SUBLIME

The dilemma that Mangan continually dramatizes in such translations is central to Schiller's essay "Naive and Sentimental Poetry" which, as Robert Welch has pointed out, often seems to be echoed in Mangan's prose articles.[18] Those echoes are the signs of his own confrontation with a dilemma that emerges in Schiller's essay. Schiller's argument is perhaps best summarized by his own remark on the difference between the ancients and ourselves: "They felt naturally; we feel the natural."[19] The loss of the immediate experience of nature causes her to "arise in the world of poetry as *idea* and *object*" (*NSP*, p. 105). In the wider field of experience, "man as nature functions as an undivided sensuous unity and as a unifying whole," but on passing into "the state of civilization and art,"

> that *sensuous* harmony in him is withdrawn, and he can now express himself only as a *moral* unity, i.e., as striving after unity. The correspondence between his feeling and thought which in his first condition *actually* took place, exists now only *ideally; it* is no longer within him, but outside of him, as an idea still to be realized, no longer as a fact in his life.
>
> (*NSP*, p. 111; original emphasis)

This progression from a presupposed actual harmony to a moral, idealized unity at first seems identical with the underlying narrative of nationalist ideology. Here also, the "naive" integration of the past comes to be cast forward as an ideal for which to labor. But the complexity of Schiller's argument derives from his observations on the fervor of our projections of the ideal into the natural:

> It is *because* nature in us has disappeared from humanity and we discover her in truth only outside it, in the inanimate world. Not in our greater *accord with nature,* but quite the contrary, the *unnaturalness* of our situation, conditions, and moods forces us to procure a satisfaction in the physical world, since none is to be hoped for in the moral . . .
>
> (*NSP*, p. 103; original emphasis)

It is thus as a representation of a former state of unity, as an *idea,* that the naive in its various forms attracts us. This is essential to Schiller's argument, insofar as it is in a moral idea that transcends the natural as self-determination rather than in regressive identification that he wishes to locate human freedom. The crucial difference between Schiller's idea of human development and that of the nationalists is this basing of its necessity in the *persisting* effects of a separation, rather than in an attempt to restore continuity by a self-identification with the national spirit.

It is exactly this point that Schiller is concerned to make in his later essay "On the Sublime," when he derives the pleasure we take in contemplating the chaos of nature from our heightened sense of independence from it. If the observer demand regularity and unity of nature,

> then nothing remains to him but to expect from a future existence and from another nature that satisfaction that he misses in present and past nature. If, however, he willingly abandons the attempt to assimilate this lawless chaos of appearances to a cognitive unity, he will abundantly regain in another direction what he has lost in this. It is precisely the entire absence of a purposive bond among this press of appearances by which they are rendered unencompassable and useless for the understanding . . . that makes them an all the more striking image for pure reason, which finds in just this wild incoherence of nature the depiction of her own independence of natural conditions.
>
> (OS, pp. 205–6)

The appropriation of nature as an image thus reinforces rather than overcomes the incommensurability and disunity that subsist between man and his objects.

The sublime consequently forms the crucial mediating principle in Schiller's aesthetic, by which "culture is to set man free and to help him to be equal to his concept"(OS, p. 194). In the passage from dependence on the objective and sensual, which is the realm of the merely beautiful, to ethical identification with the *ideally* beautiful in which subjective and objective, freedom and necessity, are reconciled, the sublime supplies the crucial educative process. And it is precisely as a *process* that the sublime must be grasped. While the experience of the beautiful remains static, ultimately dependent on the existence of its objects, and therefore on nature, the sublime derives precisely from the incommensurability of the moral and the natural or sensuous aspect. The sublime provides the "shocks" that progressively emancipate man from sensuous dependence on phenomena:

> Thus the sublime affords us an egress from the sensuous world in which the beautiful would gladly hold us forever captive. Not gradually (for there is no transition from dependence to freedom),

but suddenly and with a shock it tears the independent spirit out of the net in which a refined sensuousness has entoiled it, and which binds all the more tightly the more gossamer its weave.

(*OS*, pp. 201–2)

In this sense, both Tieck's and Rückert's poems can be understood as modifications of the sublime precisely insofar as the apparent frustration of the "sehnsuchtsvolle" striving after identification with beautiful appearances may be seen to transform into the emancipation of the authentic human subject from captivation in whatever mode. Even epistemological error becomes emancipation where the sublime is referred not to its objects but to the very process of transcendence by which, in effect, those objects are negated. As Schiller has it, "individuals of a sublime temperamental disposition think themselves recompensed for every cognitive misjudgement by this idea of freedom which is offered to them" (*OS*, p. 206).

Schiller accordingly emphasizes the necessary transition from the natural to the artificial or aesthetic sublime. If in earlier writers such as Burke the distinction had been unclear or undeveloped, for Schiller it is an inevitable stage in his argument. If the sublime is to become not merely the destructive agent that emancipates human beings from captivation in sensuous beauty, but also the constructive agent that will "complement the beautiful in order to make *aesthetic education* into a complete whole," the sublime itself must be emancipated from its dependence on natural phenomena:

> Now it is true that nature herself supplies objects in abundance on which the perceptive faculty for the beautiful and sublime can be exercised; but man is here, as in other cases, better served at one remove than directly, and prefers to receive a subject matter prepared and selected by art rather than to drink scantily and with difficulty from the impure well of nature.

(*OS*, p. 211)

Two points emerge here. The first, already prepared by the discussion of the pathetic as a mode of the sublime a little earlier in the essay, is that it is crucial to the process of aesthetic education that the experience of the sublime should not — as is the case for the beautiful — be dependent on chance (*Zufall*) or on the paradoxically "scanty" abundance of nature, but should, rather, be repeatable at will, so that, as with the pathetic, "the autonomous principle in our minds gains space in which to assert its absolute independence" (*OS*, p. 209). The second is a logical corollary of this point, that the aesthetic work that subserves this emancipation from nature should not itself depend on the natural but should, rejecting the direct imitation of nature, assert its "remove" from nature by the mimesis of *semblance*, not actuality (*OS*, pp. 211 – 12). If this notion of the nature of the artwork appears to resemble Plato's grounds for disparaging art, it should be stressed that it is precisely Schiller's point to distinguish the "semblance" (*Schein*), which is the product of "free contemplation," from the natural phenomena (*Erscheinungen*), captivation by which makes man untrue to his concept, that is, to freedom. The point is made more clearly in his more extended *Letters on Aesthetic Education,* where in the "Twenty-Sixth Letter" he argues that "aesthetic semblance" is not to be confused with "logical semblance," since "to attach value to the semblance of the first kind can never be prejudicial to truth, because one is never in danger of substituting it for truth" (*AEM*, p. 193). The aesthetic, as the means of emancipating man from nature, becomes thus not truth itself but the means to arrive at the truth of human nature.

The paradox of Schiller's argument is, however, that the means by which the semblances of art emancipate man is itself a mode of captivation. Where the contents that are natural phenomena drop away from the artwork to leave it only pure *Schein,* the process of aesthetic emancipation becomes magic (*Zauber*): "Da aber der ganze Zauber des Erhabenen und Schönen nur in dem Schein und nicht in dem Inhalt liegt, so hat die Kunst alle Vorteile der Natur, ohne ihre Fesseln mit ihr zu teilen."[20] Displacing and replacing *Erscheinungen,* the *Schein* of both the beautiful *and* the sublime becomes in turn an instrument of captivation, as if miming on a higher level the natural *processes* that aesthetic works in fact repeat. Even if the sublime, by revealing the *contradiction* between reason and sensuousness that beauty dissembles, prepares the ground for our moral emancipation, it does so only by replacing the captivation of beauty by the captivation of another magic: "precisely in this contradiction between the two lies the magic with which it captures our minds [*womit es unser Gemüt ergreift*]."[21]

Though Mangan nowhere specifically discusses or cites either the essay "Naive and Sentimental Poetry" or "On the Sublime," there is some evidence that it is this aspect of Schiller that fascinated him and that led him to return several times to translate that writer's work. In a remark that reflects upon Schiller's concern with art as the means to the realization of the subject's autonomy, Mangan comments that it is "his great individuality" that differentiates Schiller from "the Protean, Voltairean faculty of metamorphosis and self-multiplication" that characterizes Goethe, Schiller's own exemplar of the modern "naive poet." Lacking that proteanism by which the naive poet becomes what he represents, rendering his objects transparent to the reader, Schiller's lyrics have as their "great hallowing charm," according to Mangan, "the captivating, rather than faithful resemblance they bear with the realities they profess to be the images of."[22] The first of the "Anthologia Germanica" articles presents several translations of Schiller's lyrics, with Mangan's customary caveat as to the true nature of their relation to their sources: "We have (for no base purpose) disguised them to the best of our poor ability; but we should, after all, be loath to hear that they had forfeited their identity" (*AG* 1, p. 41). Comparing the translations with the sources, one finds that they indeed bear the appearance of "fidelity," the source poems being certainly more readily identifiable through their new guises than many of Mangan's later "German" poems.

Among the poems so presented is a translation of Schiller's "Die Ideale," a poem that bears a close relationship to the arguments of "Naive and Sentimental Poetry" and "On the Sublime." As such, it provides an interesting instance of Mangan's reaction to Schiller, as well as an example of the extent to which these poems are in fact "disguised."[23] "Die Ideale" is an elegiac account of the loss of Youth's "innocent" immersion in nature, and of the passage, through disappointment in the incommensurability of the actual with the desired ideal, from the "naive" to the "sentimental." That youthful immersion in nature is described by Schiller at first as a very real interpenetration of man and nature, a reciprocation of desire:

> So schlang ich mich mit Liebesarmen
> Um die Natur mit Jugendlust,
> Bis sie zu atmen, zu erwarmen,
> Begann an meiner Dichterbrust
>
> Und, teilend meine Flammentriebe,
> Die Stumme eine Sprache fand,
> Mir wiedergab den Kuss der Liebe
> Und meines Herzens Klang verstand;
> Da lebte mir der Baum, die Rose,
> Mir sang der Quellen Silberfall,
> Es fühlte selbst das Seelenlose
> Von meines Lebens Widerhall.

It is the realization that the natural is insufficient to his desire to embrace the whole that leads to disappointment and to the second stage of an ideal projection "Bis an des Äthers bleichste Sterne." This stage involves the youth in the "natural" sublime of the endeavor to embrace the totality of the phenomenal world:

> Es dehnte mit allmächt'gem Streben
> Die enge Brust ein kreissend All,
> Herauszutreten in das Leben,
> In Tat und Wort, in Bild und Schall.
> Wie gross war diese Welt gestaltet,
> So lang die Knospe sie noch barg!
> Wie wenig, ach! hat sich entfaltet,
> Dies wenige, wie klein und karg!
>
> (stanza 5)

A second disappointment sustained by the failure of the pursuit of the ideal in actual worldly life leads to the final, ethical stage of the poem, leaving the poet sustained by Friendship and Occupation (*Beschäftigung*). Notably, the drive to totalization, which characterized the stage of the natural sublime, is displaced by the ethical sublime, which is characterized by repetition and construction: "Die zu dem Bau der Ewigkeiten / Zwar Sandkorn nur für

Sandkorn reicht." An acceptance of the fragmentary nature of human understanding yet allows a building toward the eternal ideal.

English translations of this poem by Mangan's contemporaries tend to emphasize either the moral aspect of the restraining of an immoderate desire to realistic activity or the lament for the loss of boyhood innocence.[24] Mangan, picking up what is scarcely more than an allusion to the myth of Narcissus in the fourth stanza's "Von meines Lebens Widerhall" ("from my life's echo") and to the myth of Pygmalion in the third, stresses the possibility of seeing the youth's naive immersion in the natural as already a fascination with his own projections. This process is immediately signaled by the title "The Unrealities," and Mangan continues, while remaining nominally faithful, to introduce a further remove, as it were, into Schiller's representations. Even in the first lines, taking a suggestion from the German *Phantasie* (Imagination), Mangan translates: "And dost thou faithlessly abandon me? / Must thy chameleon phantasies depart?" where "chameleon," with a connotation of something taking color from that on which it lives, as well as of something unstable and shifting, replaces the German *hold*, "charming." In the second stanza, Schiller's sense of rapture and intoxication is displaced by a more sinister sense of the imagination as an entrapment in delusion (one should probably not underestimate in Mangan's work the sinister quality that attaches to "fairy" in the Irish tradition). As imagination was reduced to "phantasies," so here the "Ideals" are reduced to captivating "Imagination":

> Die Ideale sind zerronnen,
> Die einst das trunkne Herz geschwellt.
>
> Those fairy bands Imagination spun
> Around my heart have long been rent asunder.

Subsequently, the *Stein* of Schiller's Pygmalion is qualified as "the lovely statue," the "enthusiastic Prince" being "*stricken* by its charms," while the *Dichterbrust* of the same stanza becomes ambivalently a "*bounding* breast," picking up the *umschlingen* of the German, which is translated as "*pressed* in."

Schiller's relationship of reciprocity is thus being shifted toward a sense of capture, capture of and by one's own images. The "narcissistic" implications of the youth's investment in the natural world are drawn out further, and the extra remove of the representation is maintained in the translation of the stanza already quoted from Schiller ("Und teilend meine Flammen-triebe"):

> Then sparkled hues of Life on tree and flower,
> Sweet music from the silver fountain flowed,
> All soulless images in that brief hour
> The echo of my Life divinely glowed!

Schiller's "Da lebte mir" becomes the superficial sparkle of the light, the *Seelenlose,* the "soulless *images,*" which in turn glow *as* rather than *from* his Life's echo. But the most radical transformation that occurs — and it is not to be found in any other contemporary translation — appears to derive from a single word, *entfaltet,* in the fifth stanza. The idea of "unfurling," here applied to the bud (*Knospe*) in Schiller's organic metaphor, is transformed systematically into the uprolling of a theater curtain, emphasizing finally the strictly artificial quality of human appropriations of nature, as well as pointing forward to the second stage:

> This human theatre, how fair it beamed
> While yet the curtain hung before the scene!
> Uprolled, how little then the arena seemed!
> That little how contemptible and mean!

The process analyzed here for the first stage of the youth's progress is repeated for the second stage, through the sixth to the ninth stanza, as, for example, the "leap" of Schiller's youth into "des Lebens Bahn" becomes an errant and aimless "roaming"; the "wings of designs" or "projects" (*Entwürfe*) become those of an "Enchantress"; love's "süssen Lohne" a "heart-bewitching boon"; and, finally, the "finstern Weg" of Schiller's pilgrimage becomes once again a stage cluttered with "the dark images of Life's poor dream" and "dusty scenery." In each case the "remove" from nature implicit in the "semblance" of Schiller's poem is redoubled until the translation becomes both the semblance of the semblance and a representation of a sublimation that is the site of capture rather than release. This may be what is intended where Mangan in the final stanza replaces Schiller's "Bau der Ewigkeiten" with the "*Mount* of Life": participation in the work of humanity becomes a submission to the weight of the law rather than the elevation of heavenly mansions.

REPETITION AND DEPENDENCE

Mangan's translations from the German engage in a double reflection: on the assumptions concerning literature that inform his originals, and on the nature and function of translation itself. Each aspect of this double reflection sustains the other. On the one hand, that his writings are translations reflects upon and repeats the kind of critique of the originals that they embody; on the other, the nature of this implied critique suggests a rationale behind Mangan's preoccupation with translation itself as a mode of criticism. If in Mangan's translations the process of translation provides an apt general model for the process of original creation, this is no longer to be understood in the sense in which English or German theorists tended to refer all poetic work to a process of "translating" an original experience or inspiration. The "burthen of the curse of Babel" is no longer the perpetual refrain of a poetry whose function is to liberate human perception from the veils of dead metaphors and so recreate its original freshness. Translation is not simply a secondary process that repeats the primary acts of poetic creation and, like that primary process, strives to attain an ideal in order, through that striving, to represent the essential unity of the processes of the human mind. Rather, where Schiller posits the function of aesthetic semblances as being the reduction of the "flood of appearances" to order and unity, in Mangan's work translation becomes a simulacrum of aesthetic semblance that implies the possibility of a ceaseless reproduction and multiplication of semblances. The function of these semblances, in turn, is to confuse and veil the truth rather than to provide a detour through which the truth can be approximated. The process of repetition by which, in Schiller's argument, the aesthetic experience was to lead to the emancipation of man from nature and to his preparation for truth becomes virtually literalized in translations. But as soon as translation's repetition sends its reader back to the source for verification, only to belie or criticize the integrity of that source, the original poem ceases to provide either authentication or ethical replenishment, becoming instead a mere counterfeit rather than an image of truth. The irony of the false translator is not one that closes at last by relegating the duplicity of the ironized content to a secondary position in relation to the educative process that derives from error. Instead, the faithlessness of the translation foregrounds the deceptiveness of *both* original *and* translation while refusing to offer the prospect of emancipation from captivity and entry into the promised land of human freedom. That paradise is conceived already as only the projection of the despair of the deceived.

The educative process by which the captivating magic of Schiller's aesthetic semblances is justified is accordingly absent from Mangan's translations. The function of the "mimetic creative impulse," according to Schiller, is to subordinate every impression to expression, to contend with nature in the production of beautiful forms precisely by treating transitory impressions as totalities prefigurative of that all-embracing unity that is the end of aesthetic work (cf. *OS*, p. 211). Parodic translations of the kind that Mangan produces, contrariwise, refuse totalization in perpetually emphasizing the refractive nature of their relationship to a source that can never be authentically repeated. What results is the proliferation of impressions behind which there is nothing to be expressed, a mimicry rather than a mimesis. Consequently, the captivating magic of the sublime is rendered as a mode of deception rather than emancipation, since it has neither ethical purpose nor relation to any transcendent totality. The poet is represented as the magician who multiplies illusion rather than as a teacher who draws insight out of error, and the supposedly emancipating "shock" of the sublime, deprived of ethical justification, becomes reduced to the utterly repeatable and superficial effect of "astonishment" that is the essential quality of a "natural" sublime:

I should far and away prefer being a great necromancer to being a great writer or even a great fighter. My natural propensities lead me rather to seek out modes of astonishing mankind than of edifying them. Herein I and my propensities are clearly wrong: but somehow I find that almost every thing that is natural to me is wrong also.[25]

The supernatural here collapses back into the natural, just as the aesthetic semblance is constantly shown to be as captivating as the natural appearances from which it was intended to be distinct. Throughout his writings, in the prose as in the poetry, Mangan constantly evinces his fascination with the supernatural, specifically with the figure of the magician. But whether he is referring to the Oriental "genii," to Charles Maturin's *Melmoth*, or to the magician "Maugraby" of his own tale "The Thirty Flasks," his attention is perpetually focused on a play of projection, illusion, and deception whose structure is identical with that of the aesthetic process that his parodic translations lay bare. Indeed, as we have frequently observed, the products of the imagination are constantly figured as enchantments whose dissolution leaves the subject not with a higher mode of knowledge but in confrontation with the "desert and the solitude" of his own alienation.

Neither the sublime nor the beautiful aesthetic semblance can furnish an "edifying" process whereby the subject escapes from captivation into transcendence. Where Schiller defines man as "the being that wills" and understands his aesthetic powers as the highest expression of a willfulness that sets man apart from dependence on either nature or the beautiful, Mangan seems, rather, to envisage man as the captive of his will to illusion, and the aesthetic semblance as the product of that will. Time and again, the expression of the will to realize the illusion, rather than simply to remain entranced before it in static longing, shatters the illusion itself: this process, however, never reveals more than the blankness of another veil. The suspension of the will before the "charm" of the semblance seems always to be the condition of poetry throughout Mangan's writings, from the earliest to the last, until it is grasped that the appearance of suspension dissembles an underlying will to illusion.

The actual experience that provides the figure for that passivity, and, among Mangan's biographers, the discrete ground for a condemnation that is precisely ethical in its terms, is that of physical addiction. Indeed, it becomes more or less indifferent whether the addiction is to alcohol or to opium: whatever the writer's choice (or the biographer's), it comports an underlying rejection of the will to ethical self-mastery and is accordingly censured as the origin of Mangan's misery. Indeed, further consideration of the various grounds given in the biographies for his wretchedness indicates not only a remarkable homology between these biographical crises, but also the extent to which they may seem to reflect the very forms of Mangan's writing, as if perception of the insistent patterns of that writing were constantly displaced onto biographical rationalization. Even the obscure "love affair" fits, in the basic form of the accounts, with a pattern that rationalizes Mangan's unethical accidie, his deliberate lapse into a "death-in-life" of utter negativity, by way of a narrative in which dependence upon delusion — in friendship, love, or the artificial paradise of opium or alcohol — collapses in the face of betrayal or infidelity. It is a pattern crucial, of course, to the function of the "unfaithful" translation, "la belle infidèle," of Mangan's work; perhaps nowhere is the bearing of the aphorism "traduttore, traditore" more considerately elaborated than in the work of this poet who is repeatedly represented as the victim of betrayal and delusion.

The passage just cited in which Mangan declares his fascination with "necromancy" (a word whose confused etymology aptly conflates the unethical powers of darkness with the fascination of the mantic trance of the world of death) comes from a collection of fragmentary and miscellaneous remarks entitled "A Sixty-Drop Dose of Laudanum." "Drop 20" of this miscellany consists of a meditation on the entrapment of the dreamer in repetition that provides at once a paradigm for the forms of parodic writing and a means to distinguish Mangan's procedures from those of his contemporary De Quincey. Mangan's brief meditation concerns "the marvellous power which the mind possesses during sleep of *recreating the same images over and over with no exercise of memory on the part of the dreamer.*"[26] He offers as an example of such a dream one in which the dreamer is compelled to traverse and retraverse perpetually a series of chambers that are, on each return, the same as before, but always forgotten in the intervening cycle. The rooms are identified on return by the indices of enigma that furnish them, "a strange picture on the wall — a sphynx on a marble table." The dream is analogous to the cyclical pattern found in Mangan's translation of Tieck's "Sehnsucht," since the condition of the dream's recurrence is that the will "is passive throughout" and the imagination, which "is always conscious of exercising its power," is in abeyance. Both the will, which "can help to destroy" all that which it "helps to fabricate," and the imagination, whose products "are never twice the same," are principles antagonistic to the kind of "painfully conscious" proximity that allows repetition to recur and entrap the dreamer in his "involuntary pilgrimage."

Mangan, at the end of this text, remarks on the possibility that his dream may remind the reader of the "English Opium-Eater's dreams about the staircases of Piranesi" but states emphatically that between his and De Quincey's dreams there is "scarcely one salient point of resemblance"; he even doubts whether De Quincey "ever had such dreams." The point of Mangan's distinction is well taken. Piranesi's pictures, the *Carceri* series, provide for De Quincey the figure of sublime productivity, of the "power of endless growth and reproduction." Within his description, where repetition becomes a means to transformation, the figure of Piranesi is perceived in a constant, if painful, transcendence of impasse:

> But raise your eyes, and behold a second flight of stairs still higher: on which again Piranesi is perceived, but this time standing on the very brink of the abyss. Again elevate your eye, and a still more aërial flight of stairs is beheld; and again is poor Piranesi busy on his aspiring labours: and so on, until the unfinished stairs and Piranesi are lost in the upper gloom of the hall.[27]

Though the subject escapes from self-presence as the object escapes from identity with the subject, what is presented here is nonetheless a paradigmatic sublime scenario in which the subject is produced through the necessary pain of "aspiring labours"; the inevitable incompletion of the labor once again relegates the ethical work to the *process* rather than to the product. The passage is, accordingly, a synecdoche for the ethical work of the *Confessions* as a whole, where the labor of the writer to transcend the delusory paradises of opium that gradually sap his will is directed at producing an ethical subject through the educative power of pain.[28] Precisely this labor of ethical self-production is absent from Mangan's dream, where the dreaming subject is, on the contrary, suspended perpetually in the passivity of dependence.

This point can be elaborated and Mangan's modes of writing further distinguished from another British Romantic writer with whom, on the grounds that translation is a mode of "negative capability," he has occasionally been compared. The burden of Mangan's dream contrasts markedly with Keats's otherwise comparable image of the series of chambers through which one must pass in "the large Mansion of Many Apartments" that is human life.[29] In the sequence of Keats's letters, this image supersedes the idea of "negative capability," in which the poet is precisely the man who *lacks* identity, and prefigures the equally famous figure of life as the "Vale of Soul-making" through which "intelligences" come "to possess the sense of identity."[30] The image of the series of chambers has accordingly a fit place in the middle of this sequence, since what it describes is the maturation of the poet in a progress in which he is emancipated gradually from intoxication "with the light and the atmosphere" of the "Chamber of Maiden-Thought," a state analogous to Schiller's state of captivation by beauty. As the poet passes through the various chambers in the course of his maturation, each individual chamber is not, as in Mangan's dream, obliterated by the next in a series of discrete states without apparent connection. The relationship between the chambers is sequential, progressive, and, specifically, genetic:

> The first we step into is what we call the infant or thoughtless Chamber, in which we remain as long as we do not think — We remain there a long while and notwithstanding the doors of the second Chamber remain wide open, showing a bright appearance, we care not to hasten to it; but are at length imperceptibly impelled by the awakening of the thinking principle — we no sooner get into the second Chamber, which I shall call the Chamber of Maiden-

Thought, than we become intoxicated with the light and the atmosphere, we see nothing but pleasant wonders, and think of delaying there for ever in delight: However among the effects this breathing is father of is that tremendous one of sharpening one's vision into the heart and nature of Man.[31]

Keats's poetic career has become paradigmatic of the ideal moral evolution of the poet, and in turn of the cultivated individual, from immersion in sensuous experience to ironic ethical concern. This is at least in part due to the economy with which his letters, matched step for step by his poetic writings, trace out a process we might term "Romantic self-fathering." The original poet originates himself, suppressing both his old work and his old self in each new creation that he forges. In doing so he both supersedes and contains the work of his predecessors, and becomes a major — or "strong" — poet.

To pass beyond the immediate implications of Mangan's dream of repetitions, it is precisely this self-origination that his chosen modes of writing preclude. Refusing to reoriginate his original, the translator places his work in a state of perpetual dependence on his originals, recalling them even in the moment of disjunctively refracting them. Parodic writings, in their oscillation between the opposed but intimately related modes of *Beigesang* and *Gegengesang*, are resolutely undialectical and can become generative only at the point where they cease to be parodic.[32] The aesthetic of parody is one in which repetition is not aimed at producing or liberating the authentic human subject; its effect is, rather, to question incessantly the notions of authenticity, self-presence, and self-productivity, by its refusal of independence. Even where Mangan confesses to the composition of original poems passed off as translations — a move often understood as covert self-expression — he conceives of it as a kind of antithetical plagiarism and as a confusion of the order of generation, "fathering upon other writers the offspring of his own brain," as the "impersonal autobiography" puts it.

It is not insignificant that Mangan should describe the processes of his writings in such terms in the course of a dissembled autobiography in which he also stressed his own alienation from his father in childhood. The texts by Keats and De Quincey with which we have been concerned are, if only in an allegorical sense, likewise "autobiographical." In the fullest sense of that word, these texts interlock the biographical struggle of the writer to attain an identity with the process of the writing itself. Suffering and mortality become the pretexts of a writing in which their mastery and sublimation produce the ethical identity. It would, evidently, not be inappropriate to consider Schiller's "On the Sublime" as the master-text for such autobiographical writings, given the manner in which it posits generally the aesthetic semblance as the means to the production of a moral self, superior to worldly, natural calamity. In Mangan's "impersonal autobiography" likewise, an elaborate complex of relationships between the life and the writing is implied, but the relationship between writing and suffering is, like the order of generation, reversed: "His misfortunes have been very great; and he ascribes them all to his power of writing, facetiously deriving *calamity* from *calamus,* a quill" (*IA,* p. 28). Writing ceases to be a means to transcend suffering and becomes instead the site of a painful reproduction of wretchedness. In each of the autobiographical writings, all of them written in the final months of Mangan's life, this complex relationship among false paternity, suffering, and writing is played out in various ways. From these writings derive most of the mythical accounts of Mangan's life, but an understanding of the parodic dimension of Mangan's writings not only suggests grounds for suspicion as to the "truth" that they pretend to reveal but also supplies the basis for another reading of them, in relation to the repetitive oscillation between dependence and opposition that characterizes his work in other genres. This aspect of the autobiographies, and its implications for the way in which we grasp Mangan's understanding of the relation between writing and the production of identity, will be addressed in the next chapter.

6

The Autobiographies

Both Meehan's religious and Mitchel's nationalist account of Mangan's life supply the redemptive closure that Mangan's autobiographies fail to furnish. In this they are seconded by O'Donoghue's biography, which, in awarding Mangan a degree of canonical status, furnishes an aesthetic cure for his suffering. For them, writing sublimates suffering, contrary to Mangan's assertions, while the role of the father as initiator of Mangan's misfortunes is minimized in all accounts. The intricate relationship among paternity, suffering, debt, and writing that furnishes the latent structure of Mangan's autobiographical writings is consequently misrecognized in the biographies through a process that can be understood in the fullest sense as sublimation. It is, on the contrary, to the elaboration of that structure that this chapter will be devoted, with particular attention to the most extended and reflective of the autobiographies, the *Autobiography* itself. Taking literally the meaning of the word as a "writing of the self," and allowing for the parodic nature of Mangan's writings in other genres, we will focus here on the nature of the self or of subjectivity as conceived by Mangan and on the nature of self-production as it appears in his writings. Mangan's articulation of the structure of subjectivity can then be understood in relation to the ethical and political definitions of a proper subjectivity to which his "waywardness" owes its significance.

PSYCHOSIS AND THE END OF AUTOBIOGRAPHY

As an intrinsic element of Young Ireland's project for fostering cultural nationalism, Thomas McNevin could suggest "a nation-wide program of public readings stressing the 'biography of self-sustained energetic men.'"[1] The importance of biographies to the *Nation*'s Library of Ireland series indicates the unexceptional nature of McNevin's project in nationalist circles. Biography, generically including autobiography, is intimately linked to the aesthetic politics of Romantic nationalism. The biography of the national hero is, in the first instance, a repetition of the history of the nation. Through conscious identification with the nation, the individual transcends in himself the actual disintegration of the nation by coming to prefigure the nation's destiny: the total identification of the individual with the spirit of the nation is a figuration of the total unity of the political nation that is the goal of the nationalist's labors. The nationalist hero is thus doubly productive: in the mundane sense, his political labors further the cause of national unification and liberation; in a secondary, but generally more significant, sense, his life story serves as an "inspiration," enjoining and mediating the identification of each individual with the nation to which all ideally belong and without which they are incomplete and inauthentic. Nationalist biographies, like nationalist histories or ballads, gain saturation with meaning by manifesting the spirit of the nation: they represent, and partake in, the continuity of that spirit in the double sense of asserting the ideal continuity of the nation's history and the continuity of the individual with his nation.

Mitchel's *Jail Journal* sketches the paradigmatic detour of Irish nationalism: cut off from their heritage by the fault of their fathers, it is the labor of the sons of Young Ireland to forge again an authentic spiritual paternal line. This metaphor is made equally explicit in Davis's diagnosis of the effects of losing a national language: " 'Tis to cut off the entail of feeling, and to separate the people from their forefathers by a wide gulf." The resolution to this problem is found in part in a writing that is seen as suturing the ruptures of translation by way of the writer's total identification with the paternal spirit of the nation. The historical rupture imposed by the alien rule is sublated into the symbolic structure of nationalism as a willed break with one's immediate origins in order to restore a self-authenticating relation to the true origin, which precedes all difference. The rebellion of the sons against their immediate forefathers, who were corrupted and diminished by subjection to an alien law, is justified by an ethical appeal to a prior transcendental principle of paternity.

Nationalist propaganda mobilizes all the figures of a familial romance, sanctioned as often as not by the apparently archetypal figure of the motherland, Kathleen ni Houlihan. The specific conditions that determine the appeal and efficacy of such figures and, more importantly, of the family romance that defines their function, are somewhat obscure but can be inferred from the economic and social transformations known to have occurred in the first half of the nineteenth century.[2] The access to professions and to increasing economic power which the Union of 1800 allowed the Catholic population encouraged a significant movement on the part of the growing Catholic middle classes — from which the nationalist intelligentsia was primarily drawn — toward urban centers, or at the very least it encouraged a redefinition of class interest in relation to urban-oriented economic activities, whether mercantile or professional. In consequence, the extended families of rural communities came to be replaced by the urban nuclear family, a process similar to that which occurred later in rural districts as a direct result of changes in landholding practices after the Famine. Accordingly, a new familial structure enters into the symbolic configurations of nationalism, offering an ideal resolution both to the alienation of the urban intelligentsia and to the continual ruptures between father and son which characterize bourgeois familial relationships.

Given that the upward mobility of Irish Catholics involves their effective dislocation simultaneously from the land and from the Gaelic language and culture, which then come to be identified with the land, nationalism may be understood to offer a virtual reterritorialization to the new middle classes. The spiritual nation provides a sublimated territory, while the figure of transcendental paternity which ensures the nation's continuity and self-possession replaces the actual father in possession of and working the land. McNevin's invocation of the "self-sustained energetic man" reflects the injunction to self-making that provides the dynamic of the mercantile economy in those maritime fringes which were being drawn increasingly into the general imperial economy. At the same time, the nationalist project allows the familial conflicts caused by self-making to be resolved by replacing the individual's immediate identification with the family by an ethically sanctioned identification with the nation.

Biography is in consequence appropriate to nineteenth-century nationalism not only for the parabolic function of its narrative elements — the figure of the national hero, the account of his individual struggles, the representation of those significant moments of national history in which he participates — but moreover, and arguably more importantly, on account of the recurrent formal characteristics of the genre. In most general terms, autobiography, including fictional autobiography, tends to represent the ethical self-realization of the writer from a perspective of self-consciousness through which the repetition of a life endows it with the appearance of a providential or predestined pattern. But while autobiographical texts are devoted to composing the unity and integrity of a personal identity through repetition, they are necessarily devoted at the same time to producing the individual as *autonomous,* that is, as self-authenticating and as self-authorizing. In the tradition of male autobiography that runs from Wordsworth's *Prelude* through John Stuart Mill's *Autobiography* to the virtual apotheosis of the genre in Joyce's *A Portrait of the Artist as a Young Man,* the concept of paternity is mobilized in a variety of configurations that, various as they are, share a fundamentally congruent structure and function. A perpetual tension subsists between the desire for self-origination, to produce oneself as if without a father, and the awkward knowledge of indebtedness to what precedes and influences the subject. If one option, that of Wordsworth, is the sublime assertion of self-constitution and emancipation, troubled incessantly by the return of the voice of another in one's own, one alternative to this masterful pattern involves the splitting of the father into an externalized actual yet "false" father and an internalized "mythical" father who functions as an avatar of the self. Appropriately, that internalized father is, in the case of Mill, Wordsworth himself; in the case of Stephen Dedalus, it is the "old father, old artificer," the *original* Dedalus who displaces the actual and inadequate fathers of the foregoing text.[3]

Louis Renza has drawn attention to such patterns in autobiography in speaking of the "metafather" who enjoins or motivates what Renza terms the "narcissistic mode of autobiographical writing."[4] In relation specifically to the political and ethical demands that inform nationalist ideology, the "metafather" performs a twofold function. In the first instance, it enables the process of "self-fathering," which intends to reproduce the individual subject as autonomous. In the second, it appears to resolve ethically the contradiction that is intrinsic to the political theory of the bourgeois state, imperial or nationalist, namely, the perpetual opposition between the claims of individual liberty and those of association. For in internalizing a metafather the individual subject identifies with the nation's transcendental paternity, which allows him to become representative of the race itself, partaking of and reproducing both its lineage and its destiny. In this respect autobiography may be understood as the particular representation of a general paradigm for the constitution of subjectivity.

Accordingly, to approach the interlocked questions of aesthetics, politics, and ethics through a consideration of autobiographical writing is equally to illuminate the degree to which these discourses saturate the domain of subjectivity, determining the modes in which the history of its constitution is at any juncture represented and naturalized. For reasons that have been well elaborated elsewhere, the family emerges in the nineteenth century as the point of intersection between society and the individual subject. It becomes at once the realm and the limit of individual autonomy, mediating the authority of the state while privileging the relative economic and moral autonomy of the family unit itself.[5] In this mediation, the figure of the father, as both "inside" and "outside" the family, as both wage-earner and protector of the private space, takes on a peculiarly significant, if often contradictory, role as both guarantor for and block to the autonomy of the son.

As the relationship of the narrative paradigms of nineteenth-century autobiography to family conflicts indicate, Freudian analysis is at once the culmination and the moment of crisis of a tradition. It can be understood as the culmination of an

autobiographical tradition not simply on account of the importance of autobiographical elements in such texts as *The Interpretation of Dreams,* or in the quasi-autobiographical texts
ghosted by Freud in the case histories. What is of greater import here is the extent to which the *formal* qualities of that genre
enter into the technical procedures of psychoanalysis in its therapeutic aspects. Fundamental to Freudian analytic technique is
precisely that process of interpretation permitted by repetition,
"tracing and retracing the paths of its own discourse," that
is equally characteristic of autobiography.[6]

What determines this formal congruence between two modes
of self-analysis is the direction of the analysis toward the ends of
reconstruction. The ethical ends of psychoanalysis, the reconciliation of the analysand with a real that is the social status quo,
are mediated through transference, a moment that parallels
precisely the internalization of the father in autobiography.
Transference is a repetition that simultaneously spells the end of
compulsive repetition; the "bad" relation to the real father,
which has inhibited the sublimation of him as superego and has
determined the outbreak of pathological behavior, is displaced
and overcome in a structurally repetitive identification with the
figure of the analyst as father.[7] For psychoanalytic therapy,
transference produces retroactively that "catastrophe to the
oedipus complex" which Freud describes — with peculiar reso-
nance in the present context — as "a victory of the race over the
individual."[8] But it is also on account of the crucial role it gives to
transference that psychoanalysis recognizes in its very description
of the etiology of psychosis the immanent limits of its practices.
For if, as Jacques Lacan has formulated the problem in his
elaboration of Freud's interpretation of the case of Schreber,
psychosis as a condition is determined by a foreclosure of the
"Name-of-the-father," then it is not merely practically but
essentially inaccessible to an analytic practice in which the analyst
assumes the position of a metafather.[9] For obvious reasons, any
autobiographical text that forecloses rather than sublimates the
father is similarly inassimilable to the autobiographical tradition.

The first effect of the radical absence of the psychotic as the
subject for analysis is the "textualization" of the disorder:

"Since paranoics cannot be compelled to overcome their internal resistances, and since in any case they only say what they choose to say, it follows that this is precisely a disorder in which a written report or printed case history can take the place of personal acquaintance with the patient."[10] Freud's reading is devoted to the understanding of the genesis of psychosis, but it is necessarily based on a *post festum* reconstruction of the psychotic experience by a subject who has already achieved a resolution, however compromised, of the conflicts that provoked the psychotic crisis itself. In other words, as Ida Macalpine notes in her introduction to the English translation of Schreber's memoirs, what Freud is analyzing is not the condition of psychosis itself but the obsessional neurosis that is its trace or residue.[11] Moreover, the analyst is here engaged, to use Freud's own terms, upon *translation* doubly removed from the source of its truth, being a translation of "glosses" or "quotations":

> He himself not infrequently presses the key into our hands, by adding a gloss, a quotation or an example to some delusional proposition in an apparently incidental manner, or even by expressly denying some parallel to it that had arisen in his own mind. For when this happens, we have only to follow our usual psychoanalytic technique — to strip his sentence of its negative form, to take his example as being the actual thing, or his quotation or gloss as being the original source — and we find ourselves in possession of what we are looking for, namely a translation of the paranoic mode of expression into the normal one.[12]

A text that is already a translation supplemented or disfigured by quasi-translations — glosses, quotations — is in turn translated in a process that insists on taking quotation or gloss for the original itself. To make sense of a discourse that is already a translation of what is, in the strictest sense, non-sense requires that the analyst be restored to his original position, that of origin of sense, by way of a process of translation that conforms, in keeping with the philological analogues and procedures of Freudian interpretation, with that theory by which the ideal translation is always the identical repetition of its original's origin.[13]

The analysis of psychosis succumbs accordingly to the general problem of translation, namely, that it is always necessarily to be conceived as the translation of a post-script, of a supplement, beneath which the original is effaced.[14] This is not even to say that Freud's reading of Schreber's text is necessarily incorrect or false but, rather, that it cannot be a reading of the psychotic text as such. The possibility of its truth lies precisely in the fact that the discourse of truth has been restored to it by the post-psychotic's own obsessional reconstruction — one devoted, in this case, to nothing less than recognition as an ethical subject before the Law.[15] In turn, it is no accident that the truth of Schreber is found by Freud to lie in his homosexual identification with his father, since in order to make sense of Schreber's text it has already been formally necessary to replace the paternal principle at the origins of interpretation.

The question here is ultimately that which is raised by what the reconstruction of psychosis may be thought to bar: a domain that *cannot* be represented within the scope of a discourse that is predicated on the authenticating presence of the paternal figure of origination. What cannot be spoken inside a discourse that depends for its philological investigations on a poetics of composition and condensation (*Verdichtung*) is a discourse of decomposition, of non-identity, such as might precede, or seek to return to before, the institution of the order of sense through the agency of the metafather.[16] The question as to the specific truth or falsity of any particular reading of the psychotic text is displaced by the larger question posed by psychosis to the model of truth — at once ethical, aesthetic, and "historical" insofar as its narratives of identity are predicated on an evolutionary historiography both onto- and philogenetically — that psychoanalysis shares with philology, with nationalism, with the canon, with autobiography. To state what has always been implicit in previous chapters, truth is given in each of these domains as that unity or self-identity which is historically produced by the perpetual repetition of origins in the act of knowing. Though variously figured, the *formal* criterion of truth remains fundamentally the same. Foreclosing the paternal figure which is the ground of truth, psychosis is essentially relegated to a domain that precedes the opposition between the true and the false, between sense and nonsense, and in which the subject itself is no more than a simulacrum lapsing constantly in the absence of any founding origin.[17]

When, then, in the following analysis of Mangan's autobiography, the claim is made that it is essentially *anti*-autobiographical insofar as it may be read as the representation of a psychosis, a number of provisos should be made from the outset. First, with regard to the truth of Mangan's text, it can only be stressed that since it is a *representation* of psychosis, it is subject specifically to the problematic that afflicts any psychotic text, namely that it is a translation, and to the general problematic of translation raised in Mangan's own writings, that translation effaces the origin that might have authenticated it. Second, while a Freudian reading of the etiology of what Mangan terms his "moral insanity" is appropriate in relation to the field of the "family romance" that psychoanalysis retrospectively articulates, it will already be clear that insofar as Mangan's text is a representation of psychosis, its "truth" ultimately eludes the techniques of psychoanalysis and, for that matter, those of any mode of analysis predicated on the presuppositions that found psychoanalysis. At the limits of any available mode of criticism, we confront those veils that, as Mangan realizes, the resources of speculation furnish as a barrier to the insanity which impends in the lapsing of origins.

THE PATERNAL DEBT

"A heavy shadow lay / On that boy's spirit: he was not of his fathers." This quotation, which Mangan attributes to Massinger, opens the *Autobiography* with a threefold reflection.[18] It establishes the initial condition of the text, its predication on a disjunction between the writer and the paternal line; it establishes, second, the sense of woe, which may be either the condition or the sign of that disjunction; it reflects, by its status as quotation and, moreover, as a quotation that is quite radically disjoined contextually from an original that is not even named, upon the condition and effects of disjunction itself, which will become both theme and procedure of the text thus introduced. Accordingly, we could add the question as to the identity between the *name* of the author and the text to which it is appended. This autobiography is opened by a citation from the text of another, to whom the writer is accordingly indebted much as is the sermon or commentary to the text which governs it; what, then, is the status of a narrative that must be introduced by another's voice, even when the quotation claims to deliver the most intimate truth — the genesis — of the writer's own condition, namely, his having nothing to do with his forebears? If the quotation becomes autonomous in being quoted and is, like the boy of which it speaks, radically disjoined from its originating context, why the need to establish its prior propriety, even if only in the form of a residual ascription to Massinger? If a debt is thus acknowledged in the very place where it is asserted that the boy owes nothing to his fathers, does this imply that it is in the prior text that we must still seek for the truth of the text or of the subject who claims to be disjoined from his origins? In this latter case, the thematics of the text, the condition of woe that is the result as it is the sign of disjunction from the father, might be already in contradiction with the procedures, to which, as will become apparent, the ascription of origins and the use of quotation are intrinsic. While the text is "about" the effort to break with the father, the fact that it is conditioned by, and recognizes its origin in, a relation to the father makes of the text a constant elusion, rather than a sublation, of that father.

The circumstantial origins of the *Autobiography* virtually recapitulate the problematic outlined above. The actual site of writing — Fishamble Street, according to Father Meehan — involves a topical repetition. In order to write the history of his life, Mangan returns to the place of his birth. Meehan's note also claims that it was "at [his] instance" that the autobiography was composed: the *Autobiography* was, then, apparently written at the behest of a *father* confessor who was also a metafather. That Mangan was aware of the psychic identity between his own father and Father Meehan is indicated by the similarity between his description of Meehan's temperament in a biographical sketch written virtually contemporaneously with the *Autobiography* for the *Irishman,* and the description of the father in the *Autobiography* itself:

The disposition and temper of Mr. Meehan are lively, quick, and bordering on the choleric. His Milesian blood courses rather too hotly through his veins.[19]

> [Mangan's father's] temper was not merely quick and irascible, but it also embodied much of that calm concentrated spirit of Milesian fierceness, a picture of which I have tried to paint in my Italian story of "Gasparó Bandollo".
>
> (*A*, p. 13)

Meehan and Mangan senior both emerge here not only as figures of impending threat but also as representatives of the original Irish racial spirit — a conjunction which is intrinsic to the tale of Italian nationalism here cited.

The external injunction that determines the very composition of the *Autobiography* stems from a figure who repeats the "real" father, just as the site of its writing involves a return to Mangan's own place of origin. The ethical injunction itself is writ large in the opening paragraph of the *Autobiography* in a figure that subsumes both fathers: Providence itself. What Providence demands of Mangan is, in fact, an autobiography that will serve as a "memorial" of his sin and suffering and be a warning to his fellow men. But if the "conviction" of this "imperative duty" clearly impressed itself on Mangan "at a very early period" in his life, it is equally apparent that this conviction is at once the index of the sin and the nature of the suffering of which he must write: "This conviction continually gained strength within me, until it assumed all the importance of a paramount idea in my mind. It was in its nature, alas! a sort of dark anticipation, a species of melancholy foreboding of the task which Providence and my own disastrous destiny would one day call upon myself to undertake"(*A*, p. 9). The origin of this text lies not in some specific event or set of events but, rather, in the "anticipation" of the narrative itself. That "Providential" anticipation is the absolute ethical demand that produces both the "bodeful text" and its subject, a suffering which is constant anticipation. Mangan, however, is anxious not to "anticipate [his] mournful narrative" and anxious that these preliminary observations should not "appear as the commencement of a history" (*A*, p. 10). These remarks refer, instead, to the ends that precede the history, determining the shape of its reconstruction in keeping with the ethical injunction that elicits it. These ends turn out to be twofold. The first is a settling of accounts, a payment of *debts* that can, in effect, be carried out only by Mangan's delivering of himself, true and entire, to his readers: "To all I owe a debt, and that debt I shall endeavour to repay to the uttermost" (*A*, p. 11). The debt is to be repaid in the form of revealing the truth beneath an appearance, and the second, broader intent of the *Autobiography* is consistent with that purpose:

> My desire is to leave after me a work that may not merely inform but instruct — that may be adapted to all capacities and grades of intellect — and that, while it seeks to develope [*sic*] for the thinking the more hidden springs of human frailty, shall also operate simply in virtue of its statements, as a warning to the uneducated votary of Vice.
>
> (*A*, p. 11)

In the very process of writing are reestablished the two levels of understanding that seemed to be denied in the presentation of the "simple and undecorated truth" of Mangan's self. And, while in reading through the *Autobiography* we may be puzzled as to what could be read in this deeply subjective history of suffering to serve as "a warning to the uneducated votary of Vice," it is equally the case that the "truth" of Mangan seems constantly to elude us. Far from being the case that, as he claims, his self is effaced in becoming a mere representation of "the hidden springs of human frailty" ("For myself, individually, I crave nothing," *A*, p. 11), the appeal to the reader's understanding involves a pursuit of the authentic Mangan that both exceeds the apparent *ethical* intent of the *Autobiography* and fails to close the debt by *repaying* the reader's labors. We are faced with a text that in every sense seeks to make its ends meet, but never succeeds.

For the "truth" of Mangan's misery, its true origin, is never present, but always slips between anticipation and recollection:

> In my boyhood I was haunted by an indescribable feeling of something terrible. It was as though I stood in the vicinity of some tremendous danger, to which my apprehensions could give neither form nor outline. What it was I knew not; but it seemed to include many kinds of pain and bitterness — baffled hopes — and memories full of remorse. . . . I did feel that *a period would arrive*

when I should look back upon the past with horror, and should
say to myself, Now the Great Tree of my Existence is blasted, and
will never more put forth fruit or blossom.

(A, pp. 9–10; italics added)

In the "Nachträglichkeit" of his recollections, it is the event itself
that is effaced while always represented as yet to come. His dread
is based on the apprehension of a danger that is, in a quite literal
sense, prefigurative: it has "neither form nor outline," it is not to
be figured or described.

In the end, it is in his father that Mangan finds the figure of his
dread, and in a formulation that makes of the origin a site of debt:
"I have an inward feeling that to him I owe all my misfortunes"
(*A*, p. 14). What should be stressed, however, is that it is exactly
as a *figure* that Mangan's father supervenes on the objectless,
formless dread that prefigures the specific threat that he comes to
represent. This figurative status is accentuated by the deviations
of Mangan's account from what is known to be the case: contrary
to what he implies, Mangan's father in fact died before his
mother, while it appears that rather than being driven from the
house, his sister either died in infancy or remained on as one of
Mangan's own dependents till quite a late date. These radical
distortions seek to make of the father an adequate origin for the
anxiety that Mangan suffers.[20]

We begin, then, from the perspective of the father and with the
effect of the paternal figure in the constitution of the "normal"
subject. According to Freud, the "dissolution of the oedipus
complex" should occur by way of an introjection of the paternal
figure and of the moral sanction which it represents "into the
ego, [where] it forms the nucleus of the superego."[21] At one level,
the "castration anxiety" that motivates this introjection is
merely a mechanism, so to speak, that enables what is of primary
importance, the formation of an ethical identity through identification not with the real but with a sublimated father. But if the
personal identity of the subject emerges reflectively at the moment
of the dissolution of the oedipus complex, it is by way of dissolving
equally the narcissistic ego, which recognizes no difference
between itself and the other. At this juncture, the apparently
merely mechanical function of "castration anxiety" returns and

determines the more radically unsettling aspects of Freud's elaboration of subjectivity. For castration anxiety is predicated on the recognition of difference, in the first place on sexual difference since what the little boy is said to perceive is the sister's or mother's lack of the penis. An economy of identity, that of the infant's relation to the mother, is fractured by the possibility of difference. When, therefore, in the interests of anatomical identity, the little boy reconstitutes his identity by way of identification with the father, the phallus continues to make a difference. In place of a narcissistic totality in which the self-identity of the infant is assured, there comes into being a subject whose identity is always constructed by identification with an other. Far from being a guarantee of the integrity of the subject, the accession to what is, in form as in content, an ethical identity becomes a splitting of the subject between a self-identity that is necessarily effaced, persisting always as only imaginary, and an identification with the other that can never be complete, precisely because of the trace of self-identity it always leaves behind.[22]

Within this schema, the father stands as the primal representative of the subject's relation to the other in general. Moreover, precisely because the moment of identification spells the end of the "pleasure ego" and of an economy in which the infant's needs are articulated as demands to be met by the mother, another economy is established, which may be conceived of as an economy of *debt*. Given that the subject's identification with the father can never be total, he will perpetually be indebted to this figure of the other to whom he owes his very identity. Structured from the start around an insufficiency or lack in the self that is predicated on the recognition of difference, the subject's desire emerges as a perpetual striving for identification with the other that he is forever unable to achieve. While both Freudian and Lacanian analyses open out continually from the subjective domain to ones that are ethical, political, and, in the fullest sense, aesthetic, what is revealed in the very structure of those discourses that aim to produce a transcendent or autonomous subjectivity is the figure of a subject forever indebted to the other who constitutes him.

It is consistent with Mangan's work as a whole that in the *Autobiography* he articulates his relationship with his father around a *debt:* "I have an inward feeling that to him I *owe* all my misfortunes." The relationship to his father is structured in the same way as his relationship to others in general, as he indicates in the general observations in the opening chapter: "To all I owe a debt." Theoretically, then, it should be his project to pay off that debt in the writing of an ethical autobiography which would provide an alternative paternity by developing "the hidden springs" of the subject's identity. The hindrance, however, is that the father here represents not the transcendent site of identity, but one who is in his turn perpetually indebted. To identify with this father is not to enter into self-possession but to perpetuate one's own indebtedness. For Mangan's father succumbs early to bankruptcy, and in his losses the son's identity is lost.

The "fault" of the father, who should, as we have seen, be both the provider for the family and the protector of the family space, is *improvidence*. Failing to provide for the family, he spends his money and property on strangers. But if his material properties are the first to go, they are rapidly followed by those essential ethical properties, his "judgment and disposition," and he is led to exchange the trade in provisions for that of a vintner. What the father provides for the young James is in turn an atmosphere opposed to Providence: one "of curses and intemperance, of cruelty, infidelity and blasphemy — and of both secret and open hatred towards the moral government of God" (*A*, p. 14). In consequence, however, the father becomes himself the victim of "a retributive Providence" and, increasingly, a debtor. Rather than becoming the symbolic figure of Providence — source both of Law and plenitude, of "*giving*" — the father becomes a figure of privation, himself indebted and punished for improvidence.

As the political metaphors of his account suggest, Mangan's siblings enact, in the face of their father's "tyranny," a moral and political program like that of the nationalists. Mangan on the other hand adopts a strategy that might seem an intensification to the point of parody of their cultural and historical program:

> For me, I sought refuge in books and solitude; and days would pass during which my father neither seemed to know nor care whether I

was living or dead. My brothers and sisters fared better: they indulged in habits of active exercise, and strengthened their constitutions morally and physically to a degree that even enabled them to present a successful front of opposition to the tyranny exercised over them. But I shut myself up in a close room: I isolated myself in such a manner from my own nearest relatives that with one voice they all proclaimed me 'mad'.

(*A*, p. 15)

Mangan almost literally brackets the spectacle of his siblings' opposition with that of his own withdrawal. The implied superiority of their strategy appears accordingly not only to be an "indulgence" that leads ambiguously to a "*front* of opposition" but, more importantly, aligns them with the father as the "one voice" of the family that declares him mad.

Mangan's "madness" is of course itself a mode of resistance, and it is important to grasp why this chosen mode becomes, in his own words, "the seeds of that moral insanity. . . which afterwards grew up into a tree of giant altitude" (*A*, p. 15). It is a frequently repeated paradigm of nineteenth-century autobiography and autobiographical novels that the child who does not fit within the family has recourse to self-seclusion and to reading as the means to establishing a degree of autonomy outside the constraints of the family: one has only to think of Jane Eyre or Daniel Deronda, David Copperfield or Maggie Tulliver for the persistence of the pattern to be apparent. The privacy of the act of reading the novel itself becomes figured within the autobiographical novel, in the widest sense of that term, as the means to producing a private identity. If, in Mangan's case, what is produced is, rather, a kind of "idiocy," in both the etymological and current senses of the term, we need to seek the reasons for that reversal of the product of reading within the specific history of Mangan's development.

Like that of his fictional counterparts, Mangan's withdrawal may be conceived of as offering at first a double satisfaction. At the same time as it provides a negative refuge in solitude, reading furnishes a positive substitute for the investments that have been withdrawn from the family. It is possible to see this withdrawal as a regressive repetition and even an intensification of a prior moment of negation, in which the withdrawal of investments from unpleasurable objects founds at once the narcissistic ego and the beginning of the process of thought itself.[23] Those thoughts, first directed toward the question of the child's own origin, later turn toward the child's attempt to liberate himself from parental authority by establishing another parentage through his fantasies.[24] The pursuit of knowledge that his solitary reading involves satisfies at once the desire to be wrapped up in another scene and the more aggressive desire to construct another parentage, or, more radically, to deny the dependence that is itself structured around the threat posed by the father. The father as origin of self and of self-consciousness is both displaced and, in a move that becomes increasingly significant at a later stage, decomposed by the multiplicity of texts to which the child has recourse in pursuit of independent origins.

The double satisfaction that Mangan's pursuit of knowledge provides is in fact neatly recapitulated in the phrase that he uses of his schooling, which, he says, stood him "in some stead" (*A*, pp. 15 – 16), aptly condensing the complementary notions of support and replacement which his schooling represents.[25] The anecdote that he tells of his schooldays and that, he says, "will somewhat illustrate the peculiar condition of my moral and intellectual being at this period" (*A*, p. 16) embodies a similar condensation. Asked to define the word *parenthesis*, in which the word *parent* remains audible if submerged, he responds with the ready definition of the word as "something included in a sentence — but which might be omitted from the sentence without injury to the meaning of the sentence" (*A*, p. 16). He has at once displaced his parents (and indeed the "one voice" of his family: "parent-he-sis") as a contingency unnecessary to his meaning, but only at the expense of being shamed and outcast by familial "sentence."

The reasons for Mangan's inability to exceed the condition of suffering that his psychic constitution enjoins seem to lie precisely in the reversible grammar of his relationship to his family. The respect and love that the child owes to father and family are stemmed by the threat that the father represents, transforming through fear into hate. The subtle dissymmetry condensed in the difference between the phrase "to him I owe all my misfortunes" and its implicit opposite, "to him I owe all my love," the difference between that *for* which one is indebted and the mode in which the debt is to be paid back, is in a way annulled: the misfortune of which the father is the source or originator is returned back upon the father as hatred. But in Mangan's case, a further reversal ensues that prevents him from forming a "front of opposition" and that transforms his hatred of the father, and of the family that shares the father's "one voice," into the sense of *being* hated. The onset of this paranoid representation of the world shores up Mangan's interior world, disconnected as it strives to be from "relations."[26] At the same time, its very structure depends on its negative relation to the figure of the father, who is never "introjected" but persists as the excluded cornerstone of Mangan's constitution. The "severe check" that Mangan, retrospectively, finds to have been in preparation for his faults (*A*, p. 17) manifests itself accordingly when both the material conditions that provided the possibility of his withdrawal and the adequacy of the paternal metaphor simultaneously disintegrate. For with his father's economic and psychic collapse, Mangan loses the ambivalent figure who stood between him and a "world outside." The diminished father is, on the one hand, incapable of performing psychically the threatening role that furnishes the motive and the support for Mangan's inner world; on the other hand, his disintegration removes figuratively and literally the screen that protected that inner world from intrusions. The consequence is a series of breakdowns that appear to cross the "minimal split" between neurosis and psychosis.[27]

The collapse of Mangan's interior world, constructed as it was through regression into narcissistic egoism, comes about through the cessation of his schooling. With a deep sense of betrayal he speaks bitterly of being "taken from [his] books — obliged to relinquish [his] solitary rambles and musings" (*A*, p. 18), of losing, in other words, the supports of his alternative and inverted world. The paranoic affects that colored that world are realized in his expulsion into a world in which contact with others can be experienced only in the form of physical and mental assault: he is forced in the scrivener's office "to herd with the coarsest of associates and suffer at their hands every sort of rudeness and indignity which their uncultivated and semi-savage natures prompted them to inflict" (*A*, p. 18).

These claims are exaggerated if not entirely phantasmal. What is more surely phantasmal is the depiction of the "house, or, if the reader please, hovel, in Chancery Lane" (*A*, p. 19), which, as he confessed to Meehan, "he dreamt" (*PPM* 1884, p. xli n.) and which becomes the appropriate symbol of his collapsed defenses. The loss of his "close room" (*A*, p. 15) becomes represented as its transformation into a "den" through which the winds and rains "howled through the winter nights like the voices of unquiet spirits" (*A*, p. 19). It is, moreover, a most striking version of the ruins and broken towers that so frequently in his writings figure the collapse of illusory paradises and the subsequent expulsion of the poet-dreamer into alienation. The corresponding bodily image is the physical mutilation that Mangan attributes to his time in hospital, when he shared a bed with a child "who was afflicted from head to foot with an actual leprosy" (*A*, p. 12) that Mangan in turn contracted.[28]

The ruined dwelling and the phantasm of a ruined, leprous body signify more, however, than the mutilations inflicted by the subjects' identifications. They signify in addition both the effective cause of Mangan's collapse and the identification that draws him into an alienation that can never be redeemed. For if, in the first instance, it is the father's extravagance and ruin that casts Mangan out from the shelter of introversion, leaving it a ruin and himself "a *ruined* soul in a *wasted* frame" (*A*, p. 23), he is obliged in turn to take on the father's role and with it his debts. James Mangan substitutes for James Mangan, and, in identifying with the father, takes on also his economic and psychic ruin, while the parents themselves become the younger Mangan's dependents. Identifying thus with his father as debtor rather than as Providence, the "succession" of the father's debts are in turn figured in the succession of diseases that culminates in his hospitalization with the leper and subsequent contraction of an "incurable hypochondriasis."[29]

This particular crisis gives way to a work of reconstruction that takes the form of melancholia, in which a "great overcurtaining gloom . . . had become . . . a sort of natural atmosphere" (*A*, p. 24). But still wrapped in the gloom so familiar to his contemporaries, Mangan is nonetheless obliged to return to work a second time on behalf of his "indifferent" parents (*A,* p. 25). This repetition of Mangan's displacement and replacement of his father gives way again to a second, structurally similar onset of illness, commencing more severely this time with hallucinations of being "shut up in a cavern with serpents and scorpions and all hideous and monstrous things, which writhed and hissed all around me, and discharged their slime and venom over my person" (*A,* p. 26).[30] These phantasms of an insistently offensive encroachment on the incarcerated subject are aggravated "by the pestiferous atmosphere of the office, the chimney of which smoked continually, and for some hours before the close of the day emitted a sulphurous exhalation that at times literally caused me to gasp for breath" (*A,* p. 26).

The claustrophobic workplace becomes here the parodic inverse of the "close room" to which Mangan was driven as a boy by the threats of his father, and that inversion is supplemented by the "pestiferous atmosphere" that repeats the psychic "overcurtaining gloom" of his psychic state. It is certainly possible to read the "serpents and scorpions" of his fantasy as a further fragmentation of the threatening father, who was figured initially as "a human boa constrictor" and is multiplied now in the form of vermin which are in turn the inverted image of the texts that were the boy's resources. For, at the same time, we can grasp how the ambivalent structure of Mangan's psyche remains in play in the midst of paranoid delusions. If the father persists here as a threat in the multiplied and fragmented form of a venomous other, it is equally the case that the father as such is no longer a threat, having become the younger Mangan's *dependent.* Having displaced and replaced his father, Mangan is in turn harassed by the "small creatures" that depend on him economically, just as his father earlier regarded his children as mice to be chased into holes.

Mangan's phantasms thus figure quite precisely the decomposition of his identity into a multiplicity of possible and contradictory identifications. There is, first, that of the child, which has persisted throughout, his "close room" transformed, perhaps by even a further regression, into the womblike form of a cavern itself not free from penetration by phallic beasts and their foul discharges. If this is the figure of the child elicited by the parent who destroys self-identity, a further identification may be found with the mother in the figure of the younger Mangan submitting to the intrusive vermin that crawl all over him as multiple versions of the father. Such an identification may make some sense of the fact that throughout all his autobiographical writings, Mangan scarcely mentions his mother, and then only as the silent support of the father's will or desire.[31] Finally, there is an identification with the father, but one that is predicated precisely on a lack in the father and that, accordingly, cannot supersede and order the previous identifications. All remain in play at once, with the consequence that the assumption of a stable and "authentic" identity by Mangan is precluded; in a more Freudian expression, he remains fixated at a stage anterior to the dissolution of the oedipus complex.[32]

Given the impossibility of sublimating his inadequate father, Mangan's psychic investments are transferred gradually from the family to the sublime domain of religion, where the structure of his relations to the transcendental other, God, reproduce those already formed around the split between his real and his figural father. Throughout the *Autobiography,* Mangan refers to his father in terms that mingle admiration with dread. God the Father takes on the projection of precisely these qualities: on the one hand, he represents the refuge of innocents, the kindly father that Mangan lacks in his own parent; on the other, he is placed in the role of unremitting chastiser, from whom, as Mangan's break-downs perhaps suggested to him, there is no escape, and to whom there is no appeal. This double aspect of God perpetuates irrevocably the ambivalence of Mangan's disposition. At one extreme God is represented as the refuge of the innocent dead where, as has been seen, Mangan's desire remains suspended around an inviolate image of the self-sufficiency that might have been his as infant. At the other extreme, God the Father, conceived as dwelling apart in a quite exclusive transcendence, takes on the affect of dread that is transferred from the real father only to be projected into an absence which, inviolable as it is, becomes the secure pivot of Mangan's own solitude. For if the projection of God into an "interminable chasm" (*A,* p. 29) guarantees the perpetuation of his suffering, despite risk of eternal damnation, it provides more importantly the promise of an inviolable space of singularity that can have, will have, nothing to do with society. The remoteness of God in Mangan's theology thus takes on in form and motive the distance he previously chose to set between him and his real father, with whom, in his chastisement at "the hand of retributive Providence" (*A*, p. 15) and altered position as dependent, Mangan can now identify. Having taken up the place of father as provider for the family, Mangan becomes in turn the victim of Providence, a God who assumes on a vast scale the *repulsion* that was the characteristic stance of others toward the writer and who accordingly becomes, far from the source of plenitude, the abyss into which the *irredeemable* subject pours his lost self.

Mangan's impasse is finally articulated, both in "form and content," by the introduction in the last chapter of a discussion with a young Catholic evangelist that centers on Pascal's *Pensées* and in particular on "that passage in which Pascal compares the world to a dungeon, and its inhabitants to condemned criminals, awaiting the hour that shall summon them to execution" (*A*, p. 23). The discussion begins in impasse, with Mangan's assertion that he had "even then learned enough of the nature of the human mind to know that disputation hardly ever converts or convinces" (*A*, p. 23), an assertion confirmed by the "great gulf" that Mangan perceives between him and this other. Its end, like the origin of Mangan's condition, is unavailable, since the manuscript breaks off midway, with Mangan objecting to the stranger's appeal to "the goodness, the justice of God" against his own statement of "the belief of the holiest and most learned theologians" of the Roman Catholic Church "that the majority of mankind will be irrevocably consigned to eternal misery" (*A*, p. 34). Though the reasons for the manuscript's breaking off at this point remain obscure, its present inconclusiveness is an interesting encapsulation of an impasse far more deeply written into the autobiography, and it effectively highlights the absolute incongruity embedded in the attempt to accommodate the "development" of the springs of Mangan's character to the teleological expectations of a moral tale of fall and redemption to whose forms the *Autobiography* constantly alludes.[33]

In the perspective of an autobiography whose impasse is thus confirmed in a refusal of the approach to God that would complete both life and work, the allusion to Pascal reveals a backdrop through which are recapitulated all the issues of the text, but on a critically reflective plane. The allusion has manifold references. Not only is Pascal familiar as the theologian of "le Dieu caché,"[34] which Mangan has been seen to adopt as the transposed support of his psychic structures, but the unattainability of that God is reinforced by what might seem the rather invidious act of concealing "le noeud de notre condition" beyond the attainability of knowledge through reason, in order to ensure the submission of that faculty to God himself (*Pensées*, 184.434). In a distance that opens between a hidden God and the "hidden springs" of our condition, the nature of that condition constantly reveals itself to be a "misère" which is the only sign we have of our fall from some higher state (*Pensées*, 172.409).

But from the suspension-in-suffering that is for him our fallen condition, Pascal refuses to have recourse to nostalgia for a pre-lapsarian state, which is seen as a diversionary delusion rather than a true stimulus to faith:

> Qu'est-ce donc que nous crie cette avidité et cette impuissance, sinon qu'il y a eu autrefois dans l'homme un véritable bonheur, dont il ne lui reste maintenant que *la marque et la trace toute vide*, et qu'il n'essaye inutilement de remplir de tout ce qui l'environne, recherchant des choses absentes le secours qu'il n'obtient pas des présentes.[35]

But the very structure of Mangan's psychic constitution, which depends on the exclusion of the other as the only defense against total dissolution, prevents his being redeemed through accepting Pascal's ultimate injunction, to fill the abyss with the presence of God (*Pensées*, 177.425). He of necessity remains in a state of perdition. What he retains from Pascal, however, is the radical doubt in relation to origins and to any recourse to a "trace vide" for retrospective consolation. Closed out from either origin or end, the reprobate is suspended in an abyss in which he will persistently seek but never find the God to whom a sin that has preceded him has left him utterly indebted. He can see "nothing in creation but what is fallen and *ruined*" (*A*, p. 33). He remains among the lepers, the disintegrating outcasts of whom few are saved, as Massillon stresses in the sermon that Mangan quotes.[36] The young man's response, a contrary refusal to submit the autonomy of his judgment even to that of the authorities of his own church, in turns throws into relief Mangan's personal *dependent* status, that of an "infant" who has never developed his own autonomy by internalizing the paternal principle. That dependence is repeated in the dependence of his text itself on a battery of anterior texts, texts which include those with which it commences and, virtually, ends. The structuring of the texts around the obscure resources of citation becomes the stylistic equivalent of the psychic disposition of the writing subject, and the acutest possible metaphor for his conception of the production of the self in non-identity.

DEPTHS OF CITATION

Mangan's invocation of Pascal at the close of a text that purports to be devoted to "developing the hidden springs" of his condition is peculiarly apposite not only in relation to the theme of the illusory consolation to be derived from such pursuits, but also in view of the extent to which such reflections are reproduced in the formal status of citation in Mangan's *Autobiography*. Drawn as one is to follow the network of quotations and allusions that permeates the text, in pursuit of an anterior context that might permit a "translation" of the deeper truth of Mangan's writing, one is perpetually reminded by the insistence of the citations or allusions themselves that the writer remains irredeemably indebted even in the process of writing himself out: the supports of his texts constantly erode the authenticity of the self that is represented in them. In this "Iliad of [his] woes" — an expression he borrows from that other great text on "influence" and debt, De Quincey's *Confessions*[37] — the epic of the self falls back perpetually on a multiplicity of types whose formal analogue is the mannered effect produced in Mangan's prose by the recurrent intrusion of the quotations themselves.

But, as the metaphors at the opening of his fifth and last chapter serve to remind us, to trace back through the type or fragment the archetype in which the complete identity of the self might be rooted is a fruitless endeavor. In the years between any past moment and the present, "life upon life has followed and been multiplied on and within" the writer; any archeology of the self can in turn only disinter the ruins of a *present* self ("The Pompeii and Herculaneum of my soul"), which are but an "imperfect picture" of their originals (*A*, p. 31). The history of the self is that of progressive ruin. In an allusion that once again encapsulates Mangan's ambivalent identification with and resentful debt to the father, his ever-increasing indebtedness is ultimately figured in the original father of the race, Adam, at once the prototype and the source of Mangan's sufferings as of that rebellion which leads to his expulsion from the enclosure of paradise into the suffering of labor: exchange of knowledge for innocence initiates, like the parodic paradise of Mangan's reading in a close room, a debt that multiplies indefinitely by endless self-reproduction.

Mangan alludes to this myth immediately before those concluding passages that introduce Pascal, but provides it with an analogue that is characteristically disjunctive:

> It is ever and everywhere the same immemorial tale. From the days of Adam in Eden to our own we purchase knowledge at the price of Innocence. Like Aladdin in the Enchanted Subterranean Garden, we are permitted to heap together and gather up as much hard bright gold and diamonds as we will — but we are forever therefore entombed from the fresh natural green pastures and healthful daylight.
>
> (*A*, p. 32)

The fable of Aladdin's entombment boldly inverts the previous metaphor of the history of the self as one of archeological disinterment. More significantly, it introduces a crucial difference in the initial appearance of a repetition of "the same immemorial tale." Unlike Adam, who is expelled from a real Paradise by his true author, Aladdin is "entombed" in a false paradise by the machinations of a false father — an evil magician who claims to be the orphan's uncle.[38] The tale of Eden, which might have seemed the type of human experience, repeated "ever and everywhere," finds its negation in the guise of similitude and in a tale that ultimately turns out to be the ideal "family romance." Aladdin, the child who declines to labor to redeem the family's debts and who is the victim of a false father, is the self-image counter to that of Adam punished by a righteous father, so that the conjunction of citations here displays and keeps open the tension between the contradictory impulses of the psychotic subject, between love and hatred, identification and rejection.

Such reversibility of intention appears constantly to define the function of quotation in Mangan's writings, and nowhere more than in the *Autobiography*. Even the apparently innocent "Farewell the tranquil mind! farewell content!" which prefixes both chapters 4 and 5 turns out to be the cry of Othello believing himself betrayed by Desdemona but already betrayed by a "James" (Iago) who leaves him indeed with a "mind full of scorpions." The sense of betrayal infects the entire text, father betraying son, but equally, in the motivation of the text itself, son betraying father. So much is even compressed into the name Mangan inserts into the given name, which would otherwise entirely identify him with his father. "Clarence" as a *borrowed* name inserts betrayal between James and the "man" who "began" him, for "perfidious" is the epithet inseparable from the name "Clarence," false though his brother Richard's accusations, that he betrayed his father, may have been.[39] Already the expression of an ambivalent relationship to the father, both resentful and guilty, this name, like Mangan's other multiple pseudonyms, becomes the license to a perfidious writing, consisting of treacherous translations that "betray" their originals and their readers precisely by being, to use Mangan's own apt expression, "fathered upon others." One need only recall the sense of betrayal as *exposure* to have the full mechanism of Mangan's procedures crystallized in this word: Mangan's writing is devoted to the exposition of its own dependence.

Not unlike translation or parody, citation becomes, as a formal device as much as in the specific content of what is cited, the index of a deep ambivalence with regard to the demand for authenticity that is contained in the related demands for originality and the sublimation of paternity. Far from being the trace of successful assimilation of foreign matter into a uniform text, Mangan's citations recur as an index of indebtedness, in terms both of the stilted mannerisms of style and of the openings into the treacherous "depths" of other writers who are the ambivalent fathers of Mangan's own text. For citations at once efface and summon their originals, being, like parody, at once antagonistic and dependent. Like the dead father who is said to have haunted Mangan, the body may be buried but the spirit is invoked through citation itself, so that we are drawn into a tracing of anteriority that may perhaps be endless. In the space of irredeemable suffering that Mangan's indebted writing opens up ("deriving *calamity* from *calamus* a quill") as a space equally defined by the father who is its alternative source, a vertiginous sense of treacherous dependencies prevails, which is perfectly encapsulated in the phrase Mangan applies to the physical and mental disintegrations subsequent upon his supposed contraction of leprosy: "'within the lowest deep a lower deep[']" (*A*, p. 21).

The phrase derives from Satan's bitter lamentation upon Mount Niphates in Milton's *Paradise Lost,* where the rebel angel at once contemplates a paradise that is a mere parody of lost angelic joys and laments the fact that, since he is not his own original, having been created by God the Father, he is perpetually in a state of dependence:

> Which way I fly is hell; myself am hell;
> And in the lowest deep a lower deep
> Still threatening to devour me opens wide,
> To which the hell I suffer seems a heaven.[40]

The entirely paranoic reversal that ensues from these meditations — "Evil, be thou my good" — may, to the theorist of canonical "strong poetry," be mere rebellion.[41] But the endeavor of Mangan's writing is of a different and more difficult kind than this. If the sin of Pride, of which he accuses himself so often, identifies him with Lucifer, it is a strangely passive pride. For it only serves to open up the ambivalence of a relationship to the father that alternates between identification, in which case the identity of the son with the improvident provider is met by the identity of the father with the son as victim of the Father, and withdrawal, in which the excluded father is substituted for by the chain of books/citations which provide alternate origins, and in which exclusion inverts exile from any closed space. This reversibility is beautifully caught in the reversible phonetic patterns of the whole phrase: "It was *woe* on *woe,* and 'within the l*owe*st deep a l*owe*r deep.[']" The woe which is characteristically Mangan's is in inverse relation to the debt he owes.

For Satan, the means to be quit of "the debt immense of endless gratitude, So furthermore still paying still to owe" would be virtual identification with God the Father, the taking of his place.⁴² For Mangan, on the contrary, to take the place of the father is to assume the condition of debt all the more fully, a fact which is figured with deep irony in the disjunction between the tenor of the passage that he cites — refusal of debt to the author of one's being — and the indebtedness to another author that the vehicle of citation itself perpetuates. And where Satan may be seen to "strengthen his constitution" here with a view to presenting a "front of opposition to the tyranny exercised over him," Mangan's citation has as its referent the disintegrating influence of leprosy, whose "moral effects" are "incorporated with [his] mental constitution." Mangan's body, far from attaining the oppositional coherence of a rebel's or the homogeneity of assimilation is, as he puts it in the "impersonal autobiography," "all nerves"; it is a tissue of connections and cathexes just as the body of his texts is a tissue of connections with anterior texts. The paradox of Mangan's writing is crucially unresolved: initial foreclosure of the father, of any external origin, leads, with the disclosure of the father's own debt, not to the enclosed space of an authentic identity but to an abyss of indebtedness that is incarnated in the *multiple* readings that substitute for the father. The origin loses its singularity, becoming an overdetermined locus of disintegration and alienation rather than the source of integration and autonomy. Where, in that tradition which we have sketched through both nationalism and psychoanalysis, the internalization of the father confirms the subject's fiction of identity and originality, the *foreclosure* of the father prevents either the affirmation of identity or the assumption of originality. Equally, insofar as the end is predicated properly on the rediscovered principle of the origin, on the "developing of hidden springs," what is produced here is a text that cannot develop or end: the remarks that open it, bearing on the "prefigural" origin of his suffering, are not to be seen as the "commencement of a history," because what they have to do with is the abyss of an origin that never arrives and that can, therefore, never stand as the autonomous source of derivation. Hence it is that this text, a work called for initially to function as a therapeutic labor, fundamentally resists assimilation to a nationalist tradition of autobiography predicated on the cancellation of debt through the sublimation of a paternal figure of originality. Gesturing toward such a desire, it becomes, through that very gesture, implicitly parodic of such desires: falling back on origins in various ways for the truth of the self, it reveals in its sources — the father, its anterior texts — always the same repetitive problematic of prior indebtedness. The figures through which Mangan's subjectivity is composed are those in which its authenticity is dissolved into derivation. The truth of the subject, his identity with himself as origin of himself, which is the end of autobiography, is foreclosed, leaving only the self as simulacrum, produced in a writing that knows no principle on which to come to an end. The simulacrum, the contrary of the copy in which the original model from which it is derived is faithfully reproduced, is the inauthentic and operates like a symptom whose translation back toward its source can reveal only that it is the source itself that is in question. The very multiplication of *types,* which might seem to underwrite the "representativeness" of Mangan's case, becomes antagonistic to representation to a degree even more critical than those poems in which the subjects' representations collapse into falsity: we may find the logic of their association of such moments with the spectacle of the ruin at least in part here, insofar as *ruin* becomes the punning figure for the inadequacy of the relation between the representation and its original. The shelter of identity collapses into the abyss of debt, so that the adequate relation between the representation and the original form — its reproduction of the *archetype* — persists only as parody.

In Mangan's dreams of ruin, which he confesses to have no relation to reality however they figure the real, the ethical cure that nationalist ideology offers to subjective and political disintegration founders. The history of "self-sustained energetic men" is parodied in a writing of the self that is the history of indebtedness and is incapable of concluding in decisive acts. The perpetuation of indebtedness assures the repeated production of an inauthentic subject who continually eludes identification in or with his writings; the transformation of the father from the site of plenitude into the abyss of ruin precludes the sublimation by which dependence can be converted into that autonomy on which the nationalist will to political self-determination is predicated.

The consequence for Mangan individually is depicted in his response to Joseph Brenan's injunction "To live [his] poetry — to act [his] rhyme":

> Dream and Waking Life have now been blended
> Longtime in the caverns of my soul —
> Oft in daylight have my steps descended
> Down to that Dusk Realm where all is ended,
> Save remeadless [*sic*] dole![43]

Mangan's "dole," the word encapsulating exactly the configuration of split, suffering, dependence, and deceit that characterize his autobiographical writings, is indeed remediless insofar as the principles of negativity from which it derives are *historically* counter to any on which ethical consolation or social cure might have been based. The contemporary call to identify, with all the ramifications that the term has been seen to produce, can only appear, given the logic of Mangan's writings, as an accentuation of alienation and as a delusion, merely displacing the locus of dependence. As Mangan is careful to maintain, it is at one and the same time to his writing and to his "life" that he is indebted for the suffering that is consequent on the unredeemed dependence whose multiple forms in life and writings he perpetually repeats. Writing, accordingly, can provide no aesthetic cure for the suffering, nor can a reformed life emancipate his writing from its own perpetually dependent modes. As the confirmed addict or as the "reconstructed" psychotic, Mangan seems obliged to circle compulsively around the empty trace of an original moment which, as his own narrative implies, is what was always in question.

7

The Ends of Mangan

THE SINGULARITY OF THE POET

Mangan's critical difference with the nationalist ideology of his time is borne out in his radical refusal to subscribe to the paternal metaphor through which the nationalist solution to the problem of reconciling individual and state is most forcefully mediated. Most generally, this entails his rejection of any metaphysics of the identification of the individual with the whole that, presented as a solution to the individual's dread of mortality, in fact imposes on the individual the ethical injunction of dying into the whole. Mangan's rejection of the metaphysics of totality that underwrites the nationalist ideology of his moment, and his at least incipient awareness of the aesthetic forms in which the image of totality was mediated, are stated early in his writing career. In a letter written in 1832 to a certain Tynan, though apparently never sent, and which contains the remark that Mangan's practice, "like that of Pascal and the Port Royalists, is to sink the first personal pronoun altogether," he engages in an elaborate rebuttal of the conception of society as an integrative totality:

> Your ideas of society are probably juster than mine, but they do not appear to me to be so. My conception is (observe, I do not dogmatize) that every body is an unit, an "ego" as Kant has it, a figure of 1, a personal pronoun of the singular number. Society I take to be by no means one vast whole integer, but simply a perceptibly divisible aggregate of all these little units. . . . I wonder whether Bentham in his Book of Fallacies has noticed this fallacy about society; it is one that should be exploded at once. People are really prone to talk about the human race as though it were one body, animated by one soul. . . . Nobody is bound to any other person. Links and chains are all very well in declamation and poetry, but nowhere else. The Romans manacled every prisoner to

an incubus of a soldier, and Megentius tied a dead and living body together, but these were punishments.[1]

Aesthetic images of human bonds or of the organic form of society are here returned to their coercive function as a bondage that imposes integration upon the individual. Given Mangan's insistence on the unitary, on the "singular number," it becomes absurd to reduce his lifelong resistance to integration with any political movement to the mere effect of a damaged psychic disposition. His recalcitrance to identification, which gave his biographers Duffy and Mitchel so much difficulty is not simply the symptom of a prior sickness of spirit, but may indeed give rise to the *appearance* of sickness. Where so powerful a set of normative discourses on subjectivity, identity, and political culture dominates, a counter-discourse that radically undermines the grounds on which the norm is constructed can only appear as derangement. The refusal of a particular mode of social relations, predicated in general on a principle of paternity, obliges Mangan's "marginalization" both biographically and aesthetically. In the one case, that refusal appears as psychosis, as that condition, namely, that cannot be represented within the dominant discourse except as a "vacuum and obscure gulf"; in the other, it appears as a writing scandalous by virtue of its racial and subjective "inauthenticity."

Accordingly, Mangan's account of his singular subjectivity in the autobiographies corresponds to an account of "the poet" that is equally opposed to nationalist expectations that the poet identify with the nation as the highest representative type of the race. The individual's resistance to the family and the discontinuity between the unit and society are repeated in the isolation of the poet, in his refusal to find in his sufferings a source of identity with humanity. Mangan's fullest expression of this point of view is found in his 1843 essay on the German poet Ferdinand Freiligrath, whom he later castigates for reneging on his former political indifference by affiliating with the Young Germany movement, the German equivalent of Young Ireland:

> The Poet cares nothing for solitude, but he wishes to avoid Man. His predilections are few; his antipathies a legion. Anything is better for us than imprisonment within a sphere within which we

are "not at home"; and nothing can be more dreadful than compulsory companionship with beings who are sufficiently alike us to awaken our sympathies in their behalf, yet more than sufficiently unlike us to make those sympathies recoil upon our hearts, burdened with the mournful lesson, that in

> "Our wretchedness and our resistance,
> And our sad, unallied existence",

there lies a woe beyond our power to heal, a mystery our faculties are forbidden to fathom.[2]

If there is a human condition which the poet articulates, it is precisely the avoidance of that figure of "Man," in place of which Mangan insists on the origination of suffering in the ceaseless play of similitude with and difference from others. Unlike Carlyle, who insists on the capacity of the "poet as hero" to penetrate the "open secret" and to forge through the labor of suffering a voice for the nation and the image of the ultimate identity of the human and the universal, and unlike Mill or an anonymous writer in the *Dublin University Magazine* article, who suggest that in his solitude and self-communion the poet deciphers the essential identity of human passions, Mangan perceives the isolation of the poet to be an expression of his non-identity.[3] Suffering and resistance, which, as in the *Autobiography*, appear as simultaneously each other's cause and effect, lead not to any aesthetic cure but, rather, to an "*unallied existence*" in which the wound of severance cannot be healed, precisely because the original ground which precedes our suffering cannot be fathomed.

This unhealable wound or sorrow is clearly cognate with the "terrible mark" set upon Mangan in the *Autobiography* as the index of his isolation. In one of the poems that he here translates from Freiligrath, calling it one of "the really first-rate things in this volume," the isolation of the poet is directly assimilated to the crime against the family and against society. Mangan's translation of Freiligrath's "Bei Grabbes Tod," entitled simply "Grabbe," follows its original at first with unusual "fidelity."[4] This may be attributable to the fact that "poor Grabbe" is represented as already engaged upon a writing that might be characteristically Manganesque, embodying an irresolvable conflict between the sublime and its trivialization that is imaged after Freiligrath in the military camp where Grabbe died:

> This Camp! Ah, yes! methinks it images well
> What thou hast been, thou lonely Tower!
> Moonlight and lamplight mingled — the deep choral swell
> Of Music in her peals of proudest power,
> And then the tavern dice-box rattle!
> The Grand and the Familiar fought
> Within thee for the mastery; and thy depth of thought
> And play of wit made every conflict a drawn battle.

Following Freiligrath to this point with virtually transliterative closeness, Mangan introduces into this stanza only the epithet "thou lonely Tower." The figure is recurrent in Mangan's writings, and the progression that ensues is quite predictable. It is at this point that Mangan begins to deviate from Freiligrath's text, condensing the three subsequent stanzas of the original into one, as if to highlight the realization of the significance of his interpolation in the final stanza. Here, the depiction of the alienated suffering of the writer evokes the concluding image of a ruined temple, which, derived initially from Freiligrath, now appears as the correlative of the psychic ruin of a formerly self-enclosed poet:

> "Alone the Poet lives — alone he dies.
> Cain-like, he bears the isolating brand
> Upon his brow of sorrow. True, his hand
> Is pure from blood-guilt, but in human eyes
> His is a darker crime than that of Cain, —
> Rebellion against Social Wrong and Law!"
> Groaning, at length I slept, and in my dreams I saw
> The ruins of a Temple on a desolate plain.

Though the elements are derived from Freiligrath, the specific configuration and the progression are Mangan's refractions: the first crime, that of Cain against the family, initiates at once the aloneness of the poet and his resistance to a social law of which the family provides the mediating type. But the isolation and the resistance are purchased not only by the "ruin" of the poet, but — just as that ruin constitutes a debt — by their necessary incompletion, for the "isolating brand" signifies resistance only inasmuch as it continues to be perceived by the human eyes that reject the poet.

The specific conjunction of the figure of Cain and that of the ruined tower within the topic of a resistance that can never be redemptive prefigures the concerns of the autobiographical writings. Like them, it evokes Mangan's continual concern with the question of origins, mediated in this case through a quite specific set of anterior texts. It has already been remarked, in the context of the poems "The Lovely Land" and "A Vision of Connaught in the Thirteenth Century," that the collapsed towers which recur so frequently in Mangan's writings in turn figure the collapse of a myth of origins that had been associated with the celebrated round towers of Ireland. Petrie's *Ecclesiastical Architecture of Ireland*, by proving that the origin of the towers was monastic rather than prehistoric, exploded what both Thomas Davis and an anonymous writer in the *Dublin University Magazine* regarded as the middle-class faith that the towers revealed the origins in "indefinite antiquity" of Irish civilization. A more entire fatality of Petrie's findings was the antiquarian Henry O'Brien's *The Round Towers of Ireland, or the Mysteries of Freemasonry, Budhism* [sic]*, and Sabaism Unveiled*. O'Brien's argument, which Mangan would have known of if only through the extensive and scandalized review of the work in the same issue of the *Dublin University Magazine* as contained the first of Ferguson's Hardiman articles, reads like an elaborate parody of the fundamental forms of nationalist thinking, while his etymological methods seem like a burlesque of the "science of origins." What O'Brien's Vallenceyan philological researches "unveil" is not only the Oriental origin of the Gaelic language but, furthermore, the origin of the round towers in the phallic worship of Edenic man, which indicates the real meaning of the Tree of Knowledge and the cause of the Fall. The mark that Cain receives as the index of the Lord's displeasure at his idolatrous worship of the procreative principle is the phallus which is its sign. It is this sign that Cain thereupon erects "into a deified *Round Tower*" in whose phallic configuration the unity of the Godhead is comprehended.[5] Wayward as the argument may seem, its unintentionally parodic findings throw into relief the paternal metaphor that structures the less extreme nationalist or philological narratives of originality.

Where, appropriately, O'Brien reinterprets the mark of Cain as the phallus which "in the now fallen condition of man" becomes rather "a passport to acceptance, than an inducement to annoyance,"[6] he unwittingly unveils the socializing function of the phallological discourses of nationalism. For Mangan, on the other hand, in the context of a treacherous translation that denies the philological project of reproducing the original form of things, the mark of Cain is the sign of a severance from origins, and the broken tower the index of rupture rather than continuity. Moreover, insofar as the logic of originality assures the assumption of identity as an ethical identification of the individual with the universality of the law, Mangan's assimilation of the poet to the first outlaw asserts the inauthenticity and unoriginality of the poet in the fullest possible sense of those words. Byronic as the configuration may seem at first, Mangan is far from espousing the notion that the anti-sociality of the poet may derive from his identification with a fuller, more authentic humanity or with its elementary passions as opposed to petrified moral conventions and pieties. More often than not, it is the *insincerity* of the poet that Mangan stresses, and in the absence of principles it is difficult to see how the poet might provide a figure for higher ethical identifications in the form of a repetition of original humanity. Rejecting principles as the ethical phantasm of identity with origins, the poet-Cain's crime against the paternal law makes him asocial. The ambivalence that attaches to Mangan's figures applies here, however, since Cain is described in that long passage on the fallacy of locating our origins in the Orient as one who "may build cities, but abide in none of them" (*LO* 1, p. 274). Cain is not simply the pre-social nomad; the crime against the family and, ultimately, against the paternal law of originality does not constitute him as a self-originating, autonomous being: on the contrary, what it initiates is that oscillation between dependence and resistance which Mangan so frequently evokes. If Cain provides the image of the poet, it is not so much on account of his nomadic asociality as of the articulation of his nomadism within the frame of the city itself.

THE POET AS MANNERIST AND DANDY

Mangan's habit of representing himself as a "singular number" against the background of the crowd was early formed, and may be seen as an anticipation of the more sophisticated manner of his later writings in their repeated articulation of opposition within dependence. Mangan appears to require the urban background against which to appear as singular. Already unique among early-nineteenth-century Irish poets in not seeking his resources in rural Ireland or in the historical traditions which the peasantry seemed to incarnate, he plays out his solitude urbanely as a provocative eccentric, drawing the very attention that he perpetually eludes.

In part, Mangan's singularity manifested itself in his melancholy self-absorption at gatherings of the Comet Club or in the *Nation* and *United Irishman* offices, and in the silent, marginal position which McCall claims that Mangan habitually adopted during "convivial evenings" with writers and journalists at the Wexford Street saloon. But this passive and unexceptional reluctance to identify with whatever group is matched by a more aggressive singularity. In the series of dialogues set in the Editor's Room that appeared in Duffy's *Belfast Vindicator,* Mangan appears as "The Man in the Cloak," a pseudonym he frequently adopted from the *Comet* period on.[7] The choice of pseudonym was not unrelated to Mangan's own attire. All his biographers remark on his striking mode of dress: the peculiar short coat and baggy pantaloon, covered with a tight blue cloak and topped with a broad-brimmed witch's hat, supplemented by "a very voluminous umbrella under each arm."[8] Striking as this mode of dress must have been, what is most singular about it is the ambivalence as to whether it is intended to function as a mode of disguise or as a means to attract. Mangan's comments on the Irish Gothic writer Charles Maturin, author of *Melmoth,* address precisely this paradox. Discussing that writer's notoriously eccentric attire, Mangan, who claims often to have followed him through the streets out of sheer curiosity, asserts that for all his bizarre appearance, Maturin did not seek attention but kept, rather, to byways and alleys on his perambulations through the city. Mangan fails to penetrate the mystery of Maturin, but there is much evidence that Maturin became one of his models in style and concerns as in dress. Mangan's own Gothic tale "The Man in the Cloak" employs Melmoth the Wanderer as its obscure deus ex machina and, characteristically, it is the endeavor to escape debt that motivates the embezzling bank clerk Braunbrock.[9]

If the Man in the Cloak is a perplexing and, like Maturin or Mangan himself, an elusive figure, the reason lies in the fact that, attractive to the gaze as the costume is, it is impossible to say whether anything lies behind or beneath it. At one point at least, in discussing the Man in the Cloak, Mangan seems to assert that there is nothing behind it. The passage appears in the essay "My Bugle, and How I Blow It," which takes as its text Justinus Kerner's plaintive poem on the theme of *Sehnsucht*, "Ein Alphorn hoer ich schallen." This "Alphorn" or, as Mangan translates it, "mystical bugle," calls from afar but can never be located. The Man in the Cloak's jest is to claim that he himself is the source of the sound and to suggest that Kerner will find the rest he seeks only in "assassinating" this Bugle-player, by destroying, that is, the object that perpetually calls his self-identity into question. In the course of the essay, Mangan elaborates on his pseudonymic identity, suggesting that his consciousness and his cloak are identical:

> I am not *a* Man in *a* Cloak, but *the* Man in *the* Cloak. My personal identity is here at stake, and I cannot consent to sacrifice it. Let me sacrifice it, and what becomes of me? "The earth has bubbles as the water hath," and I am henceforth one of them. I lose my cloak and my consciousness both in the twinkling of a pair of tongs; I become what the philosophy of Kant (in opposition to the Cant of Philosophy) dominates a *Nicht-ich,* a Not-I, a *Non-ego.*[10]

The personal identity of the writer is *in* the cloak, not masked by it; to lose the cloak is to cease to be an "ego," a "personal pronoun of the singular number." Identity becomes disguise, and simultaneously elicits and deflects the gaze of the other, which would seek to identify the appearance with the authentic figure of man which should underlie it.

These remarks will be reminiscent of Mangan's comment that style conceals nothing anterior to it. In this particular passage, the stylistic singularities that are recurrent in Mangan's prose are the appropriate correlative to the assertion that no more authentic identity lies beneath the surface appearance. Its insistent jocularity resists the solemnity that would attach to those interpretations of Mangan's ulterior intentions, which, nonetheless, its manner constantly elicits; the deliberate pursuit of excruciating puns, which is one of the most recurrent of Mangan's indulgences, both undermines the identity of the word and inverts that hierarchy which subordinates the immediate phonetic surface of the word to the law of meaning, while the depths of quotation characteristically open here onto the equivocating witches of Macbeth, who "palter with us in a double sense" and are not what they seem.

Mangan's sartorial eccentricity is thus doubled in his stylistic mannerism, to the general despair of his commentators. Mannerism nevertheless receives Mangan's considered praise, in an entirely mannered passage, as that which raises the individual from amalgamation to singularity:

> Mannerism is a grand thing, pursued I, following the current of my reflections. It is the real heavy bullion, the genuine ore, the ingot itself; every other thing is jelly and soapsuds. You shall tramp the earth in vain for a more pitiable object than a man with genius, with nothing else to back it with. He was born to amalgamate with the mud we walk upon, and will, whenever he appears in public, be trodden over like that. Transfuse into this man a due portion of mannerism; the metamorphosis is marvellous. Erect he stands and blows his trumpet, the sounds whereof echo into the uttermost confines of our magnificent world. . . . Mannerism! destitute of which we are, so to speak, walking humbugs; destitute of which the long odds are, that the very best individual among us, after a life spent on the treadmill system, dies dismally in a sack.[11]

The inauthenticity of mannerism is called upon here, fitly, as the means to encounter a stranger in a bar who appears at first as the contemporary translator Bowring, only to be metamorphosed under the influence of Mangan's increasing intoxication into the sorcerer Maugraby. Mannerism conjoins here with translation and the deceptions of necromancy in a narrative whose theme is the inauthenticity of identities, a conjunction which allows us to grasp how the insistent mannerism of Mangan's style belongs within a more general project whose effect is to mobilize inauthenticity against the demand for identity and originality. In order to comprehend this project accurately, however, it is necessary to define mannerism itself rather more distinctly than has tended to be the case among critics of Mangan.

In its commonest application the term "mannerism" is reserved by art historians for that stylistic period between Renaissance classicism and the Baroque and includes the late "mannered" work of Michelangelo as well as that of his successors. It is characterized simultaneously by stylistic elaboration and an extreme conventionalism within which that stylistic play occurs. Mannerism is generally understood as a rejection, even a degradation, of the values of classicism, while not yet embodying the expressive values of the Baroque, and, in its most pejorative acceptation, is regarded as the type of inauthentic conventionalism.

In more recent work, initiated by Ernst Curtius's assertion that mannerism should be understood as a recurrent movement of Western art in its perpetual oscillation between classicism and its rejection, mannerism is seen, rather, as a general stylistic paradigm, valued precisely for its radical resistance to the conservatism of classical values.[12] As Arnold Hauser has pointed out, such universalizations of the term evacuate it of any real signification and obscure the specific historical junctures within which particular artistic strategies signify. Hauser himself seeks to reground the usage of the term in its original historical period and to associate the stylistic phenomenon with the social transformations underway with the rise of capitalism in the late sixteenth and the seventeenth century. Mannerism becomes both a resistance to and an expression of a new sense of alienation and reification as well as of the loss of socially legitimated values in a period of transition. The tension between convention and excess becomes expressive of the unstable relation between the individual subject and traditional institutions. Mannerism accordingly becomes the first manifestation of a modernist sensibility, and its "recurrence" as a stylistic paradigm is linked by Hauser to a repetition of analogous social conditions in the course of the nineteenth century. Artistic movements from Baudelaire to surrealism are seen to manifest mannerist tendencies precisely because they too are in reaction to a retrenched apprehension of alienation in the modern consciousness.[13]

The peculiar insufficiency of Hauser's argument lies in turn not in his desire to ground the mannerist phenomenon historically but, rather, in his failure to carry that project through consistently. Having traced the genesis of sixteenth-century mannerism in its social context and provided an account of the specificity of its traits in relation to this context, in assimilating this phenomenon to nineteenth- and twentieth-century modernisms Hauser falls back upon a more or less analogical method, in which, for example, against an unspecific background of urbanization and industrialization, Baudelaire's stylistic tendencies are ranged alongside those of Gongora and are shown to be more intense varieties of the same. What is singularly lacking is an account of the historical specificity of stylistic effects comparable to that undertaken for earlier mannerism. In the case of mannerism as such, its peculiar stylistic effects are differentiated from a classicism that is taken to be the dominant mode against which mannerism is in reaction. In the nineteenth century, however, the comparable dominant mode would instead have to be considered as "Romanticism," and, with every awareness of the problematic nature of the term, it is against the paradigms of Romanticism that a nineteenth-century mannerism would have to be differentially defined.

Hence, it is not against a classic ideal of equilibrium that we find a nineteenth-century mannerism such as Mangan's reacting, but against that striving for authenticity and autonomy through originality that his contemporaries demand as the means to reconcile the individual with the universal. But, precisely by virtue of its recalcitrance with regard to originality, this mannerism is not devoted to the pursuit of new modes of expression, but parodically "betrays" the dynamic of the dominant forms against which it signifies. Where Mangan, in his praise of mannerism, parodies the claims of sublimity to elevate man above both his "amalgamation" with nature and his homogenization in the "treadmill system" of labor, the transformation of the sublime into parody, as earlier into necromancy, in fact exhibits a dialectic inherent in the very logic of the sublime. The sublime, as the aesthetic correlative of the ethical and economic injunctions to self-making, provides in the first instance a means for the individual's elevation over and above his condition. But the fuller narrative of the sublime depends on the higher reproduction of an original identity of the human in which the differentiated individual will once again be "amalgamated." The efficacy of this model thus depends on the reproducibility of the sublime effect for all men, which Schiller sees it as the function of the artistic sublime to ensure, and, consequently, on the iterability of that supposedly most intimate and inimitable of experiences, the confrontation of the individual with the imminence of death.

The logic of the sublime accordingly entails its own devolution into the very homogeneity that it is its ideological function to deny. The counterpart to this devolution can be perceived in the familiar drive of the nineteenth-century writer for singularity, both personally and stylistically. Enjoined constantly to produce "original" work, in the fullest sense of that word, yet perpetually confronting the formal identity of the origin to be reproduced, the author is unable to find in authenticity anything but the reproduction of the sameness that underlies apparent difference. The history of the usage of the word "originality" encapsulates its consequences, as the fear of homogenization drives the writer increasingly to resort to the appearance of difference, to singularity and mannerism, revalidating in the name of originality a mode of that very literature of "shock" that the first-generation Romantics deplored. Manifestations of this literature are ubiquitous in the journals of the first half of the nineteenth century, achieving their fullest realizations, not entirely paradoxically, in the stylistic extravagances of such writers as De Quincey and Carlyle.[14] It is within this development that Mangan's peculiar version of mannerism must be understood.

However, if this logic begins to provide some historical location for the phenomenon that Harold Bloom has termed the "anxiety of influence," as inspired by the precursive original, it is still necessary to push that logic further, beyond entirely canonical and aesthetic matrices, in order to grasp the political and social configurations of which it is symptomatic. In this regard, Hauser's elaboration of modernist mannerism through a series of writers more or less associated with the phenomenon of dandyism is suggestive and assists us in grasping the political significance of both these aspects of Mangan's personal and literary style. The dandy as a social type emerges at the beginning of the nineteenth century as the self-conscious expression of resistance to the homogenizing tendencies of bourgeois society. Though represented in some views as symptomatic of the last struggles of a declining aristocracy to maintain an ideological or moral ascendancy over a rising bourgeoisie, what is striking about the dandy is his assumption of classlessness: ostensibly detached from any specific class affiliation, the dandy seeks to restore distinction precisely where distinction appears to have been abolished. As Baudelaire was to put it in "Le Peintre de la vie moderne," the dandy emerges in "transitional epochs" where democracy is not yet fully ascendant and aristocracy not yet entirely corrupted:

> Dans le trouble de ces époques quelques hommes déclassés, dégoûtés, désoeuvrés, mais tous de force native, peuvent concevoir le projet de fonder une espèce nouvelle d'aristocratie, d'autant plus difficile à rompre qu'elle sera basée sur les facultés les plus précieuses, les plus indestructibles, et sur les dons célestes que le travail et l'argent ne peuvent conférer.[15]

The dandy is situated expressly in opposition to the bourgeois values of work and money, in opposition to those values that reduce humans to identity by predicating all social relationships on equivalence in exchange. At the same time, the dandy is at once symptomatic of individual anxiety at the spectacle of homogenization and indicative of that restoration of distinction in bourgeois society which the ideology of *original* equality in identity seeks to legitimate. Honoré de Balzac suggests as much in his "Traité de la vie élégante," in which he endeavors to show how "la vie élégante," of which dandyism itself is merely an heretical form, must be understood to rest "sur les déductions les plus sévères de la constitution sociale." Fashionable life is derived precisely from the regeneration of inequalities in the wake of the revolution.[16] The trajectory of the revolution reveals the mendacity of the assertion of political equality for all men, showing it to be, quite literally, a question of pure *formality:* both freedom and equality are formally defined, as universals, while the specific content of social forms, which makes the difference, is left out of account. It is partly Balzac's point that "la vie élégante," as the expression of an aristocracy of talent or intelligence, recreates and accentuates social distinctions in contradiction to the claim to equality; partly, and more significantly, that by stressing their singularity the nonproductive men of fashion equally deny the ideology of universal humanity that underwrites the bourgeois constitution. As his ironic axioms have it: "Rien ne ressemble moins à l'homme qu'*un homme!*" and "Sont en dehors de la vie élégante les détaillants, les gens d'affaires et les professeurs d'humanités."[17]

But if the dandy is defined by his opposition to the homogenizing tendency of bourgeois democracy, the history and the immanent logic alike of dandyism betray its essentially parodic relationship to the forms it opposes. Dandyism is at once the critique and the fullest expression of bourgeois subjectivity, and nowhere more so than in the extreme "volonté formelle" which it shares with the poet.[18] For the essence of dandyism, as Baudelaire — himself no "extravagant" dandy — was to point out, lies not so much in costume as in a relation to the economy. The scandal of the dandy lies less in his attire than in his apparent idleness. His singularity is to live outside the domain of production, a characteristic which is only most blatantly figured in the unsuitability of his attire to utilitarian pursuits. The dandy becomes an aesthetic object in the strictest possible sense, representing not only a modality of the beautiful submitted to the gaze of the other but, more significantly, the type of that elevation above economic interest which is where the aesthetician would locate the essential identity of the human. If Baudelaire claims that "Le Dandy doit aspirer à être sublime sans interruption," the condition of sublimity is fulfilled as much in the disinterest required in order to "vivre et dormir devant son miroir" as in the shock that the dandy constantly offers to the man of business.[19] The sublimity of the dandy is his transcendence of nature, "qui n'est pas autre chose que la voix de notre intérêt,"[20] a fact that entirely justifies the claim, explicit or implicit, made by defenders of dandyism or "la vie élégante," that their treatises elaborate "les principes qui rendent la vie poétique."[21]

The dandy, then, according to the logic of the aesthetic, becomes representative man, all the more so in that he represents the human as achieving a higher identity in transcendence of nature and special interest. Grounded in the desire for pure difference, the urge to dandyism is, paradoxically, fulfilled in its completion of that narrative of identity of which differentiation is merely a stage. At the same time, however, the dialectic of the dandy transforms that narrative into a parody of itself which manifests both the inauthenticity and the lack of autonomy that are the actual condition of the democratic subject. The reaction of the dandy is directed at an ideology of equality whose real meaning is equivalence or substitution.[22] Revolting against aristocracy in the name of universal identity, the bourgeois measures the value of men, as of objects, according to a universal scale of equivalence whose ground is abstract labor and that substitutes for status determined by birth the infinite interchangeability of men differentiated only by an exchange value whose variations are accidental. The infinite capacity for substitution which is the economic meaning and rationale of the concept of a universal human essence annuls the original identity which is the theoretical support of the ultimate authenticity of personal identity. Where differentiation becomes merely change of place, or substitution (which in turn creates in the name of "identification" the dynamic of that quintessential bourgeois form, the novel), no essential identity is guaranteed. The dandy, who substitutes appearance for essence — "*Paraître, c'est être* pour les Dandys, comme pour les femmes"[23] — is no more than the fullest expression of the condition of the subject under capitalism, who is defined not by any human essence but by his or her economic role.

This is not to say, however, that in his apparent transcendence of the economy the dandy achieves the autonomous singularity denied to others. For the autonomy of the dandy is as much a semblance as his identity, since he is irrevocably linked to the fundamental modes of bourgeois subjectivity by the inevitability of debt. For the bourgeois subject, it is the perpetual anxiety of debt that motivates that labor which guarantees his civic identity; psychically, that debt appears, even for the "self-made man," as the irredeemable debt owed to the ethical principle in consequence of an initial break with the real father. For the dandy, similarly, and in the cases of Poe and Baudelaire quite literally, rupture from the father initiates indebtedness: singularity entails debt. The history of the dandy, from Brummell to Wilde and beyond, is littered with debtors, such that the very anti-economic principles of extravagance to which the dandy subscribes become ultimately the logic by which, not unlike aesthetic autonomy itself, the autonomy of the dandy transforms into dependence on the economy which was to have been transcended.[24] When Baudelaire remarks that the dandy is not concerned with wealth or money "comme à une chose essentielle," adding that "un crédit indéfini pourrait lui suffire," he recognizes implicitly that credit itself is merely the acknowledgment of debt.[25] The inevitability of debt in the economic sphere is replicated in the ethical sphere: if Baudelaire is a rebel, his rebellion is a recognition of the ineluctable "devoirs" imposed upon the bourgeois subject, since even when summoning the image of Satan he is, like Satan, never permitted to achieve autonomy.

MASKENFREIHEIT AND THE COLONIAL SUBJECT

With what may appear a happy intuition, Thomas Carlyle links in one passage the figures of the dandy and the poor Irish as complementary inversions of one another. The passage appears in *Sartor Resartus,* a text that is itself constantly troubled by the quasi-dandiacal style in which it masks the truth of its intentions with an irony that may have "overshot itself."[26] The specular relation that Carlyle draws between the dandy and the Irish suggests some homologies between the democratic and the colonial subject which it is fruitful to pursue, and also illuminates the anxiety about inauthenticity that afflicts the nineteenth-century writer. It will be my contention that Mangan, in adopting the position of an inauthentic writer, both plays to the full the position of the colonial subject and, in his recalcitrance with regard to the nationalist attempt to redeem the colonized, intimates the fundamental continuity between the colonized and the democratic subject.

It is scarcely accidental that *Sartor Resartus* was first published in *Fraser's,* a journal run by a Corkman, William Maginn, and sustained by like-minded Irishmen, including Daniel Maclise, who sought to integrate themselves with the British middle classes. *Fraser's* had long been running a campaign against the aristocratic dandies, particularly as personified in Bulwer-Lytton's fashionable novel *Pelham,* in a manner marked as much by its concern for ethical self-making as by its distaste for aristocratic waste and frivolity. Carlyle's own attacks on the dandiacal sect in *Sartor Resartus* were probably based entirely on his readings of *Fraser's,* as his Teufelsdrockhian reference to "some English Periodical" implies.[27] Nonetheless, he grasps immediately the preoccupation of the dandy with *appearance,* and the relation of this to the specialization of trades in general and to poetry specifically: "A Dandy is a clothes-wearing Man, a Man whose trade, office and existence consists in the wearing of Clothes. . . . [He] is inspired with Cloth, a Poet of Cloth."[28] The dandy, indeed, is gifted to grasp effortlessly "the all-importance of Clothes" which the German professor "writes his enormous Volume to demonstrate," thus embodying ironically the project of *Sartor Resartus* itself. Apart from their common failure to have yet produced a reliable or readable canon, it is this instinct for "costume" that links the dandy and the "Irish Poor-slaves," which latter "appear to imitate the Dandiacal Sect in their grand principle of wearing a peculiar Costume."[29] The costume is, of course, the polar opposite of the dandy's finery and consists of the extravagant rags of the poor.

The Dandy and the Poor-slave are polar opposites whom *Fraser's* would have wished to see assimilated into a moral middle class. Carlyle, however, intimates at once a profounder relationship of specularity between them and the possibility that they represent the essence of England's "national existence," ultimately incorporating all other classes even in their contradiction: "In their roots and subterranean ramifications, they extend through the entire structure of Society, and work unweariedly in the secret depths of English national existence; striving to separate and isolate it into two contradictory, uncommunicating masses."[30] The anxiety, which will provoke the writing of *Past and Present,* is that the bourgeois subject may have no other choice than that between identification with dandy or colonized: if these represent the "secret depths" of the nation, all other choices are ultimately inauthentic.

The irony is, then, that both poles are themselves representations of the inauthentic, the dandy in the sense that we have already discussed, and the Irish Poor-slave for reasons that are inherent in the representation of the colonized subject in Ireland as elsewhere. Carlyle remarks at one point that the Irish Poor-slaves are also known, "unphilosophically enough," as "the *White Negroes.*" The "unphilosophical" status of the term resides in the oxymoron, its appropriateness in the intimation of a duplicity and a doubleness that cannot be reduced to a true identity. If in this respect the Irish Poor-slave may be assimilated all the more closely to the inauthentic figure of the dandy, it is also the case that the representation of the Irish as a species of dandy replicates their traditional stereotyping by the colonizing power as duplicit, untrustworthy, false.

This stereotype, which is comparable to those of the "treacherous nigger" and the "inscrutable Oriental," complements the stereotype of Irish sentimentality and performs an opposed function. Both posit a primitive essence as the definition and limit of Irish identity, but while the ascription of sentimentality legitimates colonialism within a hegemonic schema of gradual assimilation, the ascription of duplicity legitimates the exercise of disciplinary power. If the Irish are defined a priori as essentially untrustworthy, as beyond the reach of ethical and political improvement, the use of violence is preemptively justified. Both stereotypes can be understood to stem from the same anxiety with regard to the alien, the one operating through the desire to make the alien more like the self, the other through the need to subject the alien totally.[31] The paradox of the stereotype of duplicity, however, is that in seeking to control anxiety it perpetuates it: not only does the stereotype dictate that it will never be possible to trust the Irish, but it precludes by definition the possibility of positing an essential Irish identity. That which refuses to submit to the law of truth while equally refusing to adhere consistently to the lie becomes the simulacrum itself, eluding the law of identity which would ground the concept of an essential and eternal principle to which the type would conform. The set of attributes that supposedly characterize the Irish nature ranges from the charming to the malevolent, and precisely in that range confirms the unstable oscillations of the stereotype. What all have in common, however, is an opposition to the laws of truth and the political economy of language: blarney, tall stories, "bulls," bombast, punning, lies, betrayal, slander, informing, demagoguery can all be referred back to the single stereotype of duplicity, and all leave the colonial power in a bog of uncertainty which the stereotype itself affirms.

This is not to say that the stereotype itself is without foundation in the actual practices of the colonized Irish. To be sure, the pretense of failing to understand English sufficiently or even the adoption of a certain charming stupidity served — and continues to serve — to establish tactically a space for the colonized to maneuver in; even more surely an instinct for simple survival motivates the apparent obsequiousness of the servant who is by night among the Ribbonmen. But, erroneous as it is to identify the tactical maneuvers of an oppressed people with the essence of their character, the necessity of appearing as if masked can transform into a strategy that would subvert the founding principles of colonial ideology in the very act of assuming its stereotypes. A tactical duplicity engaged as a means to elude assimilation may become a critical instrument that addresses that positing of original essences in continuity with which the authentic subject is produced for ethical and political assimilation. For, as the stereotype itself tends to suggest, beneath the grimacing or grinning mask there may be no single, coherent identity, only an abyss of duplicity.

Hence the importance of Mangan's differences from his nationalist contemporaries, both in terms of his habits of life and of his modes of writing. It is intrinsic to the Young Ireland program to overcome the subjection of Ireland through abolishing the ground for stereotypical denigrations of the Irish race. If the legitimation of English rule is derived from the self-validating argument that the Irish are essentially incapable of self-government, that argument must be countered by producing ethical selves in Ireland who will be unified in themselves and capable of producing and governing a united state. Accordingly, the pursuit of the principles of Irish identity is devoted to the constitution of a counter-image of the Irish as an essentially principled race, who have been perverted only by their historical exclusion from self-determination.[32] The ideology of nationalism is, in the first place, the morality of a predominantly urban middle class who have as little sympathy with rural guerrilla resistance as do their unionist counterparts. In the second place, it replicates the bourgeois ideology of the state disseminated by the colonial power within which, for writers from Coleridge through Carlyle and Mill to Arnold, the right to representative government is conditional on an ethical and aesthetic culture that alone can produce the coherent political subject.

In the course of this study it has been argued that Mangan eludes or critiques turn by turn the principles of originality, authenticity, and autonomy that ground the identity of the political subject and the representative man for nationalism specifically and for the democratic state generally. Playing out the role of the inauthentic in both writing and lifestyle, Mangan, like the habitual debtor, always appears as masked. It is, moreover, made highly questionable that beneath the mask there lies some authentic identity: Mangan's technique is, rather, to multiply personae, masks, as he multiplies the texts on which his writings depend while simultaneously converting them into the "secondary" texts of his own writing. In this respect it is proper to understand him as the urban intellectual counterpart to the rural "white nigger," refusing to assume that fixed identity which is the very condition of representativeness and of assimilation to the bourgeois state.

But it is precisely these characteristics that make it so difficult to conclude on Mangan, however provisionally, since it is the continual effect of his writing to produce an excess of ambivalence, in the form of another depth or debt, wherever one seeks to identify him. This effect shares some of the features of that nebulous concept, Romantic irony, yet in refusing both the nationalist project which his Irish contemporaries shared with their German models and the cultural imperialism that underlies most of the British Romantic and Victorian writers, Mangan equally eludes the political aesthetic through which, precisely in its notorious undecidability, Romantic irony emerges as instrumental in the production of a subjectivity that is assimilable to the state. Accordingly, he eludes still the terms of an aesthetic that has yet to progress substantially beyond its historical predication upon the production of identity. By virtue of his excluded position as a colonized subject, without the citizenship which Mitchel and the Young Irelanders sought to recompose culturally, Mangan's writings, for all the flaws and redundancies that are apparent to an aesthetic judgment, play out the founding contradictions of an aesthetic that is fundamentally colonial in its terms and determinants. The logic of that process operates through the inversion of those terms, which provides at least a partial explanation for the impossibility of Mangan's proceeding beyond a writing that, in its elusion of autonomy and authenticity, must remain dependent and parodic. The perpetuation of minority status, as of indebtedness in all its forms, provided at that juncture the most effective, perhaps the only conceivable mode of critique to direct at an imperial culture and its specular opposite, nationalism. If in this respect Mangan presciently anticipates Stephen Dedalus's castigation of Irish art as "the cracked lookingglass of a servant," it is equally his anticipation of Dedalus's (and Joyce's own) disaffected refusal to affiliate with the nationalist cause that provides the fuller explanation for the impasse into which Mangan seems deliberately to write himself. Where imperialism destroys the forms of political organization natively developed by a colonized people, nationalism, replicating the forms of the bourgeois state that emerge in time with imperialism, seeks to constitute a mode of political identity that, though represented as a re-creation of an essence, knows no precedent among the colonized. Accordingly, it assists in the obliteration of the traces of other modes of political organization in its drive to political and social homogenization in the name of an essential racial identity.[33] For the writer or intellectual critical of the process and suspicious of its metaphysical supports, no alternative political community exists, and he or she is obliged to remain in critical alienation.

But only within a schema that understands the "alien" to prefigure essentially the "best self" and the future totality of the aesthetic state can this position attain to the pathos of the heroic, a status which Mangan, in his wretchedness as in his ironic resistance, consistently rejects. Unlike the Kafka of Deleuze and Guattari's imaginings, Mangan does not seek to produce or prefigure the conditions of a possible future community in place of the one he lacks; "national consciousness" does not pass through this literature.[34] Rather, the tendency of his work is to question the possible conditions of any community insofar as the assumption is that this community will be founded upon the authenticity and integration of the individual. And if, in turn, in the minor critical tendency of his works, as in his affecting of the persona or in his adoption of multiple and parodic styles, Mangan appears with uncanny prescience to prefigure the equally alienated modernist artist, this may be quite simply because one of the effects of the peculiar conditions of Irish nationalism was to throw into relief the *institutional* function of the aesthetic domain by highlighting its equivalence to the political constitution of the bourgeois state. Thus where, as Peter Bürger cogently argues, the antagonism of the avant-garde to the aesthetic as a bourgeois institution is its defining characteristic, Mangan's specific resistance to a nationalist aesthetic politics is sufficient to produce a writing formally comparable to some modernisms, though as different in its effects as the objects of its parodies are to those of the late nineteenth and early twentieth centuries.[35]

In his resistance to the identifying drive of the aesthetic, Mangan prevents the logic of our own desire to force some neatness of identification upon him by suggesting that he is the ironic type or representative of an Ireland, or by extension of any colony or ex-colony, that, precisely by seeking its authentic identity and declaring its opposition to imperial power through the constitution of a *democratic* state, perpetuates its own dependence. Such an assertion might seem appropriate, given that in consequence of his parodic modes of writing Mangan accentuates the forms of nationalist thinking before reversing them to draw out the figure of the perpetually indebted subject which nationalism struggles to transcend for the nation and in each individual. In doing so, however, what he succeeds in highlighting is the profound formal continuity between the democratic and the colonized subject, between the purportedly most free and the most oppressed. In some respects this must be understood as the consequence of his peculiar historical situation, as a socially and culturally disadvantaged subject of an "internal colony" yet also an ambivalent participant in the early formation of a democratizing nationalist movement. What this double identity allows him to write out, however, is the intrinsic logic of cultural hegemony as it applies to both the colonized and the democratic subject.

In the tradition of writing that establishes culture as the ideological apex of the incorporative apparatuses of the state, the process of cultivation is one that must be applied in varying degrees both within the nation-state itself and in its colonial domains. The primitive condition of the colonized peoples, supposedly due to their lower stage of development in the scale of universal history, is metaphorically matched by the relative savagery of the working classes and, indeed, in certain circumstances, even of the middle and upper classes, according to the ideal scale of cultivation. The two primary criteria here are the capacity for productive work, which is at once an ethical and an economic demand, and the ability to suspend the private for the general interest, which is at once a political and an ethical demand.[36] Neither of these criteria is met by the "savage" or the worker in their present state of cultivation. Written into the logic of aesthetic culture, however, is the perpetuation of its necessity by virtue of the fact that, in its own terms, the state of culture can never in fact be realized: the process of cultivation operates through a perpetual deferral of its ends such that those who are held to be in need of culture can in theory never fully attain it. The very means that is claimed to produce the autonomous subject in free and ethical identification with the state can, by its own logic, only produce the subject as perpetually indebted and as inauthentic in relation to the absolute demand for reproduction of the essence which aesthetic culture itself imposes. In this respect, culture replicates both the economic situation of the bourgeois, enjoined to a self-making that can structurally never be attained, given the partiality of an identity formed under the conditions of accelerating division of labor, and the political situation of the colonized subject, literally "denigrated" for a lack of political and ethical autonomy that is continually deferred by virtue of his predefined and structurally perpetuated dependence. But it is, of course, precisely from this logic of deferral that aesthetic culture derives its efficacy as an ideological apparatus, promising a formal freedom which can never be realized.

Hence, neither the democratic nor the colonial subject can ever transcend the condition of inauthenticity according to the absolute measure of universal identity imposed by aesthetic culture. So much is figured, with that clarity which may belong to moments of transition, in the conclusion to the third of Heinrich Heine's *Briefe aus Berlin*, written in 1822 more or less as Mangan's career as a writer for the popular journals was beginning.[37] The letter is concerned for the most part with the popular entertainments of the city and the extensive dissemination of cultural works — including Sir Walter Scott's novels and Carl Maria von Weber's *Freischütz* — in the context of the formation of a national culture. Its concluding paragraphs concern the masked balls in the opera and constitute an extraordinary allegory of the relationship between the freedom of democracy and the loss of individual identity in which an "urgesellschaftliche Vertraulichkeit" is restored. While the court sits above in the boxes, unmasked, it is the democratic masses that swirl below, realizing freedom and equality in disguises behind which the identity of the bearer is a matter of literal indifference, being merely one more mask:

> Aber was ist daran gelegen, wer unter der Maske steckt? Man will sich freuen, und zur Freude bedarf man nur Menschen. Und Mensch ist man erst recht auf dem Maskenballe, wo die wächserne Larve unsere gewöhnliche Fleischlarve bedeckt, wo das schlichte Du die urgesellschaftliche Vertraulichkeit herstellt, wo ein alle Ansprüche verhüllender Domino die schönste Gleichheit hervorbringt, und wo die schönste Freyheit herrscht — Maskenfreyheit.[38]

The condition of democracy that Heine here ironically represents, that its ideology of equality is an assertion of identity as equivalence, "Gleichheit," undoes the belief in the prior authenticity of the individual's identity that is the theoretical counterpart of equality itself. The individual, in consequence, appears only as masked, and it is only in this inauthentic form that the identity between the individual and humanity ("Menschen") is realized. It is this condition of inauthenticity that Mangan writes and lives out, refusing ever to enter into authentic identity. This refusal of identity involves equally a rejection of the aesthetic underlying the canon of major writing that articulates the forms of universal human identity and seeks to mediate the conformity of the individual and the universal. While this refusal has meant his relegation to minor status, it determines simultaneously the remarkable prescience implicit in Mangan's work regarding the crises inherent in the democratic forms that are figured in the domain of culture. The function of a minor writing such as Mangan's, critical as it is of the canonical form of the state mediated by culture, has perhaps been overtaken by history as those crises have come to consciousness in the literature of modernism and post-modernism. If, as Walter Pater suggested on the very threshold of aesthetic modernism, the consciousness of the modern is to be defined by an historical sense that must be understood exactly as a *universal* history of the gradual realization of man's essential identity, the definitive crisis provoked by post-modernism lies in the collapse of such a sense of history.[39] The critique of identity thinking, which has been associated both with the critical recognition of the centrality of ethnocentric thinking to the very structure of Occidental culture and with the corresponding "return of the repressed" in the form of colonized writings of all kinds, allows us to comprehend the peculiar qualities of a formerly excluded minor literature, but only in the moment when our actual political and cultural situation has spelt the effective dissolution of the terms "major" and "minor" themselves. The former legitimating function of high culture has been overtaken both by a critique grounded in its own internal contradictions and by its supersession by a so-called mass culture, the efficiency of whose assimilative techniques vastly surpasses those of the aesthetic culture by which it was formally prefigured. Whether this be seen to involve the finally total aestheticization of everyday life or merely the end of the aesthetic as an effective ideological apparatus, it is clear that the predication of an autonomous domain for aesthetic work, on which the distinction between the canonical and the minor was based, is no longer sustainable. The critique of that aesthetic which has been established here as defining the nature of minor literature has effectively been realized. If the work of a writer like Mangan continues to exercise a haunting power, it is perhaps because this inauthentic ghostwriting speaks to a moment in which the only possible position for the intellectual appears to be that of unrelenting negative critique, and in which new political formations and affiliations are only just beginning to emerge out of the crises of democratic culture.

Appendix

A Brief Chronology of Mangan's Life

1803   Born May 1, Fishamble St., Dublin.

1810   Placed in school in Saul's Court, run by Michael Courtney, taught languages by a Father Graham.

1814   School moved to Derby Court, still under Courtney.

1818   Begins work as scrivener at Kenrick's.

1818–26   Writing rebuses, enigmas, etc., for Dublin Almanacs.

1825   Closure of Kenrick's. Works successively for Franks and Leland (later Murphy) as scrivener till 1836.

1829   Catholic Emancipation Act.

1832–33   Associated with the anti-tithe "Comet Club" and writes for the *Comet*.
              During this period teaches Catherine Hayes German, till her death in 1832.

1833   Founding of *Dublin University Magazine*.

1834   Begins to write for *DUM*.

1835   Death of brother, John Mangan.

1836   (according to O'Donoghue) Gives up work with scrivenery.

1838   Becomes copier for the Ordnance Survey, under Petrie and O'Donovan.
              Also at some time in this period does some cataloguing for Trinity College Library.

1842   Foundation of the *Nation*.
              Cataloguer for Trinity College Library, after closure of Ordnance Survey in 1841.

1843   Death of James Mangan, James Clarence's father.

1845   Publication of *Anthologia Germanica*.
        First year of the Irish Famine.

1846   Contributing predominantly to the *Nation*.
        Death of Catherine Smith (Mangan's mother).

1848   Founding of *United Irishman*. Mitchel, its editor, trans-
        ported for sedition.
        Abortive rising of a section of the Young Ireland move-
        ment. Mangan's association with this group and the
        United Irishman led to dismissal from Trinity College
        Library.
        Admitted to St. Vincent's Hospital for a brief period.

1849   Dies in the Meath Hospital, Dublin, 20 June, after incar-
        ceration in cholera sheds during the famine epidemic.
        Death diagnosed as due to starvation.

Notes

As is any student of Mangan, I am indebted to Jacques Chuto's exhaustive bibliography of printed and manuscript sources for the writings of James Clarence Mangan. Since this bibliography will shortly be available as a part of Chuto's doctoral dissertation for Paris University, a separate bibliography of all Mangan's works is not included here; only those writings referred to in the text are cited.

INTRODUCTION

1. Two valuable summary sources for the general administrative and social tendencies of this period are E. Strauss, *Irish Nationalism and British Democracy* (London: Methuen, 1957), book 3, and F. S. L. Lyons, *Ireland since the Famine* (London: Weidenfeld and Nicholson, 1971), pp. 59–69.

2. General studies of the movements include Robert Welch, *Irish Poetry from Moore to Yeats* (Gerrards Cross: Colin Smythe, 1980); Patrick Rafroidi, *Irish Literature in English: The Romantic Period* (Gerrards Cross: Colin Smythe, 1980); and Thomas Flanagan, *The Irish Novelists, 1800–1850* (New York: Columbia University Press, 1959). For the relation between Irish politics and literature for the nineteenth century, Malcolm Brown's *The Politics of Irish Literature from Thomas Davis to W. B. Yeats* (Seattle: University of Washington Press, 1972) is still enormously valuable.

3. For figures indicating the trend, see Jacqueline R. Hill, "The Intelligentsia and Irish Nationalism in the 1840s," *Studia Hibernica,* no. 20 (1980): 76–91, and her general comments on the trend, pp. 94–96.

4. Gilles Deleuze and Félix Guattari, "What Is a Minor Literature?" trans. Richard Brinkley, *Mississippi Review* 22, 3 (Spring 1983): 27. This text is a translation of chapter 2 of Deleuze and Guattari's book-length study *Kafka: Pour une littérature mineure* (Paris: Minuit, 1974).

5. See Louis A. Renza, *"A White Heron" and the Question of Minor Literature* (Madison: University of Wisconsin Press, 1984), esp. pp. 3–42. I am concerned here primarily with the implications of the

literary critical history of his introduction rather than with the remarkably detailed analyses of readings of Jewett's work and its historical context that occupy the body of this work.

6. Harold Bloom, *The Anxiety of Influence: A Theory of Poetry*
(Oxford: Oxford University Press, 1973), passim, esp. pp. 26–28.

7. Something of the contradiction that emerges from Bloom's argument can be registered in the fact that the autonomy of the strong poet is
necessarily found in his fixation at a pre-oedipal stage, which, according
to the logic of Freudian analysis, would imply a virtual psychosis and the
impossibility of writing. Cf. Bloom, *Anxiety of Influence*, pp. 109–10.
Paradoxically, this would also relegate the major poet to the perpetual
minority of psychic infancy.

8. Matthew Arnold, *On the Study of Celtic Literature*, in R. H.
Super, ed., *The Complete Prose Works of Matthew Arnold*. Vol. 3:
Lectures in Essays and Criticism (Ann Arbor: University of Michigan
Press, 1962), p. 395. Text cited hereafter as *SCL*.

9. Arnold drew extensively on Ernest Renan's *Essai sur la poésie des
races celtiques* (1854) and on Henri Martin's *Histoire de France*
(1860), as well as Johann Kaspar Zeuss's *Grammatica Celtica* (1853).
Wilhelm von Humboldt's *Linguistic Variability and Intellectual Development*, trans. George C. Buck and Frithjof A. Raven (Philadelphia:
University of Pennsylvania Press, 1972) — a translation of *Über die
Verschiedenheit des menschlichen Sprachbaues* (1836) — is perhaps the
classic text in the establishment of the relationship between philology
and ethnology. On this tradition and von Humboldt's place in it, see
R. L. Brown, *Wilhelm von Humboldt's Conception of Linguistic Relativity* (The Hague: Mouton, 1967), and Robert L. Miller, *The Linguistic Relativity Principle and Humboldtian Ethnolinguistics* (The
Hague: Mouton, 1968). Immanuel Kant's *Anthropologie in prag-
matischer Hinsicht* (1800), trans. Mary J. Gregor as *Anthropology from
a Pragmatic Point of View* (The Hague: Nijhoff, 1974), was originally
delivered, during several decades, as a popular lecture series. Its concern with racial types as well as with the history of the maturation of individuals and the human race provides an important and suggestive
early knotting of the complex of ideas with which the present chapter is
concerned.

On the immediate context of the Anglo-Saxon – Celtic contrast and on
the background to contemporary ethnic stereotypes, the two most valuable studies are Frederic E. Faverty, *Matthew Arnold, the Ethnologist*
(Evanston, Ill.: Northwestern University Press, 1951), and Lewis P.
Curtis, Jr., *Anglo-Saxons and Celts: A Study of Anti-Irish Prejudices in
Victorian England* (Bridgeport, Conn.: University of Bridgeport Press,
1968).

10. See *SCL*, pp. 300–301, for Arnold's "sense of native diversity
between our European bent and the Semitic bent," which are seen as
irreconcilable. Arnold is in part engaged here in a defense of Wilhelm von
Humboldt's anti-Semitism. For the further distinction between the reli-

gious genius of the Semitic peoples and the "imaginative reason" of the Indo-Europeans, see *SCL*, pp. 369–70.

11. Edward Said comments on the use of philology in the formation of racial stereotypes in *Orientalism* (London: Routledge and Kegan Paul, 1978), chaps. 2 and 3. The reliance on the written rather than the spoken not only influences the common view of the origin of language as essentially poetic speech, a view held by writers as various as Percy B. Shelley in his *Defence of Poetry* (1821) and J. G. Herder in his *Essay on the Origins of Language* (1772), but seems, moreover, to be determining for the notion of historical evolution that structures philological thinking. For suggestive remarks on this latter question, see Miller, *The Linguistic Relativity Principle*, p. 32, and Julia Kristeva, "Le Sujet en procès: Le Langage poétique," in Claude Lévi-Strauss et al., *L'Identité* (Paris: Grasset, 1977), pp. 224–26. As does Said's, Kristeva's argument here focuses primarily on the writings of Renan.

12. For Hegel's remarks on Schiller's "grasping the unity and reconciliation as the truth," see G. W. F. Hegel, *Hegel's Introduction to Aesthetics*, trans. T. M. Knox, with an interpretive essay by Charles Karelis (Oxford: Oxford University Press, 1979), p. 61. The history of German attempts to achieve national unity in the early nineteenth century can be read in Elia Kedourie, *Nationalism*, rev. ed. (London: Hutchinson, 1961), passim, and in John Breuilly, *Nationalism and the State* (New York: St. Martin's Press, 1982), chap. 2. Though the demonstration of direct influence is not essential to the argument of this chapter, both Park Honan in *Matthew Arnold: A Life* (New York: McGraw-Hill, 1981), pp. 83–97, and William A. Madden in *Matthew Arnold: A Study of the Aesthetic Temperament in Victorian England* (Bloomington: University of Indiana Press, 1967), passim, esp. pp. 9–17, detail Arnold's debt to German idealism. For general discussions of the dissemination of German thought in nineteenth-century Britain and Ireland, see Rosemary Ashton, *The German Idea: Four English Writers and the Reception of German Thought, 1800–1860* (Cambridge: Cambridge University Press, 1980), and Patrick O'Neill, "The Reception of German Literature in Ireland, 1750–1850," parts 1 and 2, in *Studia Hibernica* 16 (1976): 122–39, and 17 (1977): 91–106.

13. See Friedrich von Schiller, *Naive and Sentimental Poetry and On the Sublime: Two Essays*, trans. Julius A. Elias (New York: Ungar, 1966), and *On the Aesthetic Education of Man in a Series of Letters*, ed. and parallel trans. by Elizabeth M. Wilkinson and L. A. Willoughby (Oxford: Clarendon Press, 1967). The latter text is cited hereafter as *AEM*.

14. *AEM*, p. 7. I cite the German (*AEM*, p. 6) since it stresses more clearly than the translation the idea of the state as an *artwork*.

15. Samuel Taylor Coleridge, *On the Constitution of Church and State* (1830), ed. John Colmer, Bollingen Series 75 (Princeton, N.J.: Princeton University Press, 1976), pp. 73–75.

16. John Stuart Mill, *Representative Government* (1863), in *Utilitarianism, Liberty and Representative Government* (London: J. M. Dent, 1910), pp. 197–202, 256–71.

17. Franco Moretti has recently argued the typicality of the bildungsroman for the novel as genre in *The Prose of the World* (London: Verso Press, 1986).

18. A range of nineteenth-century essays, including William Wordworth's preface to the *Lyrical Ballads,* Thomas Carlyle's "The Poet as Hero," J. H. Newman's "Poetry, with Reference to Aristotle's *Poetics,*" and, of course, Arnold's "Study of Poetry," imply this argument. Alba H. Warren, Jr., in his introduction to *English Poetic Theory, 1825–1862* (Princeton, N.J.: Princeton University Press, 1950), p. 7, makes the point that for Victorian critics "style . . . is directly related to the poet's moral being" but fails to stress the indifference of this requirement to actual behavior.

19. Luce Irigaray's characterization of the female hysteric suggests an arresting inversion of this paradigm of mimicry within a paradigmatic model of "exclusion":

> La névrose privilégiée de la femme serait un "mime" d'oeuvre d'art, une mauvaise (copie d') oeuvre d'art. Elle se produirait comme une contre-façon, une parodie d'un procès artistique. Transformée en objet esthétique, mais sans valeur et condamnable parce que relevant de la simulation. Stigmatisée en tant que *faussaire.* Ni "nature," ni technique de re-production adéquate de la nature. Artifice, mensonge, feinte, piège, tel serait le jugement social merité pour le tableau, les scènes, les drames, les pantomimes, hystériques.
> (*Speculum de l'autre femme*
> [Paris: Minuit, 1975], p. 156)

As will be argued later, Mangan's works produce an effect of psychosis that takes this effect of hysteric production into a critical mode.

20. Peter Bürger has argued this case in *Theory of the Avant-Garde,* trans. Michael Shaw, foreword by Jochen Schulte-Sasse (Minnesota: University of Minnesota Press, 1984), esp. pp. 57–59.

1. The Lives of James Clarence Mangan

1. See Rudolf Patrick Holzapfel, *James Clarence Mangan: A Check List of Printed and Other Sources* (Dublin: Scepter, 1969).

2. Ellen Shannon Mangan is currently at work on a biography of Mangan that promises to achieve the fullest reconstruction of the writer's life since O'Donoghue's work and will constitute a valuable reinterpretation of the biographical tradition.

3. See McCall's notes for his life of Mangan, NLI MSS 7955–59. In the course of the chapter, attention will be drawn to his inaccuracies.

4. He refers, for example, to Mangan's "forlorn condition" (*Life,* p. 51) at the *Comet* period, without further substantiation, having adequately demonstrated (*Life,* pp. 15–16) that Mangan would have been relatively well off at this period.

5. Duffy 1908, p. 293. The letter to Mitchel, first published in the *United Irishman*, 25 March 1848, p. 106, is quoted in full by Mitchel, *Poems* 1859, p. 15.

6. Jacques Chuto, "Mangan, Petrie, O'Donovan and a Few Others: The Poet and the Scholars," in *Irish University Review* 6, 2 (Autumn 1976): 169, remarks on the "romantic sensationalism" that applies to the antisocial destitution of Mangan's last years to his whole life.

7. See *DUM* 33, 19 (May 1849): 650–52, and *A*, p. 13. The footnote, *A*, p. 13, giving the date of publication as December 1848 is incorrect but may, as Jacques Chuto has pointed out to me, represent the publication date that Mangan had expected.

8. It refers to his composing "The Death Chant of Regner Lodbrok," published in *DUM* 30, 17 (August 1847): 214–23, and offers material for the June and July issues of the magazine.

9. I refer to only a few of the numerous newspaper articles on aspects of Mangan's biography, as they are for the most part clearly derived from the principal sources and are, furthermore, extremely untrustworthy and notoriously difficult to verify. Those that I have made use of either throw up new evidence for Mangan's biography or are written from perspectives significantly at variance with the canon of Mangan biography.

10. The post-revolutionary waning of Duffy's fervor was encapsulated in Devin O'Reilly's nickname for him, "Give-in" Duffy. See John Mitchel, *Jail Journal, or Five Years in British Prisons* (Author's edition, Glasgow: Cameron and Ferguson, n.d.), p. 265. His fullest account of Mangan is in Duffy 1908.

11. See Appendix for a chronology of the known events of Mangan's life.

12. O'Daly's assertions can be found in *PPM* 1849, p. xiii. The revised information is derived from the parish records for SS. Michael and John, which do at least confirm the traditional date of Mangan's birth. I am indebted to my father, Oliver Lloyd, for making this discovery. See NLI Microfilm P. 7358, n.p.

13. See William Carleton, "The Poor Scholar," in *Traits and Stories of the Irish Peasantry*, second series, 3 vols. (Dublin: W. F. Wakeman, 1833), 2: 60–298. D. H. Akenson in *The Irish Educational Experiment: The National System of Education in Nineteenth Century Ireland* (London: Routledge and Kegan Paul, 1970), pp. 45–58, discusses the hedge schools and their importance to the acceptance of national schools in rural Ireland, but points out that Carleton is one of the few firsthand sources available.

14. See Lyons, *Ireland since the Famine*, pp. 24–25, on the relative prosperity of graziers at this period. Mangan's account of this trip is in a letter to Duffy, NLI MS 138, fols. 11–12. One may probably discount his claim to have had to subsist on a diet of hard-boiled eggs on account of the terrible quality of what little bread there was available.

15. See Edmund Curtis, *A History of Ireland* (London: Methuen, 1961), p. 302.

16. Still in the hands of the Smith family in Kiltale is a shop ledger that appears to have belonged to the McNally holding in Fishamble Street and is datable to 1850. Entries recording substantial deliveries of supplies from Kiltale and from the grocery to places including the Pigeon House artillery station and the fashionable Fitzwilliam Square area testify to the substance of both holdings. Interestingly, a dwindling of entries toward the end of the ledger and notes of the transfer of supplies to 3 Fishamble St. indicate a switch of interests back to the old family holding. This is borne out by *Thom's Dublin Street Directory*, which lists M. Smith as Grocer and Spirit Merchant at 3 Fishamble St. in 1849 and 1850, but P. McNally as proprietor from 1851.

17. Price, 22 September 1849; cf. *A*, pp. 14–15, 17–18.

18. McCall, p. 4. O'Daly's brief notice of Mangan's life prefixed to *PPM* 1849 merely states that "being of rather restless disposition, he removed to another locality" (p. xiii).

19. In possible corroboration of Mangan's own statements that his father exchanged the grocery business for a vintner's store (*A*, p. 14) and that "within the lapse of a very limited period he had failed in eight successive establishments in different parts of Dublin" (*A*, p. 17), *Wilson's Dublin Directory*, in *The Treble Almanack* (London, 1801–1825) lists a "Mangan and Lanson, Wine Merchants" at 20 Greek St. (off Mary's Lane just north of the Liffey) in 1813 and 1814, transferred to Lower Ormond Quay in 1815 and 1816, while from 1817 to 1825 (when the directory ceased publication) a James Mangan is listed as Grocer and Corn Factor at 11 East Arran St. None of the sources provide any information concerning Catherine Smith after Mangan's father took over the grocery, but from 1806 to 1813 *Wilson's* lists a Catherine Smith at 10 Stonybatter (in 1801 the same address was occupied by a Michael Smith), and from the same date till 1810 as a haberdasher at various addresses, and after 1807 apparently in association with a Mary Smith, who continues in the same business at least till 1824. It is, of course, difficult to establish finally whether any of these Smiths are related to Mangan.

20. See T. D. Sullivan, "Occasional Notes," *Weekly Nation*, 16 April 1898, p. 4.

21. See the two letters to Hardiman, 4 December and 8 December 1848 (RIA MS 12 N. 20, fols. 138–39), addressed from 151 Abbey St.; a postscript to a letter to Duffy (TCD MS 4629), which explains how to find his room, suggesting a new lodging; and McCall's notebook entry "Mangan's addresses," which lists Johnson's Court, 61 New St., 11 Upper Abbey St., and Bride St. (meaning, perhaps, the cellar where Mangan was found dying in June 1849), as well as those already given. Unfortunately, McCall does not give his sources (see NLI MS 7959, p. 419).

22. The Irish post–Napoleonic War depressions are described in Patrick Lynch and John Vaizey, *Guinness's Brewery in the Irish*

Economy 1759–1876 (Cambridge: Cambridge University Press, 1960), pp. 5–7, 32–34, and in L. M. Cullen, *An Economic History of Ireland since 1660* (London: Batsford, 1972), pp. 100–109.

23. Emmet Larkin, "Economic Growth, Capital Investment and the Roman Catholic Church in Ireland," in *American Historical Review* 72, 3 (April 1967): 882. In a private communication, Ellen Shannon Mangan has expressed serious reservations about the reliability of "D. C.'"s evidence on the grounds of his anonymity, but other evidence is so far unavailable.

24. Chuto, "Mangan, Petrie, O'Donovan," p. 175 n. 12, gives documentary evidence for the dates for Mangan's employment with the survey, and for his erratic hours, from the Larcom papers (NLI MS 7565). McCall cites a letter from Petrie to O'Donovan on Mangan's "scribe work" (McCall, p. 22).

25. See Chuto, "Mangan, Petrie, O'Donovan," passim, esp. p. 169, and Welch, *Irish Poetry*, pp. 96–103, for Mangan's scholarly contacts and influences; and J. H. Andrews, *A Paper Landscape: The Ordnance Survey in Nineteenth Century Ireland* (Oxford: Clarendon Press, 1975), pp. 113 and 153, for rates of pay.

26. Charles Gavan Duffy, *Four Years of Irish History, 1845–1849* (London: Cassell, Petter, Calpin and Co., 1883), p. 776.

27. See Holzapfel's *Check List*, pp. 12–13, for a full list of these. Though many are brief, their accumulation, together with the characterization of "Clarence" in "A Peep at the Comet Club" (*Comet*, 14 July 1833, p. 511) as a quirky and rather humorless punster, produces a picture of an eccentric and rather lugubrious individual.

28. See Richard Ellmann, *James Joyce* (Oxford: Oxford University Press, 1965), pp. 97–98, and James Joyce, *Stephen Hero* (London: Granada, 1977), pp. 144–47. The reference to "Mangan's sister" in the story "Araby," *Dubliners* (Harmondsworth: Penguin, 1956), p. 28, and numerous less direct allusions to Mangan throughout *A Portrait of the Artist* and *Stephen Hero* (especially his use of the Mangan lecture of 1902 as the basis of the "Drama and Life" lecture in the latter) suggest a close reading of Mangan's life and writings with attention to the development of the artist. M. Magalaner, "James Mangan and Joyce's Dedalus Family," in *Philological Quarterly* 31, 4 (October 1952):363–71, discusses the question further.

29. For an account of Father Mathew's campaigns see Elizabeth Malcolm, "Temperance and Irish Nationalism," in F. S. L. Lyons and R. A. J. Hawkins, eds., *Ireland under the Union: Varieties of Tension* (Oxford: Clarendon Press, 1980), pp. 69–84.

30. See, for example, "A Sixty-Drop Dose of Laudanum," *DUM* 13, 75 (March 1839): 267–78.

31. See Thomas De Quincey, "Coleridge and Opium-Eating," in *Works*, 16 vols. (Edinburgh: Adam and Charles Black, 1863), 11: 103–11. For further discussion of these questions, see Louise Imogen

Guiney, *James Clarence Mangan, His Selected Poems, with a Study* (London: John Lane, 1897), p. 23, and the review of this volume by Francis Thompson, "Excursions in Criticism II. James Clarence Mangan," in *The Academy* (new series) 52, 1325, 25 September 1897, pp. 241–42. Alethea Hayter, in her study *Opium and the Romantic Imagination* (London: Faber and Faber, 1968), p. 281, misreads this article as implying that Mangan was a drunkard, not an opium user. Several inferences of these last paragraphs are nevertheless drawn from Hayter's study.

32. See Charles Gavan Duffy, *Young Ireland: A Fragment of Irish History, 1840–1850* (London: Cassell, Petter, Calpin and Co., 1880), p. 297, and Mitchel, *Jail Journal*, p. 33.

2. THE SPIRIT OF THE NATION

1. James Fintan Lalor's articles "A New Nation" and "Tenants' Right and Landlords' Law" are to be found in *The Nation*, 24 April 1847, pp. 457–58, and 15 May 1847, p. 507, respectively. The fullest account of Mitchel's break with Young Ireland is in Denis Gwynn, *Young Ireland and 1848* (Cork: Cork University Press, 1949), pp. 129–51.

2. John Mitchel, "Irish Agricultural and Industrial Affairs," *United Irishman*, 19 February 1848, p. 27.

3. Mitchel, *Jail Journal*, p. 33. Hereafter cited as *JJ*.

4. *JJ*, pp. 98–99. Malcolm Brown discusses Mitchel's fascination with split personality, in *The Politics of Irish Literature*, p. 135. Such a fascination is of a piece with the desire to come to "one mind" and replicates the *political* desire to unite Ireland's divided self.

5. Mitchel, "Poetic Politics," in *United Irishman*, 29 April 1849, p. 186. On the reactionary radicalism of Mitchel's nationalism see John Newsinger, "John Mitchel and Irish Nationalism," in *Literature and History* 6, 2 (Autumn 1980): 184.

6. See, for example, Larkin, "Economic Growth, Capital Investment," p. 871; and George O'Brien, *The Economic History of Ireland from the Union to the Famine* (London: Longmans, Green, 1921), p. 569. The economic argument for repeal is at the core of the three prize essays of the Repeal Association in 1845: see *Essays on the Repeal of the Union* (Dublin: James Duffy, 1845).

7. See O'Brien, *Economic History of Ireland*, pp. 415–21.

8. See Lennox Brown, "The Use of Money in Mid-Nineteenth-Century Ireland," *Studies* 59, 233 (Spring 1970): 87–88; Lynch and Vaizey, *Guinness's Brewery in the Irish Economy*, p. 13 and chap. 1, passim. Cf. the *Nation* editorial of March 1847, quoted in O'Brien, *Economic History of Ireland*, p. 434: "Then, when the current of trade was established — Irish raw produce to England — English manufacture

to Ireland — Englishmen offered us 'free trade.' It is not more free trade but less free trade that Ireland wants now."

9. I take the phrase from Michael Hechter's *Internal Colonialism: The Celtic Fringe in British National Development, 1536–1966* (Berkeley and Los Angeles: University of California Press, 1975), which usefully applies a core-periphery model to explore the economic and political relationship between England and its Celtic dependencies.

10. See Lyons, *Ireland since the Famine,* chap. 3, for a general discussion of this trend. Hill, in "The Intelligentsia," p. 94, argues for the impact of the British State in Ireland on the integration of the population as well as the centralization of its apparatuses; Oliver MacDonagh, *Ireland* (Englewood Cliffs, N.J.: Prentice-Hall, 1968), p. 23, stresses English willingness to experiment administratively in Ireland in ways unthinkable in England.

11. On these developments see Akenson, *The Irish Educational Experiment,* and Andrews, *A Paper Landscape.*

12. See Samuel Ferguson, "Hardiman's Irish Minstrelsy, 1," *DUM* 3, 16 (April 1834): 457–478; "2," *DUM* 4, 20 (August 1834): 152–67; "3," *DUM* 4, 22 (October 1834): 447–67; and "4," *DUM* 4, 23 (November 1834): 514–42. For a discussion of this trend as represented by Ferguson, see Robert O'Driscoll, "Ferguson and the Idea of an Irish National Literature," *Eire-Ireland* 6 (Spring 1971): 882–95, and David Lloyd, "James Clarence Mangan and 'A Broken Constitution,'" *Cornucopia* 3 (1981–1982): 71–115.

13. Quoted in O'Brien, *Economic History of Ireland,* p. 585.

14. This argument is the burden of all the repeal prize essays, but see especially Michael Joseph Barry, "Ireland as She Was, as She Is, and as She Shall Be," in *Essays on the Repeal,* pp. 10–11.

15. See Owen Dudley Edwards, "Ireland," in O. Dudley Edwards, G. Evans, J. Rhys, and H. Macdiarmid, *Celtic Nationalism* (London: Routledge and Kegan Paul, 1968), pp. 107–18, on the differences between O'Connell's pragmatism and Young Ireland idealism.

16. See Hill, "The Intelligentsia," p. 89, and passim for detailed figures on the social and intellectual composition of the repeal and Young Ireland movements.

17. See Edwards, "Ireland," pp. 1312–13, for comments on Young Ireland's distance from the social reality of Ireland, and Lyons, *Ireland since the Famine,* p. 110, on its "high-principled and futile rebellion"; Lyons goes on to stress the importance of the *legacy* of Young Ireland thinking.

18. Hill, "The Intelligentsia," p. 74.

19. Breuilly, *Nationalism and the State,* p. 3, stresses the "autonomous role of politics" as central to the emergence of nationalisms. It should be stressed, however, that this autonomy is merely an appearance, belying its origin in a specific economic disequilibrium between core and periphery.

20. See, further, E. Kamenka, ed., *Nationalism: The Nature and Evolution of an Idea* (London: Edward Arnold, 1975), pp. 9–10, and Kedourie, *Nationalism*, p. 9.

21. See Breuilly, *Nationalism and the State*, pp. 349–50. It is this aspect of Hegel's theory of the state that Marx attacks most forcefully in his "Critique of Hegel's Doctrine of the State," in Karl Marx, *Early Writings*, introduction by Lucio Colletti, trans. Rodney Livingstone and Gregor Benton (New York: Vintage, 1974), pp. 90–91: rather than expressing the particular manifestation of a transcendental idea, the bourgeois state emerges, for Marx, at the point when "private spheres have achieved an independent existence," necessitating their reconciliation in a political constitution. Paul Thomas, *Marx and the Anarchists* (London: Routledge and Kegan Paul, 1980), pp. 31–40, gives an excellent account of both Hegel's and Marx's arguments.

22. This transition is most obvious in Coleridge's reformulation of Burke's constitutional theory in *Church and State*. See Lloyd, "'A Broken Constitution,'" pp. 74–83, on this transition and its influence on unionism in Ireland.

23. See, for example, the anonymous article "Notabilities of the Times," *The Nation*, 13 April 1843, p. 426.

24. I derive the term "deterritorialization" from Gilles Deleuze and Félix Guattari's usage of it in *Anti-Oedipus: Capitalism and Schizophrenia* (New York: Viking, 1977), where the effect of cultural and psychic dislocation is seen as the product of capitalism's unleashing of economic flows which were formerly "territorialized." The term's metaphoric reach usefully connects cultural and social with economic phenomena. For a general discussion of Deleuze and Guattari's concepts of de- and reterritorialization, see Vincent Descombes, *Le Même et l'Autre: Quarante-cinq Ans de philosophie française, 1933–1978* (Paris: Minuit, 1979), pp. 205–6.

25. See especially "Imports and Exports," *The Nation*, 9 December 1843, p. 136, and, on the psychic effects of imperial centralization, "The Movement of Nationality," *The Nation*, 10 August 1844, p. 696.

26. Cf. "Imports and Exports": "we *import* commodities made valuable by the labour of strangers, for a small fraction of our people; and we *export* commodities requiring little labour of our own." See also J. Godkin, "The Rights of Ireland," in *Essays on the Repeal*, p. 129, and O'Brien, *Economic History of Ireland*, p. 434, where he quotes a *Nation* editorial on the "current of trade" ("Irish raw materials to England — English manufacturers to Ireland") which was leeching the Irish economy.

27. Thomas Meagher, quoted in Gwynn, *Young Ireland*, p. 77. Cf., for this general argument concerning the difference between nationalist and constitutionalist states, Breuilly, *Nationalism and the State*, p. 62.

28. Kamenka, *Nationalism*, p. 14.

29. Joseph Mazzini, *The Duties of Man and Other Essays*, introduction by Thomas Jones, trans. Ella Noyes, L. Martineau, and Thomas Okey (London: Dent, 1907), p. 55.

30. Ibid., p. 52.

31. J. G. Fichte, *Addresses to the German Nation*, trans. R. F. Jones and G. H. Turnbull (London: Open Court, 1922); hereafter cited as Fichte. Kedourie discusses Fichte's contribution to nationalist thought throughout *Nationalism*.

32. Fichte, p. 63. Arnold, in this tradition, makes a similar remark in *On the Study of Celtic Literature*, pp. 292-93, in relation to the Gallo-Celtic origin of the French.

33. Fichte, p. 57. See S. T. Coleridge, *The Friend*, ed. Barbara Rooke, Bollingen Series (Princeton, N.J.: Princeton University Press, 1969), I: 476.

34. This analogy is made implicitly in Fichte, pp. 58-59.

35. Wilhelm von Humboldt, *Über den Nationalcharacter des Spraches*, quoted in R. L. Brown, *Wilhelm von Humboldt's Conception of Linguistic Relativity*, p. 80.

36. According to Akenson, "Irish had ceased to be the national language long before mid-century." His assertion is deduced from census figures of 1851. See *The Irish Education Experiment*, pp. 378-80.

37. Thomas Davis, "Our National Language," *The Nation*, 1 April 1843, p. 394.

38. Davis, "Our National Language," p. 394. D. George Boyce, *Nationalism in Ireland* (London: Croom Helm, 1982), pp. 155 and 187n., points out the influence of German Romanticism on Davis, as does Brown, *Politics of Irish Literature*, p. 56, who argues his relationship to other European nationalists such as Mazzini. See more generally, Giovanni Costigan, "Romantic Nationalism: Ireland and Europe," *Irish University Review* 3, 2 (Autumn 1973): 141-52.

39. Thomas Davis, "Academical Education," *The Nation*, 17 May 1845, p. 520.

40. Duffy, *Young Ireland*, pp. 153, 155.

41. Such criticisms were voiced by Young Irelanders themselves at the time: see Gwynn, *Young Ireland*, pp. 151, 191, 258, and *JJ*, pp. 143-45. For more recent criticisms, see Edwards, "Ireland," p. 144, and Strauss, *Irish Nationalism and British Democracy*, p. 105.

42. Strauss, *Irish Nationalism and British Democracy*, p. 89.

43. "Union against the Union," *The Nation*, 11 March 1848, p. 168.

44. Mazzini, *Duties of Man*, pp. 131-32. Emphasis in the original.

45. See Edwards, "Ireland," p. 83.

46. S. T. Coleridge, "The Statesman's Manual," in *Lay Sermons*, ed. R. J. White, Bollingen Series (Princeton, N.J.: Princeton University Press, 1972), p. 30.

47. Edwards, "Ireland," p. 85. Cf. Brown, *Politics of Irish Literature*, p. 55, for comments on the necessarily "amorphous idealism" developed by Irish nationalism to overcome actual division. Such a remark should not, however, blind one to the powerful *formal* consistency of Young Ireland ideology.

48. "The Individuality of a Native Literature," *The Nation,* 21 August 1847, p. 731.

49. Ibid.

50. Quoted in Duffy, *Four Years of Irish History,* p. 72.

51. On this German tradition, see André Lefevere, *Translating Literature: The German Tradition* (Amsterdam: Van Gorcum, 1977), passim, and W. W. Chambers, "Language and Nationality in German Pre-Romantic and Romantic Thought," *MLR* 41 (October 1946): 382–92.

52. Thomas Davis, "Irish Songs," *The Nation,* 4 January 1845, p. 202.

53. "Ballad Poetry of Ireland," *The Nation,* 2 August 1845, p. 698.

54. Denis Florence McCarthy, ed., *The Book of Irish Ballads* (Dublin: Duffy, 1846), pp. 12, 21–22.

55. Ibid., pp. 22–23.

56. "Recent English Poets, No. 1: Alfred Tennyson and E. B. Browning," *The Nation,* 15 February 1845, p. 314.

57. Ibid.

58. Padraic Fallon, "The Poetry of Thomas Davis," in *Thomas Davis and Young Ireland,* ed. M. J. MacManus (Dublin: Stationery Office, 1945), p. 25. On the scorn with which the street ballad was regarded, see Duffy, *Young Ireland,* p. 756. Patrick C. Power, *The Story of Anglo-Irish Poetry, 1800–1922* (Cork: Mercier, 1972), discusses the development of the street ballad out of Anglo-Gaelic crossings, pp. 116–25, and the refined character of the *Nation* ballads, pp. 33–35.

59. According to Duffy, *Young Ireland,* p. 285, a new edition was required every year between 1843 and 1880.

3. Great Gaps in Irish Song

1. See, for the most recent version of this view, Welch, *Irish Poetry,* pp. 102–3.

2. Duffy, 1908, p. 87.

3. "Clarence Mangan," *The Nation* (new series), 8 September 1849, p. 27.

4. See, for example, a letter from Mangan to Duffy, 10 November 1846, NLI MS 248, fol. 9, and Thomas Davis, "A Ballad History of Ireland," *The Nation,* 16 November 1844, p. 91.

5. See, respectively, Mangan's "The Warning Voice," *The Nation,* 21 February 1846, p. 297; "Stand Together" by "Theta," in *The Spirit of the Nation; or, Ballads and Songs by the Writers of "The Nation,"*

fifty-first edition (Dublin 1882), p. 27; Mitchel, "The Coming Meeting," *United Irishman,* 18 March 1848, p. 88.
  6. "The Warning Voice"; Mangan's emphasis.
  7. "Irish National Hymn," *United Irishman,* 13 May 1848, p. 211. See also similar references in "The Funerals," *Irishman,* 31 March 1849, p. 203, and "A Vision: A.D. 1848," *United Irishman,* 26 February 1848, p. 43.
  8. "A Vision: A.D. 1848"; it is interesting to compare these doubtful visions of Mangan's with the certain, optimistic ones that are rife in the *Spirit of the Nation:* see, for example, D. F. McCarthy, "A Dream of the Future," *Spirit of the Nation,* pp. 122–24.
  9. "Poetry of Ireland," review of H. R. Montgomery, *Specimens of the Early Native Poetry of Ireland* (Dublin, 1846), and D. F. McCarthy, *The Book of Irish Ballads* (Dublin, 1846), *The Nation,* 10 October 1846, p. 10.
  10. Welch, *Irish Poetry,* p. 130.
  11. James Hardiman, ed. *Irish Minstrelsy, or Bardic Remains of Ireland* (1831), repr. with intro. by Máire Mhac an tSaoi, 2 vols. (Shannon: Irish University Press, 1971), 1: xxiv.
  12. Ferguson, "Hardiman's Irish Minstrelsy, 4," p. 154.
  13. Ferguson, "Hardiman's Irish Minstrelsy, 3," p. 431.
  14. "Hardiman's Irish Minstrelsy, 2," pp. 154–55. See Welch, *Irish Poetry,* pp. 126–27.
  15. Ferguson, "Hardiman's Irish Minstrelsy, 1," p. 460.
  16. Ferguson, "Hardiman's Irish Minstrelsy, 3," p. 453n.
  17. For discussions of this question, see *Life,* p. 171, and Chuto, "Mangan, Petrie, O'Donovan," pp. 178–87. Peter MacMahon, "James Clarence Mangan, the Irish Language, and the Strange Case of *The Tribes of Ireland,*" *Irish University Review* 8, 2 (Autumn 1978): 209–22, argues convincingly against Chuto that Mangan's Irish was always "negligible."
  18. "Dark Rosaleen," *The Nation,* 30 May 1846, p. 521; *PPM* 1849, pp. 256–63; D. J. O'Donoghue, ed., *Poems of James Clarence Mangan,* introduction by John Mitchel (Centenary ed., Dublin: O'Donoghue and Co., 1903), pp. 85–86; *Poems* 1859, pp. 21–22. I am grateful to Professor Brendan O Hehir for helpful discussion of the original Gaelic material throughout this chapter.
  19. Ferguson, "Hardiman's Irish Minstrelsy, 2," pp. 157–58; Hardiman, *Irish Minstrelsy,* 1: 254–57.
  20. Hardiman, *Irish Minstrelsy,* 1: 351.
  21. Ferguson, "Hardiman's Irish Minstrelsy, 2," p. 158.
  22. Hardiman, *Irish Minstrelsy,* 1: 254, 255.
  23. *The Nation,* 30 May 1846, p. 521.
  24. In an excellent discussion of the poem and its various versions, Diane E. Bessai notes Mangan's effect of a "perpetual journey":

see "'Dark Rosaleen' as Image of Ireland," *Eire-Ireland* 19, 3 (Winter 1975): 77.

25. Padraic Colum, "James Clarence Mangan," *Dublin Magazine* 8, 2 (April–June 1933): 38; Welch, *Irish Poetry,* p. 102; Jacques Chuto, "Rhétorique et authenticité chez J. C. Mangan," unpublished paper delivered to the Congrès de la S.A.E.S., Tours, 1977, p. 7.

26. *The Nation,* 8 August 1846, p. 681. Cf. Hardiman, *Irish Minstrelsy,* 2: 234–43, and Ferguson, "Hardiman's Irish Minstrelsy, 3," pp. 465–66 (unrhymed) and "Hardiman's Irish Minstrelsy, 4," p. 533 (rhymed).

27. Hardiman, *Irish Minstrelsy,* 2: 409.

28. Ferguson, "Hardiman's Irish Minstrelsy, 3," p. 465.

29. Hardiman, *Irish Minstrelsy,* 2: 409–10.

30. See Genesis 47:1–6 and Exodus 1:11–14.

31. Hardiman, *Irish Minstrelsy,* 2: 401–8.

32. *The Nation,* 8 August 1846, p. 681n.

33. See, for example, the series of footnotes giving the English versions of Gaelic names in Davis's ballad "The Geraldines," or the explanation in a note of "Coirrsliabh Pass and Ard Rathain" in "The West's Asleep": "Vulgarly written Corlews and Ardrahan," *Spirit of the Nation,* pp. 98–103, and 61.

34. Thomas Davis, "A Ballad History of Ireland," *The Nation,* 30 November 1844, p. 122. Mangan's contemporary J. J. Callanan is a good example of a poet who studiously familiarized himself with local topography and lore. See Welch, *Irish Poetry,* p. 54.

35. See Andrews, *A Paper Landscape,* pp. 119–29, for an account of the vagaries of renaming in English.

36. It is the burden of Benedict Anderson's excellent study *Imagined Communities* (London: Verso Press, 1983) that nationalisms depend precisely on the extension of technological power, at this period principally the press, for dissemination. Edwards, "Ireland," p. 144, stresses the enormous contribution to Irish cultural re-union made by *English* education.

37. Thomas Davis, "National Art," *The Nation,* 2 December 1842, p. 122.

38. For an account of Maclise's career, see John Turpin, "Daniel Maclise, Disraeli, and *Fraser's Magazine,*" *Eire-Ireland* 15, 1 (Spring 1980): 46–63. Mangan's poem was published in *The Nation,* 18 July 1846, p. 633.

39. Mangan is playing here on a convention and on a genre, both of which were very familiar to him. The convention is that of not spelling out the proper names of authors, artists, etc., in titles or citations. Thus the subtitle of this poem, altered in subsequent collections, is "On a Landscape by M*****." The genre is the rebus, a riddling poem often in the form of an acrostic, many of which Mangan composed in his youth for popular magazines and almanacs. As readers we are drawn into a

rebus, discovering only at the end of the poem the identity of the painter of this unknown — and so far unidentified — landscape.

40. Colum, "James Clarence Mangan," pp. 53–54.

41. Anon., "Petrie's Round Towers," rev. of George Petrie, *The Ecclesiastical Architecture of Ireland* (Dublin, 1845), in *DUM* 25, 148 (April 1845): 381.

42. D. F. McCarthy, "The Pillar Towers of Ireland," *Spirit of the Nation*, pp. 165–68, stanza 12; quote is from p. 168.

43. Mangan, "A Vision of Connaught in the Thirteenth Century," *The Nation*, 11 July 1846, p. 619.

44. Hardiman, *Irish Minstrelsy*, pp. v–vii. Hardiman's remarks continue by connecting both Irish music and round towers with the East, a connection whose significance will become apparent in the next chapter.

4. VEILS OF SAIS: TRANSLATION AS REFRACTION AND PARODY

1. See Eoin McKiernan, "James Clarence Mangan: Ireland's 'German Poet,'" in *Anglo-German and American-German Cross Currents*, ed. P. A. Shelley, A. O. Lewis, Jr., and W. J. Betts, Jr., 3 vols. (Chapel Hill: University of North Carolina Press, 1957), 1: 54–58, for an attempt to classify Mangan's translations in this way. H. J. Donaghy, *James Clarence Mangan*, Twayne English Author Series no. 171 (New York: Twayne, 1974), chap. 2; and James Kilroy, *James Clarence Mangan*, Irish Writers Series (Lewisburg: Bucknell University Press, 1970), chap. 2, both discuss Mangan's translations at some length with similar divisions, but tend to stick to rhythmical analysis rather than critically discussing the relation of source to translated text. For some radically variant contemporary assessments of Mangan's translations, see "Clarence Mangan," *The Nation* (new series), 8 September 1849, p. 26; review of Mangan, *Anthologia Germanica* (Dublin, 1845), in *Dublin Review* 19 (December 1845): 313; and review of *Anthologia Germanica* in *Foreign Quarterly Review* 36 (October 1845): 239.

2. On "equivalence," see in particular André Lefevere and Raymond Van Den Broeck, *Uitnodiging tot de Vertaalwetenschap* (Muiderberg: Coutinho, 1979), pp. 90–94.

3. For a discussion of these earlier views of translation, see Robert Welch, "The Translation of Poetry: Some Principles," *Studies* (Winter 1972): 339–40; F. R. Amos, *Early Theories of Translation* (New York: Columbia University Press, 1920), chap. 4.

4. Freidrich Schlegel, *Literary Notebooks*, extracts translated in Lefevere, *Translating Literature*, p. 62.

5. Cf. Wilhelm von Humboldt's remarks on multiple translations as "many images of the same spirit," translated in Lefevere, *Translating Literature*, p. 45.

6. Friedrich Schleiermacher, "Über die verschiedenen Methoden des Übersetzens," translated in Lefevere, *Translating Literature*, p. 82.

7. Ibid., pp. 80–81, 73.

8. Ibid., p. 86.

9. Ibid., pp. 75, 84.

10. See André Lefevere, "On the Refraction of Texts," unpublished MS, 1980, and "Translated Literature: Towards an Integrated Theory," in *Bulletin of the Midwest Modern Language Association* 14, 1 (Spring 1981): 68–77. Renato Pozzioli argues at first a similar case in different terms, but ends up returning to concepts of equivalence under the rubric of "elective affinity" as a model of the relation of translator to source text. See "The Added Artificer" in *On Translation*, ed. Reuben Brower (New York: Galaxy, 1966), pp. 137–47.

11. *LO* 4, in *DUM* 15, 88 (April 1840): 377.

12. *LO* 2, in *DUM* 11, 63 (March 1838): p. 312.

13. "Recollections of the Arabian Nights," in *Tennyson: Poems and Plays*, ed. T. Herbert Warren, rev. Frederick Page, Oxford Standard Authors ed. (Oxford: Oxford University Press, 1971), p. 9.

14. Johann Wolfgang Goethe, *Der West-östliche Divan. Noten und Abhandlung zu besserem Verständnis des West-östlichen Divans*, Nachwort von Hellmuth Freiherrn von Maltzahn (Munich: Deutscher Taschenbuch, 1961), p. 121.

15. Goethe, *West-östlicher Divan*, pp. 243–44. Lefevere translates the passage in full in *Translating Literature*, pp. 35–37.

16. See Margaret A. Rose, *Parody/Metafiction: An Analysis of Parody as a Critical Mirror to the Writing and Reception of Fiction* (London: Croom Helm, 1979), p. 29.

17. A. W. Schlegel, *Lectures on Dramatic Art and Literature*, quoted in Rose, *Parody/Metafiction*, p. 33.

18. Rose discusses this characteristic of parody: *Parody/Metafiction*, pp. 79–81.

19. Chuto's article is to appear in *Notes and Queries*. There is no pagination given for this brief article. See also Joseph von Hammer-Purgstall, *Geschichte der osmanischen Dichtkunst* (Pest: Conrad Adolph Hartleben's Verlag, vol. 1, 1836; vols. 2 and 3, 1837; vol. 4, 1838).

20. See Barthelémy D'Herbelot, *Bibliothèque orientale*, 3 vols. (The Hague: Neaulme and Van Daalen, 1777).

21. See "The Time of the Barmecides," *LO* 4, pp. 389–90. Chuto, in his article on Mangan's Oriental sources, suggests this to be derived from a phrase in D'Herbelot's *Bibliothèque orientale*, but there seems to be a more likely source in the introductory quatrain to the first section of the *West-östlichen Divan*, p. 5:

> Zwanzig Jahre liess ich gehn
> Und genoss was mir beschieden;
> Eine Reihe völlig schön
> Wie die Zeit der Barmekiden.

22. See *LO* 3, in *DUM* 12, 69 (September 1838): 335n.
23. *LO* 5, in *DUM* 23, 137 (May 1844): 536–38.
24. Edgar Allan Poe, "The Philosophy of Composition," *Works,* ed. J. A. Harrison and C. W. Kent, 17 vols. (New York: AMS Press, 1965), 14: 193–208.
25. On this tradition, see Otto Jespersen, *Language: Its Nature, Development and Origin* (London: Allen and Unwin, 1947), chaps. 1–2.
26. "The Sixth Discourse. On the Persians" (1789), *Works of Sir William Jones, with a Life of the Author by Lord Teignmouth* (London, 1807), 3: 135. See also "The Ninth Discourse. On the Origin and Families of Nations" (1792), *Works,* 3: 185–90.
27. *LO* 1, in *DUM* 10, 57 (September 1837): 277.
28. Jones, "First Discourse," *Works,* 3. 2.
29. Jones, "Second Discourse," *Works,* 3: 13–14. Emphasis his.
30. See, for example, Charles Vallancey, *An Essay on the Antiquity of the Irish Language: Being a Collation of the Irish with the Punic Language, with a Preface Proving Ireland to Be the Thule of the Ancients* (Dublin: L. White, 1772), and "Further Vindication of the Ancient History of Ireland," *Collectanea de Rebus Hibernicis,* vol. 6 (Dublin, 1804, p. 5. Other relevant works include "A Letter from Cornelius O'Brien on the Study of Irish Antiquities," *DUM* 3, 15 (March 1834): 328–29, and Henry O'Brien, *The Round Towers of Ireland; or the Mysteries of Freemasonry, of Sabaism, and of Budhism, for the First Time Unveiled* (London: Whittaker, 1834), p. 228. There is some reason to suspect that "Cornelius O'Brien" may be a unionist parody of Henry O'Brien, whose extravagant theories are discussed in Chapter 7, below.
31. Welch makes this point with regard to the fashion for Celticism that was sparked off by Macpherson's *Ossian: Irish Poetry,* p. 12.
32. James Stam, *Inquiries into the Origin of Language: The Fate of a Question* (New York: Harper and Row, 1976), pp. 76–79.
33. See Mangan's translation from Schiller, "The Veiled Image at Sais," in "Stray Leaflets from the German Oak, No. IV," *DUM* 30, 179 (November 1847): 546–48.
34. Novalis, *Gesammelte Werke,* ed. with a biographical introduction by Carl Seelig (Zurich: Bühl, 1945), p. 403.
35. See D'Herbelot, *Bibliothèque orientale,* 2: 100–101.
36. Von Hammer-Purgstall, *Geschichte,* pp. 13–14; Goethe, *West-östlicher Divan,* p. 178.

5. Oversettings from the German: Dissembling the Sublime

1. For the vogue for German literature in Ireland from 1800 to 1850, see McKiernan, "Ireland's 'German Poet,'" pp. 39–50, and O'Neill, "The Reception of German Literature in Ireland."
2. Wilhelm Klauer-Klattowski, *Ballads and Romances of the Ger-*

234 Notes to Pages 130–40

mans (London, 1837), and Dr. O. L. B. Wolff, *Poetischer Hausschatz des deutschen Volkes* (Leipzig: Wigand, 1841), to which Mangan refers deprecatingly in *AG* 16, "Ballads and Miscellaneous Poems," *DUM* 18, 103 (July 1841): 19–20.

3. *AG* 4, "The Poems of Matthison and Salis," *DUM* 6, 34 (October 1835): 404.

4. *AG* 15, "Wetzel's Poems," *DUM* 14, 79 (July 1839): 77.

5. See the anonymous article, "English and American Translations of Schiller," *DUM* 24, 142 (October 1844): 379, for remarks that suggest that at least some readers began to catch his drift.

6. J. H. Merivale, "Some Remarks on the Principles of Translation: Followed by Specimens from the German Lyric Poets. Specimen I, Schiller's 'Song of the Bell,'" *New Monthly Magazine and Humorist* 58 (January 1840): 127.

7. J. W. von Goethe, *Faustus, a Dramatic Mystery; The Bride of Corinth; The First Walpurgis Night*, trans. John Anster (London, 1835), pp. xvi, xx–xxi.

8. *AG* 11, "Miscellaneous Poems," *DUM* 10, 60 (March 1836): 280.

9. *AG* 5, "Faust and the Minor Poems of Goethe," *DUM* 7, 39 (March 1836): 280.

10. *AG* 12, "The Less Translatable Poems of Schiller," *DUM* 12, 67 (July 1838): 46.

11. *AG* 19, "Miscellaneous Poems," *DUM* 25, 145 (January 1845): 103; Friedrich Rückert, "Und dann nicht mehr," *Gedichte* (Frankfurt, 1872), p. 381.

12. *Poems* 1859, p. 12. For an example of the persistence of this reading, see Rafroidi, *Irish Literature in English*, p. 275.

13. Marshall Brown, *The Shape of German Romanticism* (Ithaca, N.Y.: Cornell University Press, 1979), p. 121.

14. Tieck "sucht die Verlorenheit des subjektivisten echten Ausdruck der Vergänglichkeitsschwermut": Werner Kohlschmidt, "Die Romantik," in *Deutsche Literaturgeschichte in Grundzügen. Die Epochen deutscher Dichtung*, herausgegeben, Bruno Boesch, 2nd ed. (Bern: Francke, 1961), p. 311. See also the article on Tieck in Henry Garland and Mary Garland, *The Oxford Companion to German Literature* (Oxford: Oxford University Press, 1976), pp. 850–51, and, further, James Trainer, *Ludwig Tieck: From Gothic to Romantic* (The Hague: Mouton, 1964).

15. See Mangan, "Life Is the Desert and the Solitude," "Stray Leaflets from the German Oak," *DUM* 8, 44 (August 1836): 160–61, hereafter cited in the text as *SLGO* 1; and "Sehnsucht," in *Gedichte von Ludwig Tieck*, 3 vols. (Dresden: P. G. Hilscher, 1821), 1: 1–2.

16. Edward Young, *The Revenge*, in *The London Stage* (London:

Sherman, Jones and Co., n.d.), p. 9. The pair of lines by Young from which Mangan derives the title of his translation might suggest that the solution to the alienation of the subject lies in its total identification with the other, in its abeyance in death. Young opposes the individual solitude of life with the common mortality of man: "Life is the desert, life the solitude; / Death joins us to the great majority." Though many since Mitchel have argued that Mangan's longing is for "the true home of the grave," that process is more problematic and more critically addressed than writers on Mangan have generally been willing to see. Hegel's remarks on Tieck and Solger are to be found in *Introduction to Aesthetics,* pp. 66–68.

17. *AG* 10, "Tieck and the Other Song-Singers of Germany," *DUM* 9, 51 (March 1837): 273.

18. Welch, *Irish Poetry,* p. 88.

19. *Naive and Sentimental Poetry and On the Sublime,* trans. Elias, p. 105. Hereafter cited as *NSP* and *OS,* respectively.

20. Friedrich Schiller, *Werke,* 3 vols. (Munich: Hauser, 1966), 2: 618. In *OS,* p. 212, Elias omits "und nicht in dem Inhalt," thereby distorting Schiller's emphasis on the evacuation of the *content* in favor of the form of appearances.

21. *OS,* pp. 199–200; Schiller, *Werke,* 2: 611.

22. *AG* 1, "The Lyrical and Smaller Poems of Schiller," *DUM* 5, 25 (January 1835): 42. See, on Goethe as naive poet, Elias's commentary in *NSP,* pp. 3–12.

23. "Die Ideale," in Schiller, *Werke,* 2: 688–90.

24. For other translations of "Die Ideale," see: "The Ideal" by "W. P.," *Monthly Chronicle* 4 (1829): 426–28; "The Visions of Fancy," anon., *Fraser's* 10 (1834): 162–63; "Ideals," *Blackwoods* 38 (1835): 492; and "To the Ideal," in Bulwer-Lytton, "Poems and Ballads of Schiller. No. XII," *Blackwood's* 53 (1843): 433–35.

25. Mangan, "A Sixty-Drop Dose of Laudanum," p. 268. "Astonishment" is the word Edmund Burke uses to characterize the effects of the sublime: *A Philosophical Inquiry into the Origin of Our Ideas of the Sublime and Beautiful* (2nd ed., 1759; facsimile ed., Menston: Scolar Press, 1970), passim, esp. p. 98.

26. Mangan, "A Sixty-Drop Dose of Laudanum," p. 271. Original emphasis.

27. De Quincey, *Works,* 1: 263–64.

28. De Quincey, "Levana and Our Ladies of Sorrow," *Works,* 16: 22–32, describes the process of education through suffering by way of a dream vision.

29. John Keats, *Letters, 1814–1821,* ed. Hyder Edward Rollins, 2 vols. (Cambridge, Mass.: Harvard University Press, 1958), 1: 280–83.

30. Ibid., 2: 102.

31. Ibid., 1: 282.

32. This remark is in opposition to Rose's account of what she terms "dialectical parody": *Parody/Metafiction*, pp. 88, 103, 152.

6. THE AUTOBIOGRAPHIES

1. Quoted in Brown, *Politics of Irish Literature*, p. 76.
2. Some of those transformations have been described in Chapter 2, above. David Fitzpatrick, "Class, Family and Rural Unrest in Nineteenth-Century Ireland," in *Ireland: Land, Politics and People*, ed. P. J. Drudy (Cambridge: Cambridge University Press, 1982), pp. 37–75, gives some account of family and kinship networks in rural Ireland at this period, but similar studies of the urban and mercantile family are lacking. One is forced to infer the effects on family structure from more generally known economic transformations.
3. See John Stuart Mill, *Autobiography* (Oxford: Oxford University Press, 1924), pp. 124–26; James Joyce, *A Portrait of the Artist as a Young Man* (Harmondsworth: Penguin, 1960), p. 253.
4. Louis A. Renza, "The Veto of the Imagination: Theory of Autobiography," in James Olney, ed., *Autobiography: Essays Theoretical and Critical* (Princeton, N.J.: Princeton University Press, 1980), p. 289.
5. See Jacques Donzelot, *The Policing of Families*, foreword by Gilles Deleuze, trans. Robert Hurley (New York: Pantheon, 1979), chap. 3, esp. pp. 90–95.
6. Cf. Michael Sprinker, "Fictions of the Self: The End of Autobiography," in Olney, *Autobiography*, pp. 341–42.
7. This theory of pathogenesis is given in "On the Dissolution of the Oedipus Complex," in Sigmund Freud, *The Standard Edition of the Complete Psychological Works*, ed. James Strachey (London: Hogarth Press, 1953–1974), 19: 177 (hereafter cited as *SE*). The function of the psychoanalyst as taking the place of the father in transference is suggested in Jacques Lacan, *The Four Fundamental Concepts of Psychoanalysis*, trans. Alan Sheridan (Harmondsworth: Penguin, 1977), pp. 123–35, insofar as the place of the Other is that of the Name-of-the-Father.
8. Freud, "Some Psychical Consequences of the Anatomical Distinction between the Sexes," *SE* 19: 257.
9. Jacques Lacan, "On a Question Preliminary to Any Possible Treatment of Psychosis," *Ecrits: A Selection*, trans. Alan Sheridan (New York: Norton, 1977), pp. 215–17. Jean Laplanche, in *Hölderlin et la question du père*, 2nd ed. (Paris: P.U.F., 1969), p. 3, raises this problem of the "impenetrability" of psychosis and of its refusal of "intersubjectivity." These conditions are, as we shall see, fundamental to the domain into which Mangan's *Autobiography* seems to have been forcing the tendencies of his writing. The problem of transference is also central to Ida Macalpine's discussion of Schreber and leads her to a critique of transference as effecting the patient's regression to an infantile stage: see Daniel Paul Schreber, *Memoirs of My Nervous Illness*, trans. and ed. Ida

Macalpine and Richard A. Hunter (London: William Dawson, 1955), pp. 19–20.

10. Freud, "Psychoanalytic Notes on an Autobiographical Account of a Case of Paranoia (Dementia Paranoides)," *SE* 12: 9.

11. Macalpine, in Schreber, *Memoirs*, p. 12.

12. Freud, "Psychoanalytic Notes," p. 35.

13. For a preliminary study of Freud's relationship to the philological tradition—a study by no means exhaustive—see John Forrester, "Philology and the Phallus," in *The Talking Cure: Essays in Psychoanalysis and Language*, ed. Colin McCabe (London: Macmillan, 1980), pp. 45–69.

14. The English "after-pressure" (*SE* 12: 67) is a translation of the German *Nachdrängen*, literally, a pushing from behind, and is translated by Lacan as "après-coup." It conveys the sense of delay as an *active* regression rather than a mere repression, and its effect is to produce the *Nachträglichkeit* of the patient's discourse as it enters obsessional neurosis. Lacan discusses this effect in "The Function and Field of Speech and Language," *Ecrits*, p. 48.

15. Schreber's intent in composing his *Memoirs* was to achieve his reinstatement as a judge by proving his legal responsibility: Schreber, *Memoirs*, p. 31.

16. See Freud, "Psychoanalytic Notes," p. 49: "Paranoia decomposes just as hysteria condenses."

17. For discussions of the philosophical implications of the sophistic notion of the simulacrum, see Gilles Deleuze, "Simulacre et philosophie antique," in *Logique du sens* (Paris: Minuit, 1969), pp. 292–324, and Antoine Compagnon, "Psychose et sophistique," in Julia Kristeva et al., *Folle vérité: Vérité et vraisemblable du texte psychotique*, Collection Tel Quel (Paris: Seuil, 1979), pp. 174–96.

18. I have so far been unable to trace the source of these lines in Massinger's *Dramatic Works*. The titles of some of Massinger's works, and the themes of others, are suggestive of reasons for Mangan's attraction to him: *A New Way to Pay Old Debts*, or *The Unnatural Combat*, for example.

19. Mangan, "Sketches and Reminiscences of Irish Writers, No. IV, the Rev. C. P. Meehan," *Irishman*, 12 May 1849, p. 229.

20. The process is similar to that attributed to "Little Hans" by Freud, "Analysis of a Phobia in a Five-Year-Old Boy," *SE* 10: 25.

21. Freud, "Dissolution of the Oedipus Complex," *SE* 19: 176.

22. This is further elaborated by Lacan in his "The Mirror Stage as Formative of the Function of the I," *Ecrits*, pp. 1–7, as "the transformation that takes place in the subject when he assumes an image" (p. 2).

23. Freud, "Negation," *SE* 19: 233–39.

24. Freud, "Family Romances," *SE* 9: 235–41.

25. The phrasing here is reminiscent of Stephen Dedalus at the end of *A Portrait*, just as the function of the "old father, old artificer" who will

stand him "in good stead" is similar to that of Mangan's education. Mangan's misfortune was, of course, that his education was interrupted.

26. Freud analyzes the grammatical reversals characteristic of paranoia in "Psychoanalytic Notes," p. 63. In a letter to Duffy, Mangan cites with approval Goethe's comment, "Happy are they who have no relatives, for the entire business of one's life consists in getting rid of them" (NLI MS 138, fol. 13).

27. See Lacan, "Treatment of Psychosis," pp. 191–92, 215.

28. Schreber, *Memoirs*, pp. 97–98, also evokes the notion of leprosy as a figure for his sense of bodily disintegration. In this and in his account of his transformation into a body of nerves he shows a remarkable similarity to Mangan. Cf. *IA*, p. 18, where Mangan speaks of himself as being "all nerves."

29. Freud, "Psychoanalytic Notes," pp. 56–57n., remarks on the intimate relation between paranoia and hypochondria; cf. Macalpine in Schreber, *Memoirs*, pp. 408–9.

30. Once again, an analogue of these scorpions and vermin can be found in Schreber's *Memoirs*, p. 99.

31. It is worth contrasting the effacement of the mother in Mangan's texts with the function of the mother as a kind of counterforce to the father in Joyce's *Portrait* or in Edmund Gosse's *Father and Son* (London: Heinemann, 1925). Mangan's account bears remarkable similarities to Franz Kafka's "Letter to His Father," in *Wedding Preparations in the Country,* trans. E. Kaiser and E. Wilkins (London: Secker and Warburg, 1954), p. 183: "True, one could always get protection from her, but only in relation to you. She loved you too much and was much too devoted and loyal to you to have been able to constitute an independent spiritual force, in the long run, in the child's struggle." The similarity may be due to Kafka and Mangan both engaging in what Deleuze and Guattari describe as "grossir l'Oedipe" as a means to exceed paternal determination. See Deleuze and Guattari, *Kafka,* p. 19: "Inversement, agrandir et grossir, l'Oedipe, en rajouter, en faire un usage pervers ou paranoïaque, c'est déjà sortir de la soumission."

32. Hence, perhaps, the frequent references of Mangan's contemporaries to his boyish or feminine characteristics. See, for example, Price, 11 October 1849, n.p.

33. Meehan notes on the manuscript itself that he fears Mangan either lost or destroyed it, while Kilroy, its recent editor, suggests that "it was never completed, owing to the poet's sickness at that time," but yet that its ending in midsentence might imply "that Mangan had continued his account" (*A*, p. 35).

34. See Blaise Pascal, *Pensées,* introduction and notes by Ch.-M. des Granges (Paris: Garnier, 1964), 123.194 (hereafter cited as *Pensées;* the first figure refers to the page number, the second to the fragment number according to the text of M. L. Brunschwig).

35. "What is it then that this greediness and this impotence cry out to us, if not that there was formerly in man a true happiness of which there remains to him only *the imprint and the empty trace,* and which he tries uselessly to fill with all that surrounds him, seeking in absent things the aid he cannot get from present things." *Pensées,* 176.425, my emphasis, my translation.

36. The text on which the sermon to which Mangan refers is based makes it entirely appropriate to the subtext of his account. Massillon commences his sermon, "The Small Number of the Saved," with a reference to Nathan the leper, from Luke 4:27. See John-Baptist Massillon, Bishop of Clermont, *Sermons,* introduction by William M. Willett (Boston: Waite, Peirce and Co., 1845), p. 38.

37. De Quincey, *Works,* 1: 231.

38. See "The Story of Ala-ed-din and the Wonderful Lamp," trans. Stanley Lane-Poole, in *The Arabian Nights Entertainments,* trans. Edward William Lane, ed. and trans. Stanley Lane-Poole, 4 vols. (London: Bell, 1919), 4: 323–38.

39. Mangan certainly perceived the potential pun embedded in his name. O'Donoghue cites a remark in which Mangan playfully protests that Spenser's "The wretched man 'gan grinning horridlie" should read "The wretched Mangan grinning? horrid lie!" (*Life,* p. 86).

40. John Milton, *Paradise Lost,* 4: 75–78, in *Poetical Works,* ed. Douglas Bush (Oxford: Oxford University Press, 1969), p. 276.

41. See Bloom, *Anxiety of Influence,* p. 22.

42. Milton, *Paradise Lost,* 4: 51–53.

43. Joseph Brenan, "A Word to James Clarence Mangan," *Irishman,* 26 May 1849, p. 331; Mangan, "A Word in Reply to Joseph Brenan," *Irishman,* 2 June 1849, p. 347.

7. The Ends of Mangan

1. NLI MS 138, fol. 5, sheet B. A blank space on Sheet D presumably left for the address when folded suggests that it was never sent. I am indebted to Jacques Chuto for pointing this out. There is, of course, a certain appropriateness in Mangan's *not* sending a letter that contains such political opinions. Tynan has never been identified, though in a recent article Ellen Shannon-Mangan shows that McCall had concluded that "James Tynan" was one of Mangan's pseudonyms. See Ellen Shannon-Mangan, "A Letter and A Poem: New Sources for the Life of Mangan," *Eire-Ireland* 21, 1 (Spring 1986): 11–12.

2. AG 18, "Freiligrath's Poems," *DUM* 21, 121 (January 1843): 42.

3. See Thomas Carlyle, "The Poet as Hero" (1841), in *Sartor Resartus and On Heroes, Hero Worship and the Heroic in History* (London: Dent, 1908), p. 313; John Stuart Mill, "Thoughts on Poetry and Its Varieties" (rev. 1859), reprinted in Edmund D. Jones, ed., *English Critical Essays of the Nineteenth Century* (Oxford: Oxford University

Press, 1916), p. 406; and anon., "The Present State, Influence and Prospects of Art," *DUM* 23, 134 (February 1844): 216.

4. See Ferdinand Freiligrath, *Werke*, 6 vols. in 2 (Hildesheim: Georg Olms, 1974), 1: 144.

5. O'Brien, *The Round Towers of Ireland*, p. 248.

6. O'Brien, *The Round Towers of Ireland*, pp. 232–33.

7. Mangan, "The Editor's Room," *Belfast Vindicator*, 18 July 1840, p. 4; "The Editor's Room, Second Conclave," ibid., 25 July 1840, p. 4; "The Editor's Room, Third Conclave," ibid., 8 August 1840, p. 4.

8. See O'Donoghue, preface to *Poems*, pp. xxiv–xxv, for a variety of descriptions of Mangan.

9. Mangan, "Sketches and Reminiscences of Irish Writers. No. I: Maturin," *Irishman*, 24 March 1849, p. 187; Mangan, "The Man in the Cloak," *DUM* 12, 71 (November 1838): 552–68.

10. Mangan, "My Bugle, and How I Blow It," *Belfast Vindicator*, 27 March 1841, p. 4.

11. Mangan, "An Extraordinary Adventure in the Shades," *Comet*, 27 January 1833, p. 319. Welch regards this tale as symptomatic of Mangan's disabling "affectation": *Irish Poetry*, p. 82.

12. See Ernst Robert Curtius, *European Literature in the Latin Middle Ages*, trans. William R. Trask, rev. ed. (Princeton, N.J.: Princeton University Press, 1967); Gustav René Hocke, *Die Welt als Labyrinth* and *Manierismus in der Literatur*, vols. 50/51 and 82/83 of *Rowohlts Deutsche Enzyklopädie* (Hamburg: Rowohlt, 1959); more generally, see W. E. Yuill, "Literary Pot-Holing: Some Reflections on Curtius, Hocke and Marianne Thalman," *German Life and Letters* (new series), 19, 4 (July 1966): 279–86. Marianne Thalman's *Romantik und Manierismus* (Stuttgart: Kohlhammer, 1963) is suggestive of the genealogy of Mangan's interest in mannerism, since she concentrates on Ludwig Tieck.

13. Arnold Hauser, *Mannerism: The Crisis of the Renaissance and the Origin of Modern Art*, 2 vols. (London: Routledge and Kegan Paul, 1965), pp. 38–39, 355–58.

14. Cf. Theodor Adorno on the stereotyping of the genius: "Im hohen neunzehnten Jahrhundert trug man das Genie als Kostüm," quoted in Irving Wohlfarth, "*Perte d'Auréole*: The Emergence of the Dandy," *MLN* 85, 4 (May 1970): 562. Wohlfarth's article is an extraordinary contribution to the history of the dandy and has been greatly suggestive for the following pages.

15. "In the disturbance of those epochs, some men, come down in the world, disgusted and idle, but all of native vigor, could come up with the project of establishing a new kind of aristocracy, all the more difficult to overthrow in that it would be based on the most precious, the most indestructible of faculties, and on those celestial gifts which labor and money cannot confer." Charles Baudelaire, "Le Peintre de la vie

moderne," in Honoré de Balzac, J. Barbey d'Aurevilly, and Charles Baudelaire, *Sur le dandysme*, ed. and introduction by Roger Kempf (Paris: 10/18, 1971), p. 228 (my translation).

16. Balzac, "Traité de la vie élégante," in *Dandysme*, p. 48.

17. Balzac, "Traité," p. 63.

18. Michel Lemaire, *Le Dandysme de Baudelaire à Mallarmé* (Montreal: Presses de l'Université de Montreal, 1978), p. 12, comments on this "volonté formelle" that characterizes *dandysme*. On more ethical grounds, Jean-Paul Sartre criticizes Baudelaire for "the fruitless contemplation of a singularity which is formal": *Baudelaire*, trans. Martin Turnell (London: Horizon, 1949), p. 20.

19. Baudelaire, quoted in Lemaire, *Le Dandysme*, p. 80.

20. Baudelaire, "Le Peintre de la vie moderne," p. 233.

21. Balzac, "Traité," p. 56.

22. Lemaire, *Le Dandysme*, p. 31: "Puis, plus profondément, il y a le fait que la démocratie repose sur l'idée que tous les hommes sont égaux. Égaux, semblables, équivalents? L'ambiguïté est tout à fait inacceptable pour le dandy qui place toujours en avant sa différence, son altérité."

23. Barbey d'Aurevilly, quoted in Lemaire, *Le Dandysme*, p. 69. The common association at this time of women and dandies is equally not to be reduced to a question of concern with appearance or attire. Rather, their mutual exteriority to the domain of production leads to their negative representation as belonging only to the "unmanly" sphere of reproduction (the sphere of the beautiful). It only remains to be said that anxiety concerning relegation to the sphere of reproduction, i.e., concerning "emasculation," increasingly afflicts subjects under capitalism, who are caught in the contradiction between the injunction to be productive and the loss of any individual determining control over the means of production. The dandy is an early prototype of the feminized subject of modern times. Needless to say, such stereotypes are socially produced and transformed according to the demands of division and control of labor.

24. Rosalind H. Williams, *Dream Worlds: Mass Consumption in Late Nineteenth-Century France* (Berkeley and Los Angeles: University of California Press, 1982), chap. 4, brilliantly traces the history of this transformation, which culminates with Des Esseintes in J. K. Huysmans's *A Rebours*.

25. Baudelaire, "Le Peintre de la vie moderne," p. 226.

26. Carlyle, *Sartor Resartus*, p. 216.

27. Carlyle, *Sartor Resartus*, p. 209. Ellen Moers, *The Dandy: Brummell to Beerbohm* (Lincoln: Nebraska University Press, 1978), pp. 167–84, discusses *Fraser's* campaign against the dandies and Carlyle's extension of it in *Sartor Resartus*.

28. Carlyle, *Sartor Resartus*, p. 204.

29. Ibid., p. 211.

30. Ibid., p. 214.

31. Frantz Fanon, *Black Skin, White Masks,* trans. Charles Lam Markmann (New York: Grove Press, 1967), constitutes an extensive investigation of the production of stereotypes of otherness in colonial discourse. His title underlines the appropriateness of Carlyle's epithet for the Irish, as well as expressing the contradictory injunctions imposed on the colonial subject: "Be the same, be different." Homi Bhabha extends the argument in his valuable articles "The Other Question: The Stereotype and Colonial Discourse," *Screen* 24, 6 (November–December 1983): 18–36, and "Of Mimicry and Man: The Ambivalence of Colonial Discourse," *October* 28 (Spring 1984): 125–33. Where Bhabha stresses the *fixity* of the stereotype, I wish to argue its importance as a *principle,* capable of development and assimilation, in the hegemonic phase of colonialism.

32. See, for example, anon., "The Young Men of Ireland," *The Nation,* 15 July 1845, p. 632, which praises the French traveler De Beaumont for asserting that "the vices of Irishmen are of English culture; their virtues are the homegrowth of the heart—the nation's heart."

33. Frantz Fanon, *The Wretched of the Earth,* preface by Jean-Paul Sartre, trans. Constance Farrington (New York: Grove Press, 1968), chap. 3, "The Pitfalls of National Consciousness," provides a critique of bourgeois nationalism as "the tool of capitalism." James Connolly made a similar point, before affiliating with the 1916 nationalists, in "Socialism and Nationalism" (1897), *Selected Writings,* ed. P. Berresford Ellis (Harmondsworth: Penguin, 1973), pp. 123–24.

34. Deleuze and Guattari, "What Is a Minor Literature?" p. 16.

35. Bürger, *Theory of the Avant-Garde,* p. 49.

36. Cf. Mill, *Representative Government,* pp. 282–83, on the criteria for entitlement to vote. The analogy between the condition of the working classes and that of the "savage" becomes apparent in comparing pp. 197–98 and p. 216: both are entirely engrossed in the immediate satisfaction of wants.

37. On the greater clarity achieved in moments of transition, see Georg Lukács, *Balzac und der französische Realismus,* quoted in Wohlfarth, "Perte d'Auréole," p. 532.

38. "But what does it matter who's hiding under the mask? One wants pleasure and for pleasure one only needs humans. And one isn't really human till the masked ball, where the waxen mask covers our habitual flesh mask, where the simple 'Thou' restores the familiarity of primitive community, where a domino that veils all rights brings forth the most beautiful equality, and where the finest freedom reigns—the freedom of the mask." Heinrich Heine, "Briefe aus Berlin," *Sämtliche*

Werke, ed. Jost Hermand, 6 vols. (Hamburg: Hoffmann and Campe, 1973), 6: 37 (my translation). Rose, *Parody/Metafiction,* pp. 178–79, discusses this paragraph briefly. The letter as a whole touches parodically on a remarkable variety of topics discussed in this work and includes a parody of philology, pp. 27–28, and of nationalism, p. 37.

39. Walter Pater, *The Renaissance,* introduction by Lawrence Evans (Chicago: Academy Chicago, 1978), pp. 33–34.

Index

Adorno, Theodor, 240
Aesthetic culture, xi, 208, 210; and
    aesthetic cure, 191; aesthetic
    experience in, 18, 20, 151–52;
    and aesthetic judgment, 209; and
    aesthetic history, 18; and aesthetic
    unity, xiii; Celtic, 9; and Celtic
    sentimentality, 9; and communica-
    tion, 15; and cultivation, 6, 11,
    13, 129–30, 211–12; demands of,
    211–12; and hegemony, 4; and
    identity, 15, 212; marginalization
    of, 24, 214; politics of, 26, 77,
    214; prefiguration in, importance
    of, 12; and racial unity, 17; and
    reader's alienation, 18; self-making
    in, 200; and sensuous man, 16
Aesthetic education, 145–46; and
    aesthetic labor, 6, 15, 146; and the
    state, 13–19
Aesthetics: colonial, 209; development
    and history of genres, 14, 18; of
    form, 189; freedom and, 17;
    German, 13; majority, 23; and
    nationalism, 95; of politics, 18; of
    repetition, 139; and representa-
    tion, 17; Romantic, 124; and
    social bonds, 189–90; of the
    sublime, 144–46
Aladdin, 183–84
Andrews, J. H., 40
Anster, John, 135
Arabian Nights, 99, 116
Arabic poetry, 110, 126
Arnold, Matthew, 84, 105, 208, 218–
    19; as Celt, 18; *Culture and Anar-
    chy*, 10, and major literature, 20;
    as representative aesthetic man,

18; and Schiller, 13; and state of
    culture, 11, 12–13, 15; *On the
    Study of Celtic Literature*, 6–13
Ascendancy conservatives, 56–57
Asiatic Society, 122
Assimilation, 1, 7–8, 20, 24, 25, 123,
    185, 207, 209; of Irish Poor-slave,
    207–8; of Gaelic to English, 77,
    93; of Ireland to Empire, 95; Man-
    gan's resistance to, 77, 186, 187;
    by mass culture, 213; of original
    to derived text, 117; and transla-
    tion, 74. *See also* Translation: as
    assimilation
Augustan Age: modes of translation
    in, 105; verse of, 84
Authenticity, 194, 209; and authentica-
    tion, 116; and citation, 184–85;
    of identity, 102, 203; national,
    102; and paternity, 160; ques-
    tioned, 157, 212–13; and secon-
    dary text, 103, 104; of self in text,
    182; and sources, 103, 118, 128;
    and style, 196–97; and transla-
    tion, 106, 152
Autobiography, 160, 187; ethical,
    169–70, 173; and autonomy,
    162; narcissistic mode of, 163;
    nineteenth-century, 174; and
    psychoanalysis, 163–67; as repeti-
    tion of life, 162
Autonomy, 17, 25, 146, 186, 199,
    203, 209; aesthetic, 204; and art,
    147; and Cain's crime, 194; and
    canon, 19, 21; political and ethi-
    cal, 212; and *Sehnsucht*, 141; of
    subject, 139, 174
Avant-garde, and the aesthetic, 210

ference, 164, 236; and translation, 165–66; and truth-model, 166
Psychosis, 164–67, 176, 184, 218, 220, 236; aesthetic and ethical cure for, 188; and autobiography, 159–67; foreclosure of paternity by, 166–67; genesis of, 164, 165; Mangan's *Autobiography* as representation of, 167; obsessional neurosis as residue of, 165; and psychotic text, 166–67; questioning of psychoanalytic truth-model by, 166

Race: and "essence," 8; and genres, 18; and identity, 8, 164, 204; Indo-European compared to Oriental, 123; Irish, 68; and major literature, 20; and origins, 123; and poet, 190; and representative government, 18
Reading public: politics and aesthetics of, in Dublin, 129
Reconciliation, 219; and constitution theory, 60–61; and culture, 6, 10; and genres, 18–19; and origins, 11; ethics of, 79; in modernism, 23; refused by minor literature, 24
Renan, Ernest, 219
Renza, Louis: on narcissism and autobiography, 163; *"A White Heron" and the Question of Minor Literature,* 4–5
Repeal Association, 58, 59, 225
Repetition, 136–42, 174–75; biography as, 160; and dependence, 151–58; difference in, 183; and emancipation from nature, 151–52; entrapment of dreamer in, 154–55; and identity, 139; in Mangan, 138–39, 141, 142; of origin, 138–39, 194; and the sublime, 148–49; as suspension, 139; and transformation, 155; and the unique, 137–138; and unreality, 141
Representation: aesthetic, 82; antagonism to, 101, 176, 187; in autobiography, 170; and canon, 18; dandy as, of the inauthentic, 206; of Irish landscape, 95–96, 97;

Irish Poor-slave as, of the inauthentic, 206; and major literature, 20; and nationalism, 76; of past unity, 143; and political function of aesthetics, 16–17; political, 18, 208; and the represented, 103; and strategies of minor literature, 22–23; and sublimation as capture, 151; and translation, 109
Representativeness: ethical, of clerisy, 17; in government, as racial ideal, 18; of individual, 15–16; and Irish intellectual, 67; and minor literature, 22; in political theory, 17; and stereotype, 16; writer's, 20
Rhys, Jean: *Wide Sargasso Sea,* 21–22
Ribbonmen, the, 69, 207
Rogers, Samuel, 118
Roman Catholic Church, 180
Romanticism, 71, 199–200; aesthetics of, 124, 139–40; British, 156, 209; epistemology, 70; German, 114, 125, 130, 227; and nationalism, 1, 71, 160; philosophical method of, 139; poetry of, 84; and Romantic irony, 117, 208–9; and self-fathering, 157; and translation theory, 114, 139–40
Round towers, 98–99, 192–94, 231
Rückert, Friedrich: "Und dann nicht mehr," 136–39, 145

Sais, 124–26
Schiller, Friedrich, 129, 200, 219; and aesthetic cultivation, 13; and aesthetic education, 14; and aesthetic semblance, 158; "The Art of Style," 135; contradiction in aesthetic theory of, 15–16; and dependence on sensual, 144; on ethical identification, 144; and formation of German state, 13; and German aesthetics, 13; and human development, 13; "Die Ideale," 147–51; *Letters on the Aesthetic Education of Man,* 14–17, 146–47; *On Naive and Sentimental Poetry,* 13–14, 142–44, 147; "On the Sublime," 144–46, 147, 152–53, 158; and nationalist ideology, 143–44; and role of

Compositor: Skillful Means Press
Text: 10/12 Sabon
Display: Sabon
Printer: Braun-Brumfield, Inc.
Binder: Braun-Brumfield, Inc.